FIRST IN

TREVOR COULT MC

Library of Congress Control Number: 2015904890
ISBN: Hardcover   978-1-4990-9656-9
                 Softcover   978-1-4990-9654-5
                 eBook   978-1-4990-9655-2

Print information available on the last page.

Rev. date: 07/30/2015

To order additional copies of this book, contact:
Xlibris
800-056-3182
www.Xlibrispublishing.co.uk
Orders@Xlibrispublishing.co.uk
710387

CONTENTS

Chapter 1 Baghdad Support Unit...1

Chapter 2 Ranger Platoon 21

Chapter 3 First into Sangin 37

Chapter 4 Battle Preparation 66

Chapter 5 Incident Response Team 91

Chapter 6 Battle for Sangin 106

Chapter 7 Bloodiest Ever Day 118

Chapter 8 Rangers Visit 163

Chapter 9 Decompression 180

Chapter 10 Fort George 195

Chapter 11 A Living Hell...207

Chapter 12 Senior Brecon 219

Chapter 13 Back to Helmand..243

Chapter 14 A Determined Enemy 255

Chapter 15 Sapwan Quala 271

Chapter 16 Day of Days...278

Chapter 17 PB Pylae 285

Dedicated to L/Cpl Luke Edward McCulloch Killed in Action, Sangin 6th September 2006 & Rgr Justin Cupples Killed in Action Sangin 4th September 2008

In memory of Anare Draiva & Paul Muirhead

Be careful what you wish for"
"Rangers do not die they just go to heaven and reorg!

Special thanks goes to Dave Heyhoe & Treo DM without their dedication and selfless courage many of my soldiers including me would never had made it back home safely

Chapter 1

 # BAGHDAD SUPPORT UNIT

It was September 2005, a platoon from C-Company Royal Irish Regiment were relaxing in Shibah Log Base in Iraq (SLB). It was OP TELIC 7, just back from the APOD after escorting troops back to the airport, they were on their way home, some on R&R while others had just ended their six-month tour of duty.

Another very humid day, the troops were starting to call this groundhog day, one of the commanders had been warned off for a nice little trip aboard a Royal Navy vessel; this did not go down well with the guys, he wasn't even a C-Coy soldier, he was attached, he never left the tent, would not socialise, and to be quite frank, was actually quite boring.

The rest of the troops headed for the phones, to phone home. I and a few of the usual suspects went to the village to play cards. It was an air-conditioned hut, made by the Danish equivalent of our own NAAFI, and a great place to see Danish female soldiers; it also took you away from reality of patrols and constant work.

We didn't spend all day chilling out, we had timings to stick to, daily briefings that we needed to attend; this would be from the battle group battle space, we would know who was doing what, what areas they were working in, and what the intelligence picture was. We would also find out weather reports for the next seven days, who was going on R&R, and most importantly, who had been injured or Killed in Action (KIA) within our own regiment.

So far we had been lucky, there had been numerous rocket attacks into camps all over Iraq, especially up in Basra. SLB was a very quiet place, our most likely attack of any kind was going to come from a Locally Employed Contractor (LEC). There were over 1,000 of them working all over the base, many of whom were wearing our combat boots and gortex jackets (these had been supplied by their line managers) because no matter where the British forces work, we have a duty of care to look after the people that we employ.

This is always planned from the start; without these important people, we would not be able to carry out hearts and minds, which is a vital piece of our intelligence. We headed back up to camp 4, this is where my company group was situated for the operation, and my platoon sergeant had returned from the brief and started to gather the troops, so when the boss arrived to give his orders, we were already waiting.

My platoon sergeant was a friend of mine. We had gone through the ranks together; he had been promoted before me. He was a tough Irishman, and when he shouted, everyone heard him. In some respects he was not one to be messed with; he would go through you for a shortcut. He made sure that he carried out a nominal roll call, just before the boss got there.

The boss was again another Irishman. He got on well with the troops and was tactically sound at his job. He had learnt a lot from the platoon sergeant and used his experience to good effect; his brief mainly consisted of who was on the next patrol, who was going on rest, and what had been happening in our own area of responsibility (AOR).

The battalion had been quiet overall. There had been a major drama with B-Company; one of their platoon sergeants had apparently lost his mobile phone while out on patrol, but instead of reporting it to the chain of command, he took a young ranger back out into a dangerous part of Iraq, with no other call signs to support them and no countermeasures in place in case of roadside bombs. He had placed his and the young ranger's lives in grave danger, just to save face.

He was sacked on return to camp and sent back to the United Kingdom. His career now surely was over; he had been known as pockets and pouches, this due to the amount of pouches he carried on his belt kit. He had been a good soldier, but as any soldier will tell you, you are only remembered for your last contact or course, not for the years you had done superbly before.

This was to be the topic of conversation for the next few days; as the rest of the troops would go to the small village, I would start to go over to the Hospital. Not because I was injured, but because they had a great NAAFI, and let's not be naïve, that's where all the hot nurses and doctors would hang out, so it was very pleasing on the eye to sit there and just chill out.

We had started to go there most days. Well, when I say we, I mean myself and only a select three or four guys from my platoon. I didn't want everyone to spoil my guilty pleasure, so I kept this rather low key from the others.

The following day it was my turn to stand up in the coach and brief all the occupants of the actions on contact. I had all ranks on my coach; once I could see that all seats were taken, I walked up and down the coach counting every single man.

I gave the count to the packet commander and then began my brief. 'Sir, ma'am, troops, as you can already see, the curtains are closed on each coach, you are not allowed to open them at all while the coach is moving, no lights are to go on whatsoever, this will show the position of the coaches while they are moving.

'The road we are about to travel down to the airport is very dangerous indeed. We will have flank protection and the rest of my company will escort us there. If we come under attack from gunfire, you are to remain in your seat with your body armour and helmet on, myself and the ground troops will deal with the attack. If we hit an improvised explosive device, well, we have enough team medics and trauma-trained personnel to deal with the incident. I will ask you all to sit back, relax, but do not sleep during this journey. I hope you all have a fantastic leave.'

Once I had given my brief, I got off the coach to give my boss the thumbs-up. 'Boss, we are ready to move.' He turned acknowledged me and waited for the rest of the team to do the same; within a few minutes, we were off on the patrol.

It took exactly forty minutes to get to the APOD. It had felt like two hours, when you take into consideration all the stopping and starting, radio messages, and getting civilian vehicles out of the way. Again it had been a quiet patrol. I know I was itching to get into a contact with the enemy, but I did not want to say; the troops may have thought that I was a little bit mad, but that's why I had joined.

I wanted to be a soldier who had fought properly with the enemy, not who carried out a great exercise or showed leadership qualities on a course. I wanted to do something to make my family proud. I was just a boy from Ballybeen Estate, Dundonald. There were not many from there that had actually had the chance to close and engage with enemy forces, I think I was probably going to be the first. I wanted to be the first!

News came fast through the platoon that some of us were going to Baghdad as part of the protection force for a three-star general. I wanted to be a part of it. I went straight to the boss and asked to be included. He told me that the Officer Commanding (OC) was going to select the men that he thought would make the greatest impact and give the Royal Irish Regiment a good name.

I spent the next few days excited with the fact that I could be going to Baghdad, then during one of our daily briefings, the boss said, 'Speedy, you're going with the OC on a reconnaissance of Baghdad support unit, you will be leaving tomorrow at 0500 hours, start packing your kit tonight, breakfast is at 0430 hours.'

This was fantastic news. I spent most of that night sorting out my belt kit and helmet along with night-vision goggles. My kit was packed then unpacked and packed again. I had OCD and wanted everything to be just perfect. I sat outside the tent in the platoon area and began to clean my rifle; there were a few other guys there having a chat and smoking. That night I went to bed very relaxed yet excited inside.

I had a good sleep that night, and when one of the guys on duty came to wake me, it felt like I had been sleeping for about twenty-four hours, my body was refreshed and I was raring to go. I went over to breakfast with my grip bag and combat equipment fighting order (CEFO).

The OC was already there, sitting with the Regimental Sergeant Major (RSM). He just winked over at me, and with his southern Irish accent, he said, 'Yul right, Speedy son?' I just replied, 'Aye, sir.' 'Enjoy yer recce, kid.' On that note he stood up, put his plate in the bin, and walked off.

I quickly had breakfast, loaded my kit into the back of a snatch vehicle, and waited patiently for the OC to arrive; his kit was already in the vehicle. We waited for about five minutes, then he climbed in. 'Right, Speedy boy, let's get to Baghdad.'

We drove for only about ten minutes, where we met a convoy that was going to the international airport. I had done this journey many times now, this time I was the one being briefed. We arrived there in good time, collected our bags, and checked in, it was very fast.

After only a few minutes we climbed onto a Hercules transporter (C130) and started our flight into Baghdad, which took approximately two hours in total. When we came into landing, we made a very steep descent. This was to ward off any missile attacks that could be launched at the aircraft. It was also a wakeup call that we were now in Baghdad.

My nerves were on edge and my mind was thinking, 'Make sure you look after the boss.' We got off the aircraft and made our way across the runway. Everywhere I looked I could see US Marines, US Army; the place was swarming with Americans, yet only a handful of British service personnel.

We then got onto a Merlin helicopter with our kit and flew at such speed over Baghdad. Our heli was just flying above the rooftops, again this was to ward off rocket attacks and small arms; the door gunner was already made ready and scanning his arcs of fire all the way to the landing zone and into a small airstrip in the green zone. This was the safe area in Baghdad, it had over 150,000 soldiers, sailors, and airman. Once off the chopper, we drove through the green zone. I noticed a pattern that every 100 metres there was a checkpoint.

Both sides of the road were sealed off. Massive concrete blocks had been placed out to give cover from attack, mostly suicide bombers. The threat was extremely high in Baghdad. Here there had been several attacks in the past few months.

They tend to hit more than one checkpoint at a time; this causes massive confusion. Then they normally follow up with a secondary attack, to get maximum casualties and gain the upper hand. This works for a short period of time, when morale is low amongst the troops; the insurgents have won that particular battle.

We drove through a series of checkpoints, past an Iraqi checkpoint, and into Maude house. This was where the three-star general stayed. He was the second highest-ranking soldier in Iraq who worked alongside a four-star general. He was in fact a US Marine based inside Camp Victory and the only way to get there was to drive down route Irish, known as the most dangerous road in the world. You had to drive out of the green zone, onto the highway, and into insurgent territory. This I was looking forward to, yet was very nervous and apprehensive about.

So we drove into a vehicle park beside Maude house, the only troops here were part of an escort force attached to the general. There was a lot of work involved, you had to train on the blue force tracker, a system that sends live feeds to a control room that lets coalition troops know the exact location of your vehicle in case your call sign got into a contact; there would always be air support on standby when a friendly call sign was on the ground. We even had our very own special forces a few hundred metres down the road. They were on black ops mission, working well above our pay scale.

Myself and the OC went our separate ways for a few hours. He went on briefings with the officers while I went and mingled with the commanders to get a feel of the place. I took photographs of the accommodation, the cookhouse, the toilet, shower block, the internet suite, downtime area, the guardroom, and other areas of work. I wanted to go back with answers to as many questions as possible, or what was the point in taking me.

So far everyone that I had spoken to loved working at this place. They spoke of Baghdad support unit (BSU) as the perfect post in Iraq; it was also the only place in Baghdad that had alcohol. There was a strict two-can rule of course, but if you had the following day off, then guys could be a little bit more robust with the drink. Poker table was a place to mingle. They held poker tournaments once a week, and table tennis was the other main fixture of the night. I also visited the gym and was pleasantly surprised with the amount on offer.

Once I was completely satisfied with my notes and pictures, I headed to my bunk and began to put together a slideshow for a briefing for when I returned to my company. I then went to the American PX. This was a massive shop in the green zone used by all fighting troops; whether you were close protection, green berets, special forces, or just a contractor, they all used this area, so as you can imagine, the security was very tight.

Once inside and having had my identification checked, I went and ordered a subway sandwich, Coke, and just sat there watching the world go by. No sooner had we finished our meal than the radio went and requested that we return to BSU for a briefing.

I noticed on the way back that the guys were more relaxed than those on the way up. When I mentioned it to the driver, he laughed and said, 'Speedy, my old chum, outside the green zone, you can be killed in an instant.' That said it all! I just smiled and took in every checkpoint.

When we got back inside the gates of BSU, we unloaded our weapons at the unloading bay, one of the junior non-commissioned officers always gives the words of command for the rest to unload, and we put our weapons in the guardroom and waited for the brief.

It had been twenty minutes when the troops started to gather around the vehicles. A head check was carried out by all the commanders, while Spence, the intelligence senior NCO, was putting up his briefing board and maps of the patrol that was going out in the morning; it consisted of a spot map that all commanders carried while out on the ground.

Once everyone was there, we began by explaining what the patrol was, what call signs were required, what assets we had on call during the operation, then Spence began with the down report, of what had been happening over the last five days, what the threat levels were, and the incidents over the past twenty-four hours. To be honest it was shocking. Once he was finished, he just smiled and said, 'Well, fellas, it's what you joined for, so man up.' No truer word had I heard that day.

I went to speak to my commander for the patrol and he said that I would be better off doing top cover in the vehicle as I would get to see the route and it would be good as a recce element, I agreed.

The next morning I awoke to the sound of a bugle playing. It was funny but not great to hear at 0600 hours. At breakfast I could see the other guys already prepared for the patrol and in good spirits. I was a little excited but did not want the others see that I was one of those guys that loved the thrill of a contact. To be honest I think that every soldier secretly wants the same thing, we just tend to hide it.

After breakfast I headed straight for the vehicle shed and began to check all the kit inside or should I say at least familiarise myself with everything that this team did. I was shown the grenades, flash bangs, where the air horns were and what the team's drills were.

The entire electronic counter equipment was checked and in good order, weapons had been prepared, all vehicles were ready to deploy. My OC was going to travel in the front vehicle with the other officer commanding, so he could receive a live brief by the boss the whole way there and back to Maude house.

Once we had all loaded our personal weapons and got into our respectful vehicles, we got into patrol formation. The wagon I was in was given the dreaded task as tail-end Charlie, basically keeping all civilian transport back from the convoy.

My actions on attack were going through my mind and I was happy with the drills expected of me; after only a few minutes, we headed out through a series of checkpoints, most of them being our American counterparts.

On the horizon just before our convoy left the heavily protected green zone, I could see an M1A1 American tank, its barrel pointing towards a block of flats on route Irish; there were several US soldiers all facing out towards enemy threat, the sights on their weapons were scanning every possible attacking position.

Our convoy was now out heading at a reasonable pace along the road. Radio checks and situation reports were happening every time we crossed below a bridge or passed a certain spot on the map. It was running like clockwork, every man knew their job inside out, rehearsals had been done every single day, these guys were good.

I was scanning from 12 right through to 6 o'clock, my eyes hurting from the strain and pressure of not missing a single thing. Every window, alleyway, and vehicle was searched by my mark one eyeball; my air horn was used on several occasions to warn off potential threat from civilian vehicles.

We were now only a few hundred feet away from the US camp. I could see the build-up of traffic towards the entrance, it was when we were going to be vulnerable, we had to slow down approaching the American checkpoint. There were warning signs everywhere.

'Lethal Force will be used, STAY BACK.' The warnings were real, they meant business. We entered the base and straight away we all unloaded our weapon systems, making sure that we caught the ejected rounds that flew out of our rifles. We had a quick brief, the boss stated he was going for a brief, and a drops vehicle would be here in a few minutes. Our task was to escort it to BSU. That was our cue to go and grab a coffee. We had a few minutes to recharge and chat about the journey down, exchange a few ideas where it was a bit dodgy, build-up of traffic and locals.

The drops vehicle arrived and got into position within the convoy itself. We were just waiting on the boss's vehicle to return and we would be on our way back to the green zone. It was just a few more minutes and we were all in formation, the radio checks again got carried out by each vehicle, we had to give a radio to the drops vehicle so they could have running commentary of the patrol and keep in the know of any situation that occurred.

I got myself into position back to back with Tam, the other guy doing top cover with me, and we headed back out of camp onto route Irish. Again the atmosphere was strange, we drove down the road for approximately one kilometre, the convoy stopped. I could hear shouting from the front, I had a quick glance, my arcs did not afford me to get drawn into the situation. I did manage to see a white vehicle parked at the side of the road. It looked static, the convoy then began to move again, just at the same time the white car began to reverse towards the convoy, and my personal role radio was going berserk, people shouting orders across the net.

I then heard air horns followed by warning shots. These went into the engine block; the car was gaining speed. I turned and noticed what it could only be classed as insurgents running with a heavy weapon. They began to assemble it, I aimed my weapon and began firing it, informing the others that we were in contact. I gave a quick steer to the others. I was approximately 200 metres away from the enemy and it took me a few rounds to get on target.

I gave a steer for the driver to move his vehicle alongside the other call signs. They were taking incoming fire. I thought if I could get our vehicle alongside theirs, it would cover their extraction. It worked. I could see the strike marks as the rounds bounced off the road to the front of me, Tam the other top cover sentry had been controlling the other side of the vehicle at the time, not being drawn into the situation and remaining focussed throughout.

It seemed like forever, we had a vehicle stall on the central reservation and it needed to be bumped from behind to get it over. Another snatch vehicle helped with that. After a few more minutes, we were extracting back to the same US camp that we had just left.

We needed to regroup and discuss what had just gone on. As we were the last vehicle in the convoy, it was left to me and Tam to give covering fire for the rest of the convoy; it had been a scary few minutes. I was scanning the unclear flats to our front. There was gunfire coming from the top floor, but I was looking for the flash from the muzzle 'not seen' as soon as I could identify it, I fired a burst of two to three rounds until the flashes stopped.

All in all it had been well controlled by everyone involved. We parked up the vehicles near the PX. I noticed a few of the guys did not speak, the commanders were all at the OC's vehicle getting a de-brief. Everyone else was smoking cigarettes and writing down notes about the contact. We all knew that statements would have to be written as soon as we got back to BSU.

And this was just meant to be my recce of Baghdad! It turned out to live up to its reputation, I was going to have to give a fantastic brief on my return. We had time to reflect the situation. Everyone in the patrol had now re-bombed their magazines and we were all ready to go.

The boss gave quick battle orders and we started to leave the US camp again, this time we were slightly more observant than usual. Everyone, including me, was on edge as we drove onto route Irish. I was amazed that the white car that had driven at the convoy, which had quite a few magazines of ammunition fired into it, had now disappeared. This is in fact a normal routine with insurgents, they never want coalition forces to recover their dead; in a lot of respects, their casualty evacuation is fantastic, almost as good as our own.

We arrived back at BSU, the journey seemed very quick this time as we had a lot to do as part of the after-action review. Once we had all unloaded, packed away our kit, and changed the radio batteries (we had specific timings to stick to), the boss was in the guardroom taking notes from every patrol member, and he wanted to know who had fired what and how many rounds they had expended.

I was the sixth soldier to give my statement, and when I had explained that I had only fired nine rounds of ammunition during the contact, he just laughed at me. I then explained in great detail where every round I had fired had went. He just said, 'Fair one, Speedy.'

The next day was spent mainly in camp. I got to walk around Maude house and see what goes on in there. I was amazed to see that it had a fully functional operations room, computers and maps everywhere, a computerised global positioning satellite that follows every vehicle. They had in fact watched the whole contact that we had just been involved in. I felt very proud how I had handled it.

That afternoon myself and the boss were on a flight back to Basra. We had seen everything that we needed and gained enough intelligence to brief the company on the layout and operational side of how BSU actually worked in a day-to-day basis.

We were met at the airport by troops from our own company. They had heard of the ambush that we had been involved in and wanted to know every detail. To be honest, I just wanted a few hours' sleep before I was sent for and had to talk about the contact again.

It wasn't long before the company sergeant major wanted to see me. He spoke with me and praised me for my professionalism and leadership that I had shown in Baghdad. I said, 'Cheers, sir', and made my way back to my tent. I then loaded up my laptop and tweaked my presentation, it was ready to go.

I only showed the commanders that we're actually going to Baghdad; no one else needed to see or hear what it was like. That's how the army works. If it does not involve you, then you will never hear how others are getting on or what they are up to. It's all part of operational security or OPSEC as we call it in the forces.

We had only been back from Baghdad a few days, the OC had made his list of which personnel he was sending to Baghdad. He wasn't sending the best there. He had to equally split the company to make sure he had good commanders at every outpost that the company had to guard or patrol. I was just happy that my name was on the list as a team commander.

The days seemed to drag on and on, groundhog days had started again, patrols around SLB doing ground holding and snap vehicle checkpoints (VCPs). There was the odd escort patrol thrown in for good measure. Those convoys to umm quasar were hard on the eyes.

There had been occasions that I had drifted off while reading the map, and in fact on one particular occasion, I awoke to find my driver fast asleep. While Bryan, my top cover, was screaming at the top of his voice, 'You two idiots, wake up', he was banging the roof trying to warn us that we had driven off the road.

We started to find a way to keep our interest. We kept 100% on the job, but when there were opportunities to relax, we did. I happened to mention that one of the checkpoints was like a ramp in the road. It was in fact two oil drums dug into the ground to act as a speed bump.

No sooner had I said it than across our personal role radio, the platoon sergeant dared my driver to hit it as fast as he could. My driver looked at me and said, 'Can I, Speedy, please?' I nodded. 'Yes, mate, go for it.'

I made sure we were both wearing seatbelts. I then shouted to Bryan to get down from top cover and put on his seatbelt, but he refused to do so, he kept shouting in. 'He has no balls, Speedy,' the driver just smiled at me. There was no turning back now.

The engine revved, he laughed and sped down the road. I could see the ramp approaching fast and I closed my eyes. I could hear Bryan scream at the top of his voice. I felt the snatch lift; I looked out of the window and could see that we had lifted quite high off the road, then we bounced three times after we landed. Bryan had flown all around the back of the vehicle, his box of 200 rounds of ammunition went all over the wagon and loose kit went all over him. We stopped the vehicle and opened the doors. Bryan could hardly walk; he was saying, 'I have broken my bum.' We couldn't stop laughing at him.

It had been the funniest thing I had seen in a while. Everyone was laughing and even the platoon sergeant burst out laughing across the net. It was just what I needed; it gave me a chance to let out a little emotion that had been building up.

The names of the company that were going to Baghdad had officially been published. A list was with each platoon commander and they would let us know at the daily brief. We had to wait all day but it was worth it. I already knew I was going, the other guys now found out. A friend of mine, who himself was a commander, felt a little dejected to find his name not even on the list. I explained that his experience was needed elsewhere. He sort of understood, but it didn't stop him from wanting to go.

My boss was going to be a decent guy. His father served before him and now it was his turn. He was already a jungle warfare instructor, and to be honest, he was tactically sound as a commander, a good guy to lead your men. I had worked with him before. He knew I was professional and we had mutual respect for one another. It was going to be a good few weeks.

The days seem to drag until we were all assembled and ready to fly up to Baghdad to do a Relief in Place (RIP) with D-Company, also known as the delta dogs. They were the most senior company in our battalion and had a lot of knowledge and very experienced. It was the only company left who had soldiers that deployed back on operation grapple 1, and soldiers from a Bosnia tour were very few and far between these days.

It was in fact B-Company who had taken over escort tasks and had the privilege to take us to the plane that awaited us at Basra airport. It took a few hours to process us through, as we had a lot of baggage to get through.

It was in fact going to be the last thing we did during our tour, so we had to take our time and get it done right first time. The bags all needed to be scanned, and the Royal Air Force (RAF) were a little bit anal when it came to the movement of tobacco products. We argued that we were not leaving theatre but just moving up the road to Baghdad, but that did not sway them one bit.

Two hundred cigarettes, the rest was going to be burnt. Well, that's what they tell us. I've never ever seen thousands being burnt. I'm sure it must be done behind closed doors.

We all got aboard the Hercules C130 transporter; we placed the seatbelt on and waited for the in-flight brief to start, same old brief, windows to remain closed, no light within the cabin, and on approach we would have helmets and body armour on. This was the same everywhere you flew in Iraq; it had become standard policy.

I had fallen asleep along with most of the troops aboard. It was a much-needed rest, then after only a few hours, the captain came on the speakers telling us we were approaching Baghdad and to prepare ourselves. Fifteen minutes later, we started our descent onto the runway, it was frightening, very steep, in fact it felt like we were just dropping from the sky, thank God our seatbelts were fastened. That's how it's done in the RAF, and they were very slick with their drills.

Once we had all disembarked the aircraft, we walked a short distance to where we would be flown the rest of the way by helicopter to another remote landing strip. It was a small place in the green zone called Washington DC, quite a good name for an airport, especially when most of troops there were in fact American.

It took a couple a shuttle runs from Washington to BSU to get everyone in and our baggage sorted out, but we were all now finally here. In the heart of insurgency land, it was going to be a very testing time for everyone involved especially the command element.

We were given about an hour to settle in, before the briefs and actions on attack were drummed into us, I was shown my accommodation, it was a porter cabin, it had two bunk beds in each room. I picked the bottom bunk and used the top bunk as my admin area. I started to unpack my grip bag, due to the fact I have OCD, I could not leave the room until my bed was made and I had my own personal space sorted out. It took me about ten minutes to carry out my ritual.

I was now ready for some food. I went over to the cookhouse and grabbed a snack. We all gathered in the smoking area and awaited the boss to collect us for our first of many intelligence briefs. The insurgents were strong in Baghdad, this was in fact their back garden and they did not want us in it.

The main threat here was from suicide bombers. The possibility of shoot and rocket attack was likely, and vehicle convoys were very easy for them to strike. We stuck to specific roads and routes, where as they knew every road and alleyway, their means to escape were massive. One of the most deadliest methods of strike was from roadside bombs, and these were happening all over route Irish.

Route Irish and I had already met; I knew first-hand how deadly it could be, I just hoped and prayed that I could get my team through this tour with no fatalities or even a casualty.

Spence was there again to give us up-to-date intelligence on the insurgency within our Area of Operations (AOR), and from personal experience, there was no better soldier within our battalion that could not only give a brief perfectly, but had done and could do the job better.

He was tactically a good commander and had bags of experience, everyone that knew him said the same, he should have gone Special Forces, and he had the knowledge, only he knows why he chose not to.

After that initial brief, we got our weapons out of the guardroom, put our kit on, and proceeded to the crossed swords. This is a place where Saddam Hussein used to watch his army march past. It was now were the British forces and close protection units practised their vehicle manoeuvres and anti-ambush drills. It was only a kilometre away from BSU.

We spent the next few days here going over every possible scenario, what if this happens and what if that happens, until we had exhausted every avenue.

This would be our new home. Every spare minute, we would get our multiples together and take a drive over there. Yes, multiples, our platoons had now been split in two multiples. Three platoons now meant six multiples; this was a better way to run efficiently. It meant that we now had time off and could relax. It all was making sense.

Guard duty was in fact very relaxing. We got to see everyone that came into BSU. This would mean US Marines that wanted a beer, the occasional nurse or doctor that wanted to let their hair down. Our very own task force black (special forces) and a mad US Cavalry officer who wore a cowboy hat and played a guitar, he had his own songs to sing, and the more beer he drank, the better he sounded. They all had to book into the guardroom, many of whom had to hand over their personal protection weapons (PPW).

I would get to spend a lot of time over the next few weeks either at the poker table that was 6 foot by 4 foot, with a proper blue felt across it, and the internet suite. This is where I would keep in contact with the outside world. My thirty minutes a week was quite enough to get to find out what everyone back in the UK was doing with their time. Patrols seemed to come and go with ease at BSU. Everyone was professional and it ran like clockwork. There was the odd day that I felt nervous, especially those escort tasks to the Ministry of the Interior.

We had to drive slowly through the town and it gave potential attackers the upper hand. We were going so slowly at times, we may have been static. It was hard to keep crowds back from the vehicles. With everyone doing top cover using the air horns like they were going out of fashion and the screams of 'GET BACK' by the time the patrol was over, we needed new horns, and more than anything, we had in fact lost our voices due to the amount of shouting.

On another day and after a long patrol and lunch at Camp 'VICTORY', we were making our way back up route Irish and there had been another incident involving US Marines. This time in particular the place was swarming with soldiers.

Bradley tanks were facing potential risk areas, while Blackhawk helicopters flying low over the buildings, there had been a white Toyota pick-up driving too close to the convoy so the call sign closest to it had just fired their .50 calibre weapon system at it, killing everyone within the vehicle. That's how the Americans dealt with would-be attackers.

One of the scariest nights that I had in Baghdad was when Iraq had been playing an international football match against Iran. They had beaten Iran 3-1 away from home, and to be honest, what came next was totally unexpected. There was automatic gunfire all over Baghdad.

The noise was deafening, the sky was lit up with green and red tracer rounds, you could see the coloured bursts of fire, then came the fall-out—rounds of 7.62 mm and 5.56 mm were now falling all over camp. At one point we thought that we were under attack.

No one knew at first what had just happened, and then across the net we were all told that it was celebratory gunfire and that we were not to react to it, just as well, as none of us would have known where to start the next morning after another escort task. I was sitting watching the news when a surprise visitor had popped in to see me. It was in fact my old recce friend 'Fish'. He had left the army and became a close protection officer.

He was earning a fortune working in Baghdad. He wanted to know if I fancied a spin in his black Humvee. I had to go and seek clearance from the CSM. He knew Fish and said, 'Go ahead, but don't be long, Speedy.' We only went to the PX and had a chat; it was good to catch up on old times. He dropped me back at BSU then went back to work. That was the last time I ever saw him. He is still alive today; we just lead different lives now.

News started to circle that the battalion were putting together a platoon. This platoon was going to be full of the best soldiers within the battalion. It was going to be hand-picked by the commanding officer. If anyone wanted their name put forward for selection, then now was the time.

The only drama was that no one knew what for and for how long. The information slowly got drip fed across the battalion. The platoon would be full strength and be attached to the Third Battalion the Parachute Regiment and be based in Colchester. It sounded great; I made sure my name was on the list that was put forward.

Then the truth started to come out. The boss briefed a few of us and said, 'Guys, this will be very hard, but you will be trained up to fight in Afghanistan, it will be the first time troops have entered a place called HELMAND.

'It is ruthless, one of the Taliban strongholds within the Middle East, and where the poppy fields lie. They get their opium from the harvest of the poppies and they will fight very hard. Without the opium, they cannot buy weapons, so prepare for a battle.'

We had heard all this rubbish a thousand times before. We just nodded and smiled. 'Yes, sir,' that was all officers wanted to hear, and one of my default settings.

Anyway we still had three weeks until the end of this tour. It was on everyone's lips for the entire time. We all wanted to know who the commanding officer and his team had selected. It was not long before the OC had an orders group (O Gp) and explained what was going to take part.

He explained that the chosen platoon would in fact leave theatre a week early and proceed for three weeks' leave on their return to Fort George. Inverness they would begin training on conventional warfare.

Sergeant Spence would in fact be dealing with the training side of things and would be the platoon sergeant. Straight away the platoon had been given the best sergeant in the battalion. The section commanders were going to be Robbie, Strainer, and myself. I was over the moon.

I knew that we were in fact the three fittest corporals within the battalion, and without a shadow of doubt, we were all tactically sound commanders.

The platoon commander was going to be Sean. He had been a ranger before and he knew all of us. The command element of the platoon was looking very strong indeed and the fact that most of us that had been picked were already in Baghdad was amazing stuff. It was hard not to smile for the remaining time in Baghdad. Not only was our time here coming to an end, we now had something else to look forward to.

I got to know Spence a little while out in Baghdad and asked him what he thought it would be like in Helmand. He said, 'Not sure, but I can tell you this for nothing, we will be prepared for every eventuality.'

It wasn't long before the new brigade started to arrive and begin their handover with us. We had already made out new orbats, and this would include their commanders. We had to take them out with our patrols in order to let them see how we conducted ourselves. They could carry on what we were doing or change it to suit themselves.

The handover was terrible. The Royal Scots were not living up to their name, they were rubbish, their basic drills at private soldier level were not what was expected, they lost rounds of ammunition during the unload at the entrance to Camp Victory, an NCO had left his weapon in the cookhouse in the US camp.

They had crashed the only two close protection wagons for the general, while practising their driving skills at the cross swords.

And to top it all off, one of their officers had pushed in front of me to unload his weapon fast and had in fact fired a round just past my head. He had a negligent discharge with his weapon, right in front of everyone. I wanted to punch his lights out. I ended up having to write yet another statement. The general got wind of all these mistakes and wanted to get rid of this unit.

Baghdad had come to an end for the selected few. We were flying home for a few weeks off, then back to work for preparation. I got a flight back to Northern Ireland and arrived at the Belfast City airport where I was met by my parents, as per usual they were pleased to see me. I got the third degree from my mother on why I looked so thin, but this is what mothers do, they tend to insult your weight so that you let them fatten you back up. I enjoyed it, my mother's cooking was fantastic. The first thing I asked for was an Ulster fry. She was great at them.

My dad just smiled, he knew that if I was getting one, then so was he. The journey home only took ten minutes and that was long due to the amount of traffic at the bottom of the Sydenham bypass. It was good to see the place again once we pulled up on the driveway.

I could see the garden looked great. It always did. My parents loved to work in the garden. Everything had been pruned and cut to perfection, and the colours of the flowers looked great.

My parents smiled at me, as they knew it looked good. I'm sure they were both just waiting for me to comment on how good it looked, so I fulfilled their wishes. 'Mum, the garden looks great,' I said. I could see her face light up. She unlocked the door and said, 'Right, coffee with two sugars.' 'Yes, Mum,' I replied.

That's when I knew I was home; I headed straight up the stairs and began to unpack. The room had not changed a bit. My parents liked to leave it the way I had left it. I had a look in the wardrobe and there in a box were all my old trinkets, badges, and certificates that I had won running road races and cross-country events.

Some of my clothes that I had left hanging up still smelt fresh. I think my mother kept washing them in order to keep them smelling fresh. As soon as I had finished, I went downstairs for that Ulster fry. It smelt great; my dad was already sitting in the dining room waiting for me. We had a chat and I told him about my next project. He just looked amazed.

I was home for a few weeks before I started training again for Afghanistan. I explained that it might be better in the sense of a combat environment and I might actually have a chance of getting into a proper engagement with the enemy. He thought my head was full of sweetie mice. Being home was very relaxing, but no sooner was I home than I was starting to feel like I should be doing something. I was used to having timings to stick to and places to go.

I spent a lot of my time sitting at home and chatting to my parents. I missed the fun we had. My mum always wanted a cup of coffee, so we took it in turns to make it, and I never really asked my dad if he wanted one. His automatic answer was always 'NO, I DON'T.'

I travelled up the Newtownards road a few times just to visit my sister and her family that was always good crack. Her husband always wanted to place a wee bet on the horses, and to be honest, I would place the odd one on also.

I never won though. My two nieces were starting to grow up fast, one was always getting into trouble by doing silly things, but that's what teenagers do.

I had spent two weeks at home and it was time to travel back. My parents gave me a lift to the airport. It was a hug followed by a few tears this time. I hated these goodbyes, they left a sour taste in my mouth each time I had to say bye. Thank God they did not last too long. My parents never wanted me to go and I never wanted to leave.

At the airport I bumped into a few guys returning from their leave. We had a beer in the bar while we waited for our flight. The conversation was all about what we had done on leave and how we were both on edge and needed something to do. I think deep down they were slightly jealous of what Ranger Platoon were about to embark on. I could not explain to them what it felt like, but I knew I was excited about leading a section of men into a combat environment.

Chapter 2

RANGER PLATOON

Our flight was departing in thirty minutes, so we started to make our way to the departure gate. It was Easy Jet, so we were at opposite ends of the aircraft, not much room for manoeuvre either.

The flight from Belfast to Inverness only took one hour ten minutes. At the airport I got a taxi to camp; even though it was only four miles from there to the camp, it still cost ten pounds, but it was worth it. I got into camp and rear party was still on. They did not realise that our platoon were all returning to start work, and because we had been on leave, Spence needed to properly thrash us for a few days in order to blow out cobwebs and build on the fitness.

The platoon was assembled the next morning outside C-Company block. We got to see who was in it. The sections were still not put together, but over the next few days the boss had started to put the platoon Orbats together. There were some good soldiers in the platoon. Others I did not comment on, as I had never worked with them. A guy from A-Company called Dougal was a robust individual. I had heard that he was a good soldier.

I decided to wait to pass judgement on these individuals. If they could do the job, then that's good enough for me.

We started off with lots of endurance runs, to build up our stamina, then running with weight started to make an appearance. Soon we were running with full Combat Equipment Fighting Order (CEFO), the platoon was starting to take shape. Along with the patrolling across ground, and the contact reaction, it was all good. The one thing that I hated was casualty extraction, and we were running with casualties for about three miles, and then being told the Helicopter Landing Site (HLS) had been moved.

He was teaching us break contact drills, lifesaving drills; we were all starting to perfect the drills the way he wanted. Spence was starting to get the platoon gelled the way he wanted, and it was with blood, sweat, and tears.

We spent nearly two weeks going over all kinds of scenarios, and when he was ready and had been given the thumbs-up by the boss, we were ready to get on the coach and travel to Colchester. We were now **RANGER PLATOON**, and we were part of C-Company 3 Para. This is where we would remain until the operation was over; our new camp was waiting for us some fourteen hours' drive away.

Next stop, Colchester. Everyone just wanted to sleep. O,Driscol was on the phone trying to organise a date at the end of the journey; let's just say he went for the more mature woman.

We arrived there late at night. Once off the coach, the colour sergeant directed us to C-Company block. Our rooms were not bad actually. All the commanders had their own room. My room was right next door to Rob's, so that was good. We used to go out together and he was one for the ladies. At 6 foot in height rather tanned and boyish good looks, he was always guaranteed a girl at the end of the night.

We had to get up the next morning at 0500 hours, not what we had expected, especially as we did not know where the cookhouse was, so it was follow the leader. We eventually found it. We got some weird stares from the paratroopers, to them we were just hats.

We began the morning with a little bit of kit issue from the Quarter Masters (QM) followed by introductions from the OC and CSM. They were very pleased to have us on board, and we couldn't wait to show them what we had brought to the party.

The company started to go for endurance runs. I think we surprised the paratroopers, with Strainer Robbie and myself always coming one, two, and three, closely followed by O,Driscol. He was another fit guy that we had. He was always at the front of a run, or as near to it, we showed them that we were very fit indeed. The rest of our platoon was of a decent standard as well. With the competitor streak inside all three of our section commanders, we all wanted to win, neither of us wanted to let the paratroopers beat us at anything.

We started this off during the basic fitness test, all three of us breaking eight minutes for the run. We carried this onto the Brecon 2 miler. We each came first, second, and third. The platoon was running on pride. We had not let ourselves down, in fact the CSM had indeed told the other platoon sergeants that he would rather have three Royal Irish platoons, he was embarrassed at their lack of determination.

I think we caught everyone by surprise. We stepped up to the plate and showed we could go toe to toe with any unit if you pushed us. It was still early days, but the platoon was bonding very well. The rapport was fantastic and we now looked out for each other.

We made up for our hard work in camp by even harder play down the town. We went out most nights and had a great time. We wanted to adopt the town of Colchester. It was a great night out, the women were stunning—or maybe that was the alcohol that was making them look better.

On one occasion when I had in fact returned drunk to camp, I could hear noises coming from support company block. I was now feeling a little better due to the walk back having sobered me up slightly. I walked around the camp only to discover between two of the blocks was in fact a fire.

There was a paratrooper sitting by himself with a few cans of beer. Once he had noticed me, he wanted to know if I had anything to burn. I went to the bin area and grabbed some rubbish and placed it on the fire. He handed me a can and introduced himself as Maz; we both sat there drinking beer until we decided to go to bed.

After only two weeks in camp, we got a brief that we would fly to the country of Oman and begin final training preparation for Afghanistan. Its terrain was very similar and the temperature was of realistic training value to us. We were looking forward to the final test to see if we could cut the mustard against the elite paratroopers. The amount of firepower on show here was going to be exciting. It would be the first time ever that we got to work with the assets that would be available to us in Afghanistan.

The new Apache helicopters were going to be on show, doing their thing with hellfire missiles. We would be calling them into targets.

We had javelin missiles and fast jets flying low. If this is what we were going to be doing in Afghanistan, I could not wait to get out there.

When we got to RAF Brize Norton. We had to wait a few hours for time to board the aircraft. It was a Tri-Star. I had been on many in the past, but this was my first time going to Oman. The only thing I knew about Oman was that an Irish ranger called Labalaba, who had joined the Special Air Service (SAS), had been killed there at the battle of Mirabat. He had been trying to ward off hundreds of enemy fighters and had been killed still firing his gun. He was posthumously awarded a mention-in-despatches.

And ever since that day, he had been a hero within the Fijian community, and rightly so, we were able to pick our own seats on the aircraft that made life a little easier. I sat beside Robbie and Dougal. It was a very relaxed trip, one of which I managed to sleep most of the way.

Once in Oman, I could feel the heat come through the cabin. I began to sweat rather badly. It got worse when the door opened. I could feel the dry yet humid air. I wanted a drink, bottled water was now being supplied by the cabin crew, and was well appreciated by everyone. The airport looked very clean from the steps. The numerous coaches at the steps of the plane would mean that we were not allowed to walk out in the open here, especially as we were all in desert combats.

The battalion had now landed in Oman and we were ready for the final exercise. The brigade commander was already here waiting on the commanding officer Lt Col Stuart Tootal. We got on the coaches, bags loaded onto the four-ton vehicles, and we drove to what only can be described as a circle of barbed wire with numerous tents erected inside it. Once inside the tent, it was pleasantly surprising. With the air-conditioned units working, it was the best place to be, only problem was I could never acclimatise if I stayed inside.

We began to sort out our kit. Training would begin in the morning. There was a little shop there being run by the locals; it had a good selection of drinks and food. I must have spent £30 in that shop, buying rubbish. We used to sit there at the end of each day drinking coffee and chatting about how we could improve for the following day.

We began doing section drills building up to platoon break contact drills. We tweaked everything we could and utilised the time we had there, then came a section competition within the battalion. We were at the top of our game, the fittest we had ever been and hungry for success, we managed to finish first, second, and third again. I don't think the Paras really tried to be honest. The commanding officer wanted to speak to us all, so we were assembled in the cookhouse.

He started by telling us he was extremely proud to have us there working alongside his beloved paratroopers, and that he realised that it was St Patrick's Day, and if we were back at our own battalion, we would be celebrating it, so he promised to buy us a bottle of whiskey once this was all over.

It was a nice gesture; he didn't have to say that. To be honest it lifted our spirits, as if we needed them lifted. We were already on cloud 9. Spence and the Boss gave us a little pep talk on how they were so proud of us and to keep up the good work. We just had the final platoon attack to get over. We were the last platoon to do it. One of the platoons in A-Company had done it in 44 minutes; another platoon had done it in 53 minutes. We sat in the forming up point (FUP) for quite a while waiting on our turn to run the gauntlet.

Then the boss sent for the commanders—right, guys, shake out, let's go, we were gone, assault, suppress, reserve, we had this down to a fine art, we flew through the positions in no time, the whole thing completed in 34 minutes. Even the directing staff, who were all in fact paratroopers, gave us praise. We now had earned the respect of the guys that we would be working alongside ourselves in Afghanistan, and that is a hard thing to gain from them.

The last attack was shortly followed by a show of force demonstration, the fast jets showing the troops on the ground what they could expect to get from them, when called upon for air strikes, this was followed by the Apache gunships, who gave a good account of themselves, then javelin patrols alongside of us gave a good demo of their firepower. It all worked together and it was shocking to see what we could achieve if we needed to take out positions.

I dreaded to see what the outcome would be if we needed to bring this deadly arsenal together on the battlefield.

We had a day off before returning to the UK. We all chose to go to the beach and relax. There was a cliff jump into the sea that was over 25 feet in height. I watched the other guys do it, to see if it was safe, once I was happy I had a go myself, it was a little scary but at least I did it and had saved face in front of the troops.

Having had a day off from training and feeling rather chilled, we all got back aboard the coach ready for whatever was waiting for us. The flight home would be in the morning and we were all looking forward to the operation in Afghanistan, whatever it was going to be.

The flight home had to stop off and refuel in Bahrain. The only drama with that was that we were not allowed to leave the aircraft wearing military clothing, so it was a scramble to get together a tracksuit top or a pair of sports bottoms. I managed to scrimp a few things together.

Well at least I looked okay, the only place to go was a bar. We had been briefed not to drink alcohol, and when we sneaked to the bar, we found everyone else there drinking, so what was the point in the brief?

After a short stay we made our way back to the departure lounge. The security surrounding our party was a little over the top. We were being ushered onto the coaches in double time speed. It looked and felt like they wanted us to be on our journey.

The flight was again long and boring. I wanted it to be as short as possible. I reckoned that if I tried to sleep most of the way, then it wouldn't take as long. Well it is true, when we landed back in the UK, it was weird. This time we landed at RAF Brize. There was hardly anyone there to meet us, it was like a ghost town. But then again why would there be anyone to meet us.

The old rumours had already started going to and from the battalion that we were doing outstanding work with 3 Para. We had now earned the respect of the guys and we were enjoying how they carried out their business. It was more relaxed than our own unit. Everyone had a professional attitude and the bullshit that goes with everyday battalion life was less than what we were used to.

All in all everyone was a winner; the main emphasis was on shooting and fitness, and that was quite apparent when you looked around the unit. They were in fact a lot more robust than our own unit. They cared that little bit more about the end product. Okay, they looked well groomed, but on the other hand, when it came to soldiering nothing else mattered, they wanted to win the battle, and nothing was going to get in their way, we wanted this feeling to carry on back at our own unit, if only!

The next few days back at Colchester would be on immediate notice to move, with all our kit washed and now re-packed for deployment, it was now just a matter of time until we were on the coaches and driving for the flight. Most of us knew deep down inside that these next few days could very well be our last time to speak to family and have a beer or just do what we wanted, so we did not let ourselves down.

For the next three days, we just went on parade at ten o'clock each day for a head count and followed by keep your mobile phones on troops and do not leave Colchester, oh, and if any of you turn up drunk for the flight, you will feel my full force on top of you, that was not what any of us wanted from Spence.

He was quite a hard guy. The drama we had was it was the second of April and one of the guys' birthdays, so we had a few beers to celebrate, then on the third of April, it was someone else's birthday. When we returned on the fifth of April slightly drunk, Spence was going to kill us.

I had to explain that last night was my birthday. At first he did not believe a word I was saying. Until he got out the platoon nominal role and there it was a list of birthdays (DOB)—April 2, 3, 4, 6, and 8—he was starting to get pissed off now.

He got the whole platoon on parade and explained that we had come a long way and that he was proud to be leading such guys into battle and he did not want us to let ourselves down.

You are all adults, warriors amongst men, big boys' rules, you turn up too drunk for my parade, and you're on the first bus back to battalion, which was all he had to say. We did not want to return to our unit, especially after all the training we had gone through to get us to this stage.

After two false starts and driving towards the aircraft on edge, only to be told not this time turn the coach around, there is a problem with the aircraft, we were all starting to get fed up, then the call came,

'It's a go.' We now felt the hairs on the back of our necks stick up, it was now the real deal.

Every single one of us was more than ready for what lay ahead. The main thing was getting to a place that had not even been built yet. It was called Bastion camp, strategically placed out in the middle of the desert. We landed in Kabul first, where we dropped off some passengers, then it was off to Camp Bastion.

It was going to be our home for the next. Well, to be honest, we did not know for how long. We just knew we were probably going to have to build it. We had already had some of our guys fly out on the advance party. It was Luke, my section second in command, he had been out here for a week already and had helped set up a few tents, one of which was our accommodation.

He was there with a vehicle and the colour sergeant (CQ). We had a chat then we drove at 2 kilometres an hour to the new camp. The runway itself was just a strip of desert that had been soaked with water to prevent the fine sand from ruining the aircraft engines.

We got off the four-tonner and made our way down black plastic flooring. This had been placed down to stop everyone from kicking up the sand, and after only an hour or two, we were sick of tasting the sand. It was dust-like particles; the smokers amongst the platoon were finding it extremely difficult to catch a breath.

The fitness was soon on the go, with the acclimatisation part, and that only took a few days before we stopped running. It was impossible to run as a squad due to the fine sand. It just became a dust cloud and we could not see 5 metres in front of us. We started to run in groups of two or three, it made a lot more sense.

The boss spent the next two days on briefings at the Joint Operations Cell (JOC), and it wasn't long before maps needed to be waterproofed and marked up. I was given over twenty maps to sort out, as we did not know what areas we were in fact going to. We had to spend time on every map. It was all getting serious very quick.

Spence had taken the sections' second in command with him plus one other from each section to collect stores and ammunition. The amount he brought back was colossal. It was enough to start a small war. We would be self-sufficient if caught out by enemy forces, so that was one less thing to worry about.

The thing that was starting to annoy me was the fact that I couldn't get a wash properly, or even have a decent shave. The showers came in the shape of bottled water, so it was a case of man the hell up. The next few days in bastion were fast and furious, with mine awareness training, zeroing and Arabic lessons, along with our own patrolling skills and basic field craft, we were very busy over the next few days.

When we got a spare minute, it was trying to work out where to find the medical tent, or the armourer, well certain things you keep to yourself, but a spare gas plug and cylinder for my rifle was top of my list. Along with any spare First Field Dressings (FFD), these would turn out to be life savers in the right situation.

Then came the lessons on Rules of Engagement (ROE) and the flying lawyer. They wanted to get drilled into us that they were in fact on our side. If we needed them after an incident, then they would make their way to our location, or if needs be, we would make our way to them.

It was now 10 May and orders had been received that we were moving as soon as possible. Myself, Robbie, and Davy started to get amongst the guys. Pressure was starting to build on the platoon. It was natural, especially when you did not know where you were being sent to.

The next day we were flown by Chinook to Forward Operating Base (FOB) Price, this was a small camp on the outskirts of Gereshk. Our task was to take over the running of the base from A-Company 3 Para, they themselves had been tasked to move somewhere else. The camp was very small with a super Sanger that overlooked the area for kilometres, a joint British-American forces base with a lot of history.

We worked out which section was going on notice to move first. We had to track down the Motor Transport representative (MT rep) and find out which vehicles were ours, in case we got crashed out to deal with an incident.

We got the drivers within the platoon to sort that out. The radio operator in the platoon took a few guys to help him with the communication side of things, while the boss is off jacking up some more Arabic lessons. It isn't long before we have section tents, this makes it a lot easier to admin the section, and I have two good

Non-Commissioned Officers (NCO) within my section, I already have a plan on how to get the best out of them.

If Spence allows me, I would like O,Driscol to do all the administration side of things within the section. He has OCD, and to be honest, that's the type of NCO that I need. Someone who is passionate about his work, he is very reliable and dependable when it comes to timings. On the other hand, he does tend to get frustrated, but I would never swap him in a million years.

Then we have Luke, he is a nightmare when it comes to timings and admin, in fact his admin is terrible. When we told him to pack his room up back in Fort George, he threw his television out the top-floor window in recce block, that's what he called packing away kit.

However I must say, putting all that to one side, he was a great commander. I had learnt to trust him while in contact. We knew how each other worked when I was moving in to take the last position.

I did not even have to ask for the rates of fire to be lifted. He was already doing it, a very trustworthy commander, so I wanted him as my section 2 i/c out on the ground and O,Driscol as my section 2 i/c back in camp.

I knew it was wishful thinking, but Spence was never going to go for it. I did pluck up the courage to ask him, only to wish that I had of kept my thoughts to myself. Spence had a way with words that made you wish you had put together a defence. When you digested his response, he always had a point and was usually right.

The boss and Spence had come up with a cunning plan. The platoon was going to be split while in camp. It would be broken into two multiples. This would give maximum rest to the guys and make sure the work was evenly spread amongst the guys. It was eight hours on guard, followed by eight hours on Quick Reaction Force (QRF), then the eagerly awaited eight hours' rest.

My multiple were in fact on QRF first. We had drawn the short straw, but it meant we would get to sleep at a decent time. The boss had sent Ralf back to the platoon area and requested the commanders all meet at the operations room. The only drama was that we didn't know how to get there. We asked Ralf to guide us all there. He had nothing better to do, he so walked us there, and it was through camp and past the pathfinder platoon.

As soon as we got there, we were introduced to certain personnel that were part of our company group. We were then given spot maps of Gereshk town centre. It had been colour coded for easy pinpointing and reference points. This was the main map that we need while here in Gereshk. After a brief and current threat update, we were given a dos and don'ts brief for the camp life.

We were told to stay away from the pathfinders' compound, as they get rather upset. The US Rangers were living across from them and ate in our cookhouse. With exception to delta force and other departments and agencies (ODA), well, they ate in their own cookhouse.

I found myself having to get Robbie to take my maps back for O,Driscol to mark up and fablon. It wasn't the fact that I was passing the buck. I had just been given a duty in the operations room from 1900 hours until 2300 hours, so it didn't make sense to keep the maps with me.

By the time I had come off duty, everyone in the section would be asleep, and I didn't want to have to turn the light on.

The next day we were on QRF. This time my duty was not until eight at night, so I had all day to catch up on either sleep or personal admin.

I got to phone home, the time difference was a few hours, but it was nice to hear a friendly voice. My parents were doing well, they were still making the garden nice for when they had visitors. It also kept their minds occupied and off the fact that I was out here.

Well, if this was going to be home for a while, we might as well make it look nice. I detailed Luke to go on the search for wood. We wanted to have seats and a table out the back of our tent. I had ideas of a relaxing area, somewhere that I could read a book and sunbathe at the same time.

It wasn't long before Luke returned with decking. I couldn't stop laughing at what he managed to find. He was pretty pleased with himself to say the least. We started straight away in placing the wood down. It looked good, the drama now was that once Luke gets his teeth into something, there is no letting go.

The garden, well, it started to look like a garden and was now taking shape. Everyone was adding a piece of magic every day. It even had a sign with stones shaped into a shamrock.

I managed to get every member of the section to hand over $20 each. I put this all together and bought a fridge for our tent. It was only two feet tall, but it was pure bliss, it held up to fifty tins of pop, and when it started to go empty, we had a roster of whose turn it was to replenish the fridge. This was one of the few things that actually worked the whole entire tour.

It was now 17 May and my niece's birthday. I would try and give her a ring to wish her happy birthday but I doubt I would get the chance. The boss asked to see all commanders in the cookhouse after breakfast. He explained that we were going on our first patrol into Gereshk at 0930 and we would be back in camp no later than (NLT) 1300 hours, well, if everything went smoothly, that is.

I returned to my tent and asked Luke and O,Driscol to assemble the troops for a quick brief. They were sitting outside the tent already. They came in while I gave a few minor details.

I explained that we were going on patrol. That was followed by a mighty roar of thank God, okay, guys, weapons oiled up. 'Yip.' Water bottles and camel backs filled. 'Yip.' Radio and countermeasures batteries all fresh. 'Yip.'

Maps marked up. 'Yip.' Right, we are going out for approximately two and a half hours, it's scorching hot out there. Make sure you all stay hydrated throughout the patrol, buddy, buddy, watch your spacing moving through built-up areas.

Luke, you should have the stretcher and medical kit, keep it at the top of your daysack. Make sure every man carries night-vision equipment, as we do not want to be caught off guard.

The patrol was very testing. It got rid of the cobwebs. We knew our fitness was of a good standard, but the heat made it a lot worse than we had expected. There were signs of dehydration in some of the guys, but overall, it was a learning curve.

The spot maps were making it very easy to navigate. The locals seemed a little curious why we were patrolling around their neighbourhood. Tomorrow will be a lot better, and we will take on-board lessons learnt from today.

Well today is 18 May and only our second patrol. We have taken on board how yesterday's patrol had panned out. So today will be a lot different, well, for a start, we are travelling by vehicle. The other platoon dropped us off on the outskirts of Gereshk.

It would be another challenging day, due to the heat. Today was going to be over 40 degrees. We were all hydrated enough to last the length of the patrol. I just did not know how we were going to react in a contact situation. I wondered if we would be able to go in hot pursuit of enemy forces, only time would tell.

We found out later that day the Taliban had fought two fierce battles with coalition and Afghan forces in the southern part of Afghanistan, leaving thirteen police and one Canadian soldier and nearly sixty insurgents dead. British gunship helicopters and Canadian artillery were called in to lend close air support during one of the clashes, which is only a few weeks before NATO-led peacekeepers are due to take over.

The patrol had again taken its toll on the guys. We were now on guard, and to be honest, it's what we had needed. It gave the platoon a chance to sort out blisters that had been gained on patrol.

We had settled into a routine now and I was actually starting to get a little bored with this sequence we were doing. I had been hearing that A-Company 3 Para was getting into a few battles and getting to close and engage with enemy forces, that's what I wanted to do.

Spence heard me talking about this and was not pleased. He made it quite clear. 'Be careful what you wish for, Speedy, you might just get more than you bargain for.' He was right as per usual.

Word came back from the daily briefing that the French had four soldiers killed in action (KIA) and two more had been reported missing in action (MIA). The police station in Gereshk had been attacked by the Taliban, there had also been a blue on blue; the Afghan Army had opened fire onto an American Humvee.

This place that is known as Gereshk and quiet is starting to hot up. The insurgents are moving into key areas throughout the village and it's only a matter of time before we get completely smashed by them. They have superior numbers than us and know the terrain very well. Let's just hope we are ready when they decide to strike.

We gathered at the back of my tent for a quick chat. The commanders amongst the platoon knew that deep down we were ready for anything that came our way. The only problem was morale was slowly going downhill, all we seemed to get from the briefs was bad news.

The Taliban killed six here, they killed nine there, so many KIA, there was never any good news, and it was making the guys nervous.

Another day started in Gereshk with gunfire in the distance, personnel running past you with their full fighting order on, word came back that the pathfinder platoon were in contact. The QRF platoon were on stand-by to be crashed out and assist. There were also three other contacts just north of our location, not sure who it involved.

B-Company had now been flown out to reinforce the troops that were in contact with the Taliban. The battle group that day had nine casualties, and it had not been a great day all around for the brigade.

Hopefully tomorrow will bring some good news and a boost that is needed for the fighting troops, some mail would be good, I don't think anyone has had a letter in the platoon yet. The boss wanted to speak to everyone again in the cookhouse, so we all went in and grabbed a seat. He was already there with Spence, and he told us about a recce patrol that we have been tasked to carry out near a school in the middle of Gereshk.

I suppose it got us out of camp for the day, and it might even help us build up an intelligence picture. The platoon had not been to that part of the town before, so I was sure it would again be just like the rest of patrols.

It started off well, the movement of the guys across open ground was very good as per usual; 3 section, which was my section, moved into secure (Papa 11) so the boss and his tactical group could move freely without the possibility of enemy fire onto his call sign.

Robbie then moved his section through mine and was now providing a satellite to the east. This would make it very hard to take on our call sign. We were covering each other's blind spot, and all those rehearsals were now coming into good use.

Davy then moved his section through Robbie's call sign and proceeded to secure Romeo 1 and Romeo 2. Once he had completed that task, he was to satellite out to the east of the school, this would free up Robbie and he would be free to move onto the next task.

The patrol seemed to go well. The boss commented on the movement over ground, the radio chat was mentioned by Spence. He wanted more situation reports, and if a call sign was not receiving or sending messages, then another call sign is to relay messages to them. He wanted things tweaked to a fine art.

He did give us a pat on the back. He knew we were all working hard, and especially running the sections rather well.

Once back in from the patrol and the debrief was over, it was time to relax. I gave my brother and sister a quick call. They told me they had heard on the news that we had now lost fifteen soldiers within the battle group.

I knew we had lost a few, but I was not counting. When I came off the phone, I went and had a shower and just lay on my bed for a while. I couldn't even be bothered to open the fridge and grab a cold tin of pop.

The next day, 24 May, was spent carrying out personal admin, obviously with a few Arabic lessons thrown in. I now knew key phrases that would come in handy—'lasuna porta', hands in the air. I thought it might come in handy one day.

The boss gave us a heads-up that we would be taking over the Immediate Response Team (IRT). This was not a job that any of us wanted to do. It was a job that no soldier could ever do and feel the same again after. Basically we would only ever fly out to collect fellow soldiers who had been involved in enemy activity. They would be wounded in some sort of way.

There was always a chance of a Non-Battle Injury (NBI), but that was just wishful thinking. We had to have a member of the platoon sitting within the Joint Operations Cell 24/7. He would find out what had happened radio us back at the tent. By the time the pilots had started the helicopter engines, our guys would be on the runway waiting to board.

We had only really settled into the role, still finding our feet, when we got crashed out to recover a pinz vehicle by Chinook, then dropped off at FOB Robinson to help reinforce it. Well, we were in fact meant to be on IRT, now we were in an FOB protecting it from attack. We only had our belt kit with us.

The next day we were still in FOB Robinson. This was an old American base, set right at the foot of the Sangin valley, the place known as death valley. This was where the Russians had lost 100,000 soldiers during the Ten-Year War, trying to defeat the Taliban.

Now I had a platoon in a deserted base and it didn't look good. God knows when we were going to leave this place. It was very vulnerable from attack.

We started to break the platoon down into fire teams. This meant the sections were halved into four man teams. It gave us a lot of scope to cover more ground. The only drama was that we would be spread over a vast distance, and we began to carry out sentry duties at each of our locations.

I noticed that there were ISO containers dotted around the base, all of which had their doors opened. I went for a quick look and discovered that they were full of American rations.

Meals Ready to Eat (MRE), I spread the news across the net and one guy from each location arrived to take some back to their position. It was a good find, when we all started looking deeper into the ISO, there were crates of Coke, Sprite, Diet Coke, the list was endless, and it was like the shops back in the UK.

We surely would not starve over the period we had to spend defending this place from attack. There was enough food and drink for a company group.

All we had to do now was find somewhere to store it. I know I wanted to have a couple of MREs packed away for emergency rations.

We stayed there throughout the night, it went without incident. If anything we should have been extracted back to Bastion for IRT duties, it was all going pear-shaped. We then received word across the net that an Afghan army outpost was going to be attacked tonight by a strong Taliban force.

Chapter 3

FIRST INTO SANGIN

Well, the orders were it was going to take place over the next twenty-four hours and we were to make our way to that location and to conduct an offensive operation. We drove there by snatch vehicle, not the most robust of vehicles, but at least it got us from A to B. It was only a short drive from FOB Robinson, so we waited until it was getting dark and made our way there.

We pulled up at the side of the road. There were old Russian tanks parked up rusting away, the compound that we were going to enter had old gates on it. They were 10 feet in height and wide enough to drive a lorry through. Each wagon had dismounted their troops, so we could react if fired upon. Someone opened the gates to let us in.

The vehicles now started to space out within the compound. Myself, Davy, and Robbie went with the boss. He was given his orders and then proceeded to take all three of us commanders with him. He climbed up onto the compound roof and started to dictate where he wanted our sections to take up arcs of fire.

He pointed over to the western side of the compound and told me that he wanted my section to cover from seven o'clock through to one o'clock. I was happy with that. But just as I was going to move across the roof to check my arcs, Robbie moved in front of me. He said, 'That's not bad, Speedy.'

He walked over to have a look at where his arcs would overlap mine, then there was a loud bang and Robbie disappeared. The roof had collapsed beneath him. Robbie had fallen a good 15 feet onto his back. He was not moving. The boss was in shock. We looked down through the hole Robbie had left, and we could hear his cries of pain.

This was not going well. I climbed down to see if he was okay. I needed a medic, our combat medic technician (CMT) came across to check him. Robbie had only gone and fallen into a toilet. Now he stank of shit. The medic made us strap Robbie to a stretcher.

He had damaged his back and needed to be casualty evacuated back to Bastion for proper medical attention. Until that time came, he was to lie still on a stretcher and hopefully not scream. We gave him painkillers. I also handed him L109 grenades.

He was only to use these if we began to be overrun by the Taliban. I prayed that it didn't happen. The intelligence was coming in fast across to our platoon, and they were now within 400 metres of our position.

The boss told me to take my section on a patrol outside of the compound and walk the 150 metres up the hill to the old petrol station and report back what I could see. My section, including myself, was feeling a little bit nervous to say the least, but an order was an order.

I gave a quick brief to Luke who was also not pleased. O,Driscol was already annoyed at being sent out to be slaughtered like lambs. The patrol went without incident, our night-vision goggles were scanning the area like men possessed, and I noticed movement on our left-hand side.

I ordered the section to go firm and listen. I could see something moving. I got on the net and asked if there were any friendly call signs in the area. I was told NO. So I fired a flare up at an angle. It ignited and lit up the American special forces, who had not made themselves known to our own forces, and now I had compromised them. I could hear them shouting and screaming at me.

But that's what you get if you don't inform others of your whereabouts; we got up, began to space out, and made our way best speed back into the compound. I informed the boss of what had happened. He seemed pleased that we were back in one piece. I then took my section to cover arcs, the boss then told us to make a sentry list for each section location. This meant we could start to get some rest. We now slept when and wherever we could.

That night seemed to drag by. Robbie had fallen asleep at last, but only when he knew he was out of immediate danger.

The following day we were told again to move locations. This was becoming the normal thing to do, it felt like we were chasing a fire fight. We were told to move to the district chief's house. This was in Sangin, one of the most dangerous places in Afghanistan and a hotbed of Taliban activity.

This time the intelligence had been that four hundred Taliban fighters were making their way to Sangin DC, this was going to be the battle that we had wanted. Spence, for the first time, was just wondering what the hell was going on—were we being used as bait by task force Helmand? It felt like we were just being thrown at everything that moved.

Before we could drive into Sangin, we had to go to the HLS at FOB Robinson and wait for the helicopter to arrive. We had to get Robbie extracted back to Bastion. It took thirty minutes to arrive, but I was glad that Robbie was safe.

It felt weird, moving through Sangin. There were no people about, the buildings looked unoccupied, the roads were in a terrible state, and to be honest, it gave me a bad feeling. I pointed out to some of the others a building near the bridge, it said Taliban headquarters above the door, then it had writing in Pashtun, the local language.

We drove over a narrow bridge, this time we had more dismounted guys than normal. The place was deserted, the building looked like it was being built. We parked up our snatches in reverse order, it forded us some sort of protection, but not much.

We all dismounted. The boss gave a set of quick battle orders to the platoon. We entered that house. Davey took his section up onto the roof, and he placed his men out then gave them arcs of fire. They had a sniper rifle along with the 51 mm mortar. My section was tasked to stay in the middle floor, and I split the section up so we could cover three separate directions and cover the rooms.

Getty was told to keep his men on the bottom floor. He would remain there throughout the battle, and his orders were to deal with the casualties, if we took any. Ammunition resupplies to both sections and most importantly to protect the vehicles, thank God, I didn't get his task, as it was a lot to deal with. No sooner had we spread out, the messages coming across the radio were that the Taliban had eyes on the building we were in, 'Well, at least one of us could see the other.'

We started to place our night-vision sights on. The guys on the roof could now see a snake of vehicle lights in the distance, and they were approximately only 1 kilometre away from us. The boss got onto the net and asked if we could change our rules of engagement to card 429 (war fighting) and was ordered to remain on card Alpha until fired upon.

This was not what we had wanted to hear. What was wrong with pre-empting the strike? We were in Sangin valley, Helmand province. Sometimes you have to love our idiotic government, and they make these decisions from their nice offices in London.

We were starting to get a little nervous. The lights were getting closer, now only 500 metres away, then the lights all went out. We were scanning our night-vision sights. We could see all the vehicles. But no Taliban, it was a nervous time, all I could hear was O,Driscol moaning, 'Speedy, I have left my night vision in the back of the vehicle, I need to go and get it.' 'NO, OD, leave it there, it will be daylight soon.'

I could hear him cursing himself, with all the confusion and rushing around and making sure everyone else was okay, he had left it on the backseat. Not to worry, the boss was now speaking to a Forward Observation Officer (FOO) in Fob Robinson. He wanted them to fire up illume so we could see what was happening. The FOO then started arguing that he wanted to send the fire mission. My boss was saying he could give it more accurately. It became another bun fight over the radio. Everyone wanted to take the glory for the work of someone else and with the thought of being able to say 'I fired the first fire mission' was obviously on his mind.

Then the FOO who was based up at Fob Robinson fired the illume. He got his grids wrong and fired it above our location. This now highlighted every single soldier on the roof, what an idiot that FOO was. Why don't people listen, if anything he had now placed us in grave danger.

It wasn't long before we heard two barrels being fired from Fob Robinson, then we heard the shell go over our heads. We all got onto our belt buckles and faced into the area of threat. The illume was up over the top of the building, the platoon were all pissed off. Not only were we all confined to this building, everyone could now see the guys spread out on the roof.

Getty had a laugh at this stage as the job he had been given, not only was keeping him from getting some trigger time with the enemy, he was now not the one lit up like a Christmas tree.

I was spending my time walking between my sections asking if anyone could see anything. The guys were all sitting well back from the window area scanning like mad, nothing seen so far. Just as I was about to go and sit down, I could still hear O,Driscol complaining about his night vision. Well, at least that brought a smile to my face. Spence was also on the roof, he and Spidey were firing illume into the suspected area. After three hours the Taliban decided to withdraw from the area.

That night seemed to pass without incident, just as well really. We now knew that we had to stay on card Alpha; we knew that the FOO based up at Fob Robinson was a complete idiot.

This was already starting to become an operation like no other. We had so far been moved all over the battlefield trying to interdict Taliban movement. We had been close to getting overrun on two separate occasions now. The only thing that had stopped us was luck, but that was bound to run out soon.

By this stage the platoons Bergans had arrived by helicopter and were at Fob Robinson. We took a chance by sending two snatch vehicles and a few guys to collect them. No sooner had we got onto the 611 Main Supply Route (MSR) than the radio message was to return to the platoon house. This was the new name that we decided to give to our building. It would forever be known as the platoon house.

The activity and movement over to our east was very alarming. We spent that night like many more to come, on edge not knowing what was around the next corner.

Today is 1 June, we have been tasked again to take a drive up to Fob Robinson, and we were being moved back to Gereshk. I'm sure there were reasons for this sudden change. We felt a little relieved once we had gotten inside the FOB. The only problem was the fact that we didn't have long enough to relax. In the distance we could see a Chinook helicopter making its way to our location.

We then got told to get into two lines (known as chalks) and sit next to the HLS. The chopper came in and turned to face the re-entrant, the door gunner was looking slightly alarmed. We ran on the back of it, not being able to see where the hell we were going. The down draft from the rotor blades had thrown up that much dust and debris, it was a matter of holding the guy in front to see where he was going.

Once we had all strapped ourselves in using the seatbelts, I could feel my heart pounding, it was going to explode. The amount of weight in my bergan was unbearable. With the water, ammunition, and now extra rations, it needed to be filtered and all the non-mission-essential kit off loaded.

I sat there just staring at the rest of the guys. Around my mouth I had hard pieces of dust, it felt like dried blood. I tried to lick it off, but need to use the bottled water. I could see that my combats were soaked in sweat now. This was becoming routine now, I was getting used to wearing dirty combats.

The flight was just what we needed. It gave us all some time to have a sleep, even if it was for only thirty minutes. The time was golden. We got dropped off on the HLS and walked straight to our tent. It felt good to be back in what was now home.

We had been given that night off to carry out administration. Most of mine was done in the first hour of being in the tent, as all good soldiers very well know. The first thing I did was to strip and clean my weapon system. It needed a pull through and oiling, the barrel was now full of sand and dirt.

Once I was happy with the weapon, I gave it light oil then placed it in a bag; this would at least keep the dust off it while I was in camp.

With an early night on the cards, I found the whole section were actually in bed at the same time as me that night. The last man in our tent always got the job of turning out the light. Once the tent was in darkness, I could hear someone laughing. He made everyone laugh. I asked what he was laughing at. Luke then said, 'Sorry, Speedy, but O,Driscol complaining the other night keeps making me laugh.'

'What do you mean, Luke?'

'Well, when he said, "Ah noo . . . shit, I've no night vision, where are they coming from, someone tell me", I really wanted to laugh out loud, but because of the situation I felt it wasn't the right time, but now it is.' He was right, now was the right time.

We could all hear O,Driscol moaning in the background. Shortly after that, we all fell asleep exhausted. I had a dream that we had gotten into a fire fight with the local militia, and it had not been a good outcome. That was one of my worst fears, being left isolated with very few rounds of ammunition left.

The next morning the guys were back on guard duty. It wasn't arduous work, it was just long hours rotating around built-up positions dotted every 50-60 metres around Gereshk camp. There were log books in each position, these needed to be maintained by the troops on duty. It also was a record of who was on what sentry and for how long. This kept the guys awake along with the fact that the enemy would in fact kill them if found monging it on duty.

Being killed was always a good incentive to stay awake and work hard.

We were only on guard for a few hours when 8 Platoon came over to relieve us; a guy called Grovesy informed me that we had been tasked to go on a long patrol the next morning so we had been given the rest of the day to sort out admin.

Grovesy was trying to wind me up. We got on well with each other. There was mutual respect. He was a corporal in the Parachute Regiment, known as the elite. Everything about him oozed professionalism. If I wanted to know something about the military, he was the guy who would know the answer.

The boss came into our section's tent and gave the commanders a brief on the patrol that we had been tasked to carry out. The brief started off by explaining what had been happening within our own AOR, A-Company 3 Para had been involved in a deliberate operation to our west. The Pathfinders (PF) had been ambushed by the Taliban. This resulted in one of their vehicles being badly damaged.

The machine gun platoon had also been involved in hostilities with enemy forces. Today the count was only five Taliban KIA. It had been a good day for ISAF, no one killed within the battle group, a few casualties here and there but nothing serious.

We knew what was happening during the patrol. Our job was to secure a crossing point for a convoy to roll through without incident. It was vital that this convoy got to each location in one piece. It was carrying ammunition, water, spare parts for weapons, and so on, the list was endless, and this wasn't just for our own location, it was for all camps along the MSR.

The radio messages were being relayed from call sign to call sign on the progress of the convoy. We were sending steers so it could not get hit by enemy fire. We spent six hours on that one location, almost too long. We never liked to stay static for long periods of time, especially in a place like this.

Once the convoy had passed through our location, we collapsed our cordon and made our way back to the camp. It was a few kilometres, but no one seemed to mind, especially as we could have a rest properly this time and the fact that we would be in time for dinner was an added bonus.

On return from tasking, there were a lot of contractors near the HLS. I could see they had flat pack buildings and electronic equipment still sitting there in bubble wrap. We were too tired to help them move it, and by the looks and size of them, I didn't think they would need our help. It turned out to be the internet system starting to be installed. This would surely lift morale through the roof.

This was now the turn of 8 Platoon. They had been given a task to patrol through the busy streets of Gereshk. We could hear how the patrol was going over, it was going rather well until their fill had dropped in the radio. The normal routine for this would have been discussed prior to deploying out on the ground. They would get our platoon to drive out to a Rendezvous (RV) at a specific time. The only problem was, they were now in contact, they could not get us, and it was now an intermittent message, with static and white noise.

They managed to send an Emergency Close Air Support report (ECAS), and two Apache gunships were now engaging positions in order for the platoon to break contact and return to our location.

My platoon were a little disappointed that they had missed out of such a nice contact. Spence did not like the attitude within the platoon. He quickly rounded us up and began to give his advice. 'Listen, troops, I don't like what am seeing within the platoon, let me tell you this. Don't go around moaning that you haven't had any action yet, because it's coming and it's coming right at you, in fact you will be begging for it to stop once it starts.

'Remember this, be careful what you wish for, it might just come true.' When 8 Platoon returned from their patrol, you could sense an air of achievement throughout the platoon. They knew they had a lucky escape. They had now exchanged rounds with the enemy and made it back for tea and biscuits, they had done well.

The internet had now been installed, no sooner was it up than the queue was starting to grow, and I would wait until I had come off duty. It would be late here, but I knew that everyone would be in bed that was the best time to send an email anyway.

The next day I was asked to go to the operations room, there was an officer who briefed me on what to expect on my next patrol. Apparently the Gereshk patrol later that day would be by our platoon. We would get dropped off by vehicle near to the town; the vehicles would remain on call throughout the duration of the patrol.

The only drama I could foresee was the fact that the British Broadcasting Corporation (BBC) would be part of the patrol. I was to wear a microphone on my shirt, they wanted to film what we did and see how we actually interacted with the locals, and it would be fun if nothing else.

After only an hour into the patrol, I stopped a white Toyota pick-up truck. I expected to see a family or someone with bad teeth smile back at me, but I did not expect to see four men with weapons. I cocked my rifle, pointed it at the driver, and was about to extract them from the vehicle when I heard one shout out that they were Afghan National Police (ANP). He was wearing civilian clothing with an AK-47 across his knees on the backseat.

After my initial shock of nearly putting a bullet into him, and totally forgetting I had a microphone on my combat shirt, the reporter was glad that it had ended peacefully. He had the footage that he needed for his news bulletin, and I had what I had needed, a nice little walk around the town.

When we returned to camp, we carried out some personal admin. O,Driscol was already sorting out the sections radio and countermeasure batteries. Luke had taken it amongst himself to go around the section and replenish everyone's water. The only thing we need to do now was clean the weapons. We did that anyway; it was ritual to complete that task before anything else was done.

We decided as we had some time to ourselves that we would have a game of poker. Robbie, Dougal, and Luke joined in; we each placed $10 in the middle of the table and played Texas hold 'em, that would mean that the winner walked away with $40, whoever won would buy a crate of pop for the fridge.

This time it was Luke that won the money. He decided we in fact needed 5 crates of pop, so he put one in the fridge and two below each of our beds. Luke was generous that way, someone who was a little bit mad, but you loved him for it.

The next day was one with waited anticipation. England was playing Paraguay at football, a lot of the guys wanted to watch it, the problem was it wasn't possible for everyone to see it. We tried our best to rotate the guys through the welfare tent, the result was a respectful 1-0 to England.

We got to know another operation quite well while we were there. It was called 'OP MINIMISE', this would be on most days. It was when we had taken a casualty on the battlefield or a fatality had occurred within the battle group, all means of communication were cut off to the outside world.

No one was given that opportunity to tell anyone of what had happened before the family had been informed first.

What had happened was an Unmanned Aerial Vehicle (UAV) had crash-landed in Sangin of all places. It had no vital intelligence on it, as it gives live feed and it's made of nothing special. Yet again a wrong decision was made to send troops out and retrieve it, in a place like Sangin that should never have been an option. It had resulted in two soldiers from the Royal Horse Artillery (RHA) being wounded in action (WIA) and one of the soldiers being Killed in Action (KIA).

Well, at least I had now served enough time in Afghanistan to receive my Herrick medal. We were all now past the twenty-eight days mark and still going strong.

Today being 12 June we went on a forty-eight-hour patrol. We would deploy by snatch vehicle along with the machine gun platoon. They were going to escort us out into the middle of the desert; we had to drive around the outskirts of Gereshk to get to our RV.

The journey out to our new location was very long, with all the stopping and starting, and due to it being a busy time of the day, we had to have dismounts to walk us through some of the Vulnerable Points (VP). We eventually made our way out of sight of any habitation or buildings. We passed a 60-foot mast; this was a fantastic reference point for any navigational errors.

We started to park the vehicles in a circular harbour. This gave us maximum protection from any possible attack, and my platoon had dismounted and were not facing out towards potential threats. I had given my section arcs of fire and then were overlapping into the other two sections arcs, so we had that covered.

Spence then told us to take it in turns with making a brew and getting nosebag on the go. Once we had that all squared, the boss sent a runner to collect me for a brief. That's the weird thing about the army, even knowing he could have turned around and spoken softly, and I would have heard him, he still got someone to get up and come and get me.

I walked across to the bonnet of his snatch and started to get a complex brief about taking out a standing patrol. I was to take my section out towards the outskirts of a village called Zumbelay. It was renowned for its non-compliance with the West.

Every single time US soldiers got over a certain northing on the map, they were contacted by the Taliban, and it was like a hornet's nest. A very strong Taliban resistance lived within the village, and they were not going to let anyone enter their homes without a fight.

I went and briefed my section that we would be leaving in fifteen minutes. They had already been fed and watered, and that was one less thing to worry about. We got our kit together and proceeded to the boss. We told him we were now leaving on task. We all gave a quick communication check and left the vehicle harbour.

I made sure that our spacing was sorted and that we all knew the direction of travel. I got Craig to check pace, just in case the weather changed for the worst. Zac was also checking pacing; when you want to work out the distance of travel, it's best to have more than one, it helps with a squad average.

By eight o'clock we had made it to the area of over watch, the only drama was that we had lost communication with the rest of the platoon. Lost communications in a place like this was dangerous. I got up and moved around trying to get the boss or any friendly call sign. This was starting to get to me. We should return to the harbour, it would be embarrassing to return empty handed.

So I got the spyglass set up by Luke and began to scan the target area that I had been briefed to do. We stayed there for approximately fifteen minutes. I had at least something to return with.

We packed up and began to make our way back the same route that we had travelled earlier that night. We still had no comms with the patrol. I moved up towards that mast that we had passed on the way to the harbour, and finally I managed to get the boss. He gave strict instructions to burn the rubbish that they had left at the harbour, then head east towards them.

I was starting to get frustrated with this whole mess. We arrived back at where the harbour used to be, only to find four empty ration boxes and a pile of rubbish, bigger still, I didn't have any friendly call signs to help me out if I was to get into trouble.

All I had was a six-man section and willpower. We were moving across the desert looking for a convoy of vehicles. My comms were total down. How the hell were we meant to find anyone?

We continued to move for another hour. After that I heard a faint message across the net. It said move towards the Infrared (IR) light. I got the whole section to put on NVGS, we were now all standing on the side of a hill, looking in every direction, neither of us could see anything that resembled a convoy or even any IR lights. It was becoming very dodgy. We headed towards the low ground. We would give one last-ditch effort to find the call sign.

O,Driscol was getting nervous. He had every right to be. We had now walked past the place that we had been over watching from. The village was getting closer as we approached it. I closed the guys in for a brief—right, troops it's about 10 kilometres back to camp, my plan is to get past this village in one piece and head towards the Afghan National Army (ANA) checkpoint. From there I will try and get comms, if all else fails, we patrol back to Fob price. Anyone got any questions?

There was a pause. Everyone was now pissed off. As we were moving past the village, I could hear dogs barking. Just as the last man was moving through, O,Driscol fired a round at the dog, now there was more than one dog barking.

I turned and could see lights and generators being turned on. I made the decision to run the section out of sight from anyone. We moved in fire teams across the open ground.

We finally reached the main road. I could see the checkpoint ahead. I got a signal. I spoke with the boss, I explained what had happened and told him what I was doing. If he wanted me, then he was to bring the vehicles to our location, I was not being messed about.

I had briefed the guys to split into fire teams and face the checkpoint. I was going to approach it with my rifle in the air. I would speak Arabic to them and inform them I was a Britannia soldier. If they fired at me, well, it was up to Luke and O,Driscol what they would do next. I had instructed them to open fire.

Fortunately they welcomed me with open arms. It was a relief for everyone in the section, and I got the section to close in, but kept them in fire teams just in case. The ANA were well-known for corruption and working alongside the Taliban. We didn't have to wait long, I could see a convoy approach from the south, and they would not come into the ANA checkpoint.

They called us over to them. After being in good spirits and finally being able to relax, I started to feel my blood boil over. I wanted to know what idiot had made the decision to leave my call sign out in the open. I was starting to swear at the boss. He said he was only carrying out orders given to him.

I knew by his tone and body language that he was annoyed with someone for causing such a panic. I think he knew how close we had come to being killed. The village was now swarming with locals, and from what I could remember from the intelligence briefs, they were all surely Taliban fighters.

The vehicle convoy were still sitting static. All the top cover were observing alternative arcs and there seemed to be a lot of confusion on the radio, because the convoy had come to my location. It gave the pathfinder platoon no option but to use the route that we were supposed to take on return to base location.

We in return used their route back in. We had been driving for only 10 minutes when we heard 'CONTACT call sign MAYHEM'. They had used our route and had been ambushed on the way back into camp. Again we had been extremely lucky. It was fate that every time something was going wrong, there was actually as reason for it. I was starting to feel like a cat, and my nine lives were starting to be used up.

The pathfinder platoon had escaped without a single casualty. One of their vehicles had a lot of strike marks on it, but their morale was not even tested, in fact they seemed to enjoy it.

The contact near the village of Zumbelay had started to play on the OC's mind. He started to have meetings with the Special Forces commanders based next door from our own operations room. He wanted to show the surrounding villages that we were in fact a force to be reckoned with. A plan was put together to carry out a patrol into the village. This would take place once we had gathered as much intelligence as we possibly could.

The next night being 13 June was going to be one that I remembered forever. It started with Spence sitting on the end of my bed and telling me what the plan was. We were going out on patrol again, this time being dropped off on the outskirts of yet another village. But far enough away that the vehicle engines would not be heard. It seemed exciting stuff. He explained that after I was up and dressed, he would properly brief me.

I sorted myself out and went to Spence's tent. He had his belt kit emptied over one of the spare cot beds, and it looked like he was packing it again a certain way. He heard me come in and started to chat about how it would benefit him later that night. I was a little confused about what he was trying to say, though curious about what the plan to be was.

He began to tell me about a patrol into a village named Jonno. It was known for Taliban safe houses and enemy activity, and we were going to move the platoon into a position of over watch. They would move around the village, taking notes and logging all activity. We needed to gather as much intelligence as possible. It would be a starting block for the patrol into Zumbelay. We had to start somewhere.

This village Jonno was just one of many that we needed to get into and gain the trust of the locals. It would guarantee our safety if we need to extract into it from Zumbelay, and if we have already conducted a recce of the village and possible VPs, it would in fact prevent us from being channelled into a killing area.

Spence told me that once we had the platoon safely on the ground, we would move forward to an area of over watch, and then cut-off teams would move to pre-designated areas on the ground and remain there; four guys from my section would remain in reserve behind Spence and me.

We were going to put a screen around the village. Our task was to move forward under the cover of darkness. We would be wearing night-vision goggles and camouflage cream over our faces. This would help keep the shine from the moon hitting our faces and more importantly help us to keep stealth while moving.

We moved into position. All commands now being carried out by use of hand signals. Spence and I would not talk until the patrol was over. We knew hand signals for everything that we needed. In fact as we are not machines, we had both been rehearsing these in our tent.

He pointed to me and then placed his hand on his head. I nodded at him and moved to his position. I knelt down beside him, and he was applying cam cream to his neck. He pointed to his watch and then held his hand up at me with fingers spread. I knew we were moving in five minutes,

We carried out last-minute checks, all my pouches were closed. I was moving across the ground in light order, no helmet on my head, yet it was attached to my belt kit. We spaced out a little. There was only 10 metres between us now. When he knelt down, I knelt down and vice versa.

We were now moving forward in slow time, weapon up at the ready, a round was already in the chamber, just in case things got too hot. We moved forward beyond the trees and out into the open. I signalled back for the rest of my section to bound forward slightly. I wanted them close enough to provide support, but not too close as to compromise us.

I looked at Spence. He was hard to locate due to him moving into the shaded areas as he moved forward. I was moving slowly, almost ghost walking across the ground. I now had a compound wall behind me. I could hear my own heartbeat and my eyes were now sore, due to my straining to take in as much of the ground as possible.

We started to move up a street. There were small buildings to our left and right. We could see some shrubbery in the middle, and we moved to the extremities of the shrubs and began to move forward. I could see a small light on the side of the building. The last thing we needed now was a dog to start barking.

Spence stopped moving forward. He placed his thumb in the air and then held it upside down as to inform me of enemy. He then held up two fingers. I stopped, looked at him, then moved forward a further 5 metres. There they were, two men who were probably supposed to be on sentry were fast asleep below a massive Afghan rug. It was slightly surprising that these guys were in fact so laid back.

Then again I'm guessing they had no idea that two British soldiers were going to drop in for a visit. Spence signalled for me to move in and conduct a search of their belongings. We wanted to know if there were in fact any weapons.

I moved a little closer, got down onto one knee, I kept my finger on the trigger guard of my rifle, and with my other hand, I slowly began to lift the blanket. They had cuddled up to one another. They looked dirty, their clothing was old and smelt badly, they had a dish-dash top and trousers on, prayer mats were neatly placed behind their heads, and prayer beads had been wrapped around the wrist areas.

Just as I was about to stand up and let Spence know that I could not identify any weapons, one of the locals sat up. He looked scared. I thought he was about to shout. I looked directly at him, and with my finger up against my lips, I said, 'Shhhh.' I then rolled my hand across my eyes and beckoned him to go back to sleep. I didn't know who was more surprised, I was just happy that he did exactly what I had asked.

We made our way back to the guys, giving them the generic compass in left-hand scenario. They knew who we were. We had a quick chat about what we had seen, and notes got exchanged. Then we moved back a further 50 metres to a pre-designated RV. It wasn't long before the cut-offs made their way to our location.

We radioed for the cordon troops to move in and collect our call sign, and made our way back to Gereshk camp. It would be hard to explain to someone what actually had just taken part. It was only Spence and myself that would ever know we had carried out a proper Close Target Recce (CTR). Nowadays they are only ever carried out by Special Forces soldiers.

We arrived back into camp at 0130 hours, a patrol report would be put together with all the information that we had gained throughout the patrol. Each member of the platoon was given a specific task. This needed to be complete by the morning.

By this stage, I was on top of the world. After having done a live CTR, Spence telling me that it was the first CTR that had been carried out by the Royal Irish since the Second World War. It made the both of us feel very proud inside, every day now we were breaking records from previous battles. It was the first time a platoon from the Royal Irish had been in a contact with enemy forces since Korea. The list just got bigger each day.

The next morning we were give an admin day. It gave us time to sort ourselves out again after getting back at 0130 hours earlier in the morning. We didn't clean our weapons, so this gave us that time to properly de-gunge them.

We got asked to put together a wish list. This would comprise of things that would make our life more comfortable while in camp. The amount of work we were producing and the type of work being carried out. It would be nice to be able to relax a little more when having a stand-down period.

More internet terminals, twice as many phones, and a better shop were the main things on our lists, but to be honest, we didn't really care. We were here to fight and we really itched for it to be sooner rather than later.

The next day was almost here, and today we were getting a visitor. It was going to be the commander of Task Force Helmand (CTFH). He was on his recce to see what would make it a better camp. That wish list we had to write was now making sense. When he had his brief with the officers, they now had some feedback from the troops what we actually needed and what we wanted. They were two different things, the commander agreed that this camp need a place of calm, somewhere to socialise and maybe have a coffee would be nice.

As he was being walked around the camp, his team were discussing the infrastructure and how they could add more real estate and utilise old ISO containers. We heard across the radio that the local ANA base was under attack. The Taliban had walked right into the base dressed as ANA soldiers and began to open fire into the rooms. This did not even raise an eyebrow. We were now used to this happening.

17 June now and another day where things didn't seem to go to plan, just been briefed that the MSR into Gereshk was being used by the Taliban as their resupply route. You have to ask yourself where these intelligence people get their information from, some of it was laughable.

So we were in Gereshk, a place that was ripe full of insurgency, a place where they lived with their families, a place where we had built a base to interdict Taliban movement, and after all this intelligence had been gathered, I was now being told that the only metal road through Gereshk was being used by the Taliban. Now I'm no genius, however, I had already made that assumption.

It didn't matter anyway. We were going out on task to conduct Vehicle Checkpoints (VCPs) along the MSR. This would be in the form of five snatch vehicles. We would spend most of the day driving up and down it. This would probably keep the Taliban away for as long as we were there only. It wasn't that bad and it got us out of camp for a while. It felt strange though. It was starting to sound like every other call sign had in fact now been involved in a contact with the Taliban except us.

I'm sure we were going to be soon. The next day we conducted yet another patrol. This time on foot into Gereshk, it was to show the locals that we were in control. The problem we were having was that the locals had not taken to us, we kept trying to gain their trust, but it came with a price. They only wanted money.

We were trying to gain trust with them, in fact we were working on the children in the hope they spread the word to their parents. We were giving sweets to the children, and when they approached us with cuts and bruises, we were carrying out first aid. I think they just wanted us to go. We were alien to them.

We got back to camp only to discover that we were taking over the QRF in the morning, and it would be for a minimum of forty-eight hours. Well, that suited me. I got to sleep in my own bed for a few days. I was starting to enjoy this relaxed life too much. I needed something that's out of my comfort zone a little.

During the handover/takeover of the QRF equipment, we noticed that there needed to be some sort of crash-out box, so Davey started to put that together. Browner went to see the MT rep and get a few florescent vests for the box. This would be used at night if we were walking the vehicles through camp, though I was sure with the amount of lights in camp it would not be needed.

The daily briefing had brought about another way to gain the trust of the locals. We had been given permission from higher authority to start to conduct an outreach program. It's just another way to say 'Hearts & Minds'; 8 Platoon had been given the glorious of driving into Gereshk to deliver pens, pencils, and footballs to the children, the patrol would stop at the local school.

The school used to be thriving with children who wanted to learn, but after the Taliban had killed the teachers and any man or woman who had an education, it fell by the wayside. Today would hopefully bring the community together, and well, that's what the plan was.

While they were out winning hearts and minds, we had two new members arrive in our platoon. It was Tam and Shankill, two good soldiers, they had been sent out by the Royal Irish Regiment. The boss had asked for some reinforcements to be sent, and these two guys were what we got. They would turn out to be assets to the platoon; it was also great to see a new face about the place.

Tam was a member of recce platoon back at camp, you had to be of good quality to be in that platoon, and they are a cut above the rest back in battalion. So he would bring his knowledge with him. Then you had Shankill, he was in fact from the Shankill road, back in Belfast. Isn't that a surprise. He was part of mortar platoon and also brought his knowledge with him. Every man brought something to the party. That's what made the platoon so great.

It was now 24 June and frustration was beginning to show within the platoon. We were all itching for a contact. After all it was why we were there, and it got annoying listening to the copious amount of contacts each day on the radio. Yet we were waiting out for our chance to see if we had what it took, could we live up to the reputation of the paratroopers, or would we fall apart in the face of the enemy, only time would tell.

We were next to carry out the outreach program. This time we headed to the far side of the town, it again was a school, only difference was that we would have a television crew arriving and with them would be the commander of British Forces in Afghanistan (CBF). He would be filmed laughing and playing football with the children as the teachers clapped away, a few soldiers would join in to make it look like that's what we did every day. Meanwhile there would be soldiers and flanking call signs all over Gereshk, helicopter gunships circling above like vultures waiting to strike on their prey. My section were spread out over 50 metres, their task was to keep the rest of the locals away from the school,

My section did not need someone telling them what to do every five minutes, they were a mature robust bunch, just sitting back and watching them go about their business was humbling to see. There were a few young boys turning into men, their self-confidence had grown so much in such a short space of time.

I walked across to have a chat with Spence. He was standing beside the driver's door fixing the strap of his helmet. I stood at the commander's door and began to talk through the wagon, and he looked at me then carried on putting green tape on the strap. I spoke to him, then in a matter of seconds I had disappeared. He wondered where I went to. I could hear him say, 'Speedy, where the hell did ye go?'

I managed to pick myself off the ground. I was seeing a white flash. My head was all light and now I had blood on my hand and a little seeping out the corner of my eye. What had happened was the local children had begun to throw stones at us, and due to the fact that we were in a soft posture approach, we were easy targets.

Spence told me to get into the back of the vehicle and the boss ordered the platoon to put helmets on. No sooner was I in the back of the vehicle than Luke was wanting to take over command of the section. He was insisting that I stay in the back of the vehicle and rest. I thought he actually cared about me. Then I discovered that the minute I said, 'YES, Luke, take over', he wanted my helmet to wear, because he had forgotten to bring his helmet.

It was a little funny that I had been hit by a stone, but to be hit right on the eyeball was very painful. I sat in the back of the snatch with the door opened slightly. I was actually feeling a little sick, then the CBF walked past the wagon with his entourage. He stopped and asked who I was and if I was okay. I explained what had happened to me. He just laughed at me and said, 'And it's not even the twelfth of July', as if I had this happen to me back in Belfast on a regular basis.

We were only there for about an hour this time, as the television crew were on a tight schedule. Everything was about media coverage now. We needed to get the message out that we were here to help and not hinder.

Back in camp the boss got dropped off at the ops room. He was talking about the patrol and what we had actually achieved. He was briefed in return that OP MINIMISE was in force. Due to two members of the Special Boat Service (SBS) having been killed in Sangin, they had their equipment stolen by the Taliban and now a radio was in the hands of the enemy.

As I was having trouble focusing, due to being hit on the eye, I was told to stand down on the next patrol. Spence asked to borrow my radio and night vision. I didn't actually know why he asked. He could have just said, 'I want now', but he did have manners after all, only then he told me that the patrol was going to Zumbelay. I was gutted, he just smiled and said, 'Well, you will play with stones.' That made me feel like a twat, but hey, there would be other outstanding patrols to come.

I lay on my bed just relaxing. British Forces Broadcasting Station (BFBS) was playing some great stuff. It had only felt like five minutes when I heard running and the echo of get the f—king vehicles running. I grabbed my weapon, put on my softie jacket, and ran to the operations room. 'What's going on, boss?' I said to the 9 Platoon commander. He said, 'Your platoon are in contact.'

At this stage, the 8 Platoon was now in the vehicles and ready to deploy as QRF. The messages coming across the radio were frightening. They had been surrounded and were now split to the four winds. A lot of the troops had fallen into deep irrigation ditches, and due to the amount of weight they had been carrying, they now could not get out. The cut-offs that were Getty and Stella had been caught out. They didn't have enough manpower to put in a sustainable assault, the platoon's radio operator was stuck in an irrigation ditch, and he had no comms to zero.

He just sat at the bottom of the ditch weapon ready to strike anyone who looked like a threat. My platoon was putting down a heavy rate of fire towards the enemy. The Fire Support Platoon was trying to steer the Taliban away from us and was now taking heavy fire. There were rocket-propelled grenades flying through the air and exploding near the troops.

The reporter that had gone on the patrol because she was an expert on Afghan culture was now stuck in a ditch with a Royal Military Police (RMP) soldier and a radio operator. The only good thing about it was the fact that the Rad Op was Alan Baxter and an ex-marine and had bags of experience. The reporter was Christina Lamb. She had never been through anything like this before. Her cream trousers were now soaking wet, she had urinated all down her legs, and she was scared.

The RMP had started to cry. He was insisting that he did not want to die. He had a wife and son at home. Everyone was trying to suppress the enemy. It was getting late now, and the fire fight had now lasted close to two hours. We used 51 mm mortars and called in 81 mm mortars, the only drama was that we could not call upon our own fast jets. They had been tasked somewhere else, priority was not us. Our guys had done well; ladders were being passed from ditch to ditch so the guys could get out.

During the whole incident, Nafrue had been at the snatch vehicles doing rear protection and came under enemy fire. He had not moved from the position, he did not want anyone to get the vehicles, he had stood his ground and fought back the Taliban, that was pretty brave from his perspective.

It had been Ranger Platoon, with the OC tactical group the plan was to have a Shura and begin to talk with the village elders and start hearts and minds. The atmospherics had changed when the children left the area. After the contact was over, the village was on fire, there was thick black smoke coming out of most compounds, well, we had been warned not to go there by the US Rangers.

Once the contact was over, I walked back to my tent. I sat out the back waiting on the platoon to come in. It was a further thirty minutes, and when they came, in they were black, they looked completely worn out. Every man was soaked from head to foot in sweat, their skin was black from smoke, and they smelt of carbon from the amount of ammunition they had fired. All grenades had been thrown used up and it looked like a fantastic battle.

The morale within the platoon was now through the roof. They had proven they could cut the mustard with the Taliban and had given them a bloody nose; big browner had his skin burnt and was in need of medical attention. His General Purpose Machine Gun (GPMG) had expended nearly 1,500 rounds of ammunition; while he was running, the barrel was so hot that it stuck to his skin. His glove would not come off, but he was just sitting there having a cigarette laughing at how dangerous it had been.

I did feel a little jealous of the fact they had now passed the self-test and knew they would not falter under extreme pressure. I still felt that I had not been tested and was screaming inside for a good contact.

The daily down reps were beginning to sound grim; casualties were starting to mount up within the battle group. While this was going on, three hundred Taliban fighters had surrounded the ANA compound in Sangin valley. They had not yet attacked, but it was building up to be a big battle.

We continued to carry out patrols into Gereshk and try to win the hearts and minds of the locals, but as soon as we had left the town, the Taliban would carry out their own patrols, so it was starting to look as if we were actually going around in circles.

The news reports were putting us in a bad light also; the headlines read, 'AFGHAN STRIKE KILLS DOZENS'. Up to eighty Taliban rebels and at least sixteen civilians were killed on Monday during a coalition air and ground attack on a village in southern Afghanistan, officials and witnesses said.

The US-led coalition said it called in warplanes after troops who were trying to capture insurgents in Kandahar province came under fire, while a governor said some of the militants had hidden in local people's houses. The air strike came amid some of the worst violence since the 2001 fall of the Taliban in Afghanistan. Around three hundred people had been killed in the past week, about twice the number reported killed in Iraq.

Today is a very important day in the Royal Irish Regiment calendar, 'IT'S RANGER DAY' out of respect for the rangers within the platoon. Spence wanted all the NCOs within the platoon to do sentry duties, so the rangers could have the day off. This news went down well amongst the platoon.

The day passed without incident, this was a welcome sign of things to come. I was sure it's only because they were bringing weapons across from Pakistan, that was the normal pattern.

Today is 2 July. We were on QRF again, but we were getting relieved later on by a composite QRF. This would consist of anyone that was not on essential duties in camp, then coy it's going out to conduct a task near a power station just on the edge of the town.

OPERATION MINIMISE had now been called again; we knew it has to be something bad. News came in that A-Company had been in contact most of the day in Sangin. Two soldiers KIA and five casualties, that was a blow to morale, it was hard to stay positive when this type of news comes in.

We were now out on task. It took us nearly an hour to drive to what was the RV point. It's dark now and night vision was going to be deployed soon. We drove to an old compound, the walls were over 15 feet in height. When doing top cover in the snatch, you could just see over them. We started to dismount the vehicles and stack up against the wall.

The drivers were still trying to park everything up neatly, when the boss started to try and brief Robbie, Davey, and myself up on what tasks he had for us.

We all moved over to him and he began to tell us that he had seen three separate locations that he wanted us to take our sections. The rest of the guys were now under the command of Spence. He was more than capable of looking after them.

The boss began to walk all three of us commanders to different locations. He was working out what positions he wanted us to go to and then who he wanted in each one. Just as we moved across open ground, we heard a motorbike engine being revved up. We stopped and scanned about, but no one knew where it was coming from.

Then I heard Robbie shout, 'Guys, it's over there.' We all looked across at Robbie, so we could see what direction he was looking at. He had his weapon raised up and pointing it at a bloke who was sitting on a motorbike at the top of a small incline.

The bloke began to move slowly down the hill towards us. All three of us now had our weapons raised and pointing them at him. However reality was setting in. As we pointed our weapons, we were all desperately trying to find cover. This could well be a suicide bomber, the bike then sped up and came down the hill.

Robbie fired aimed shots at the guy, followed shortly by Davey and myself. He must have been hit a dozen times. I remember seeing the tracer rounds bounce behind him. They had penetrated him, it felt weird from where I was standing, it looked like he wouldn't die.

We then shouted and dived for cover. There was no explosion. The boss shouted for me to move in and check for breathing. I moved in, got down on one knee, and checked his pulse, there wasn't one. There was no rise and fall of the chest either. The guy was dead, and I could see a few holes in the guy's chest, at least our grouping of shots were accurate.

Right now we had to extract from the area. We had given away our position and compromised the whole mission. The stand in CSM was crying out for someone to give him a sleeping bag, this was so we could put the body in it for the travel back to Gereshk.

So far everyone was telling him that they didn't have one. I for one was not letting him put a dead body into my sleeping bag, and he eventually gave up and now was asking for an American blanket. Again I was not letting him have mine. He was getting rather frustrated now, he started to grab blokes and fling them away if they said no. We eventually gave him black rubbish bags, these would have to do.

He began to double the bags over, in order to strengthen them, then with no remorse whatsoever, began to fold the body in two, it took him a while. I tried to help him, but he was in the zone. By the look on his face, it was apparent he was in a dark place. I walked away from him in shock.

The Estonian soldiers had brought their vehicle into us. At the start of the mission they were in fact providing our flank protection, but because of the incident, they had closed into us. Dean asked if he could put the body into the back of the Estonian wagon. I was also going back to camp in the Estonian wagon, so he threw the bag into the back of the wagon. It was right below the hatch that I was going to put my head through. There was only one thing for it.

I forced my feet into the body until I had a good firm grip. I then popped my head through the hatch. By the time we had driven back, my feet were in fact very warm. I had used the warm dead body to not only balance, but to keep my feet warm.

On return to camp, we drove past the medical centre. The Estonian wagon that I was in pulled over so the CSM could get the body out. He grabbed in with both hands and threw it onto the bonnet of a snatch vehicle. He then waited for the doctor to arrive, who then carried out the proper procedures and informed the local authorities of the fatality.

It had been another interesting night. The next morning we all had to produce statements for killing that individual on the motorbike. It was not difficult. I got the RMP to talk me through the statement, he became a great friend. I got to know him as Grant, little did I know, but I would need Grant a lot by the end of the tour. He would become a platoon asset.

Most of the day was spent learning about the local KIA, that we had brought about. It turned out that his family came to collect him this morning; they stated that he was deaf and dumb.

It sounded like someone was laughing at us. At the end of the day, it was my honest belief that he was a suicide bomber. I fired until the threat stopped, that was all I had needed to write in my statement.

We decided to try and give the platoon, including the section commanders, as much time off as possible. We broke the guard duty into three separate timings. Each corporal would do eight hours on and sixteen hours off—that was fantastic.

The dreaded OP MINIMISE was being enforced again. This time it was B-Company 3 Para. They had lost one guy in a contact in Sangin, and the numbers of deaths were surely starting to mount up. The battle group were now into double figures with casualties, and the media back in the UK were starting to put pressure on the Prime Minister for us to withdraw before it became our Vietnam.

It was now 7 July, we had been in a few scraps but nothing completely overwhelming yet. I was sure something had to come. We got tasked to go and pick up a UAV, and this did not go down well with the troops. We knew what had happened previously to another call sign. We carried out the task but were weary of what might happen. It turns out that the locals have stolen the UAV. We returned to camp empty-handed. Only to be briefed that we would take part in a deliberate operation in Sangin. This was going to be scary. It was what we all deep down had craved for, now it was coming true.

All FOBs were now on lockdown. More ammunition was to be flown in for the operation. As the day went by, more and more information was drip fed through. The Estonians and HCR were in fact on the move already. They were moving into position on our flanks as we spoke. They were beginning to take up arcs of fire. The rest of us were preparing our kit for battle. Morale was very high knowing the operation was coming up.

The media back home were still running with headlines of soldiers fighting for their lives and another death in air assault brigade. The defence secretary was considering sending extra troops, he had told MPs on Thursday that a decision would be made 'very soon', and that they would be the first to know when it was taken. The *Sun* newspaper claimed on Thursday that nearly 1,000 troops from 16 Air Assault Brigade would be deployed to the increasingly violent Helmand province on Monday.

The defence secretary said he had received advice on sending extra troops to Afghanistan and was considering it as a matter of urgency. This came as the sixth British soldier had been killed.

We got our kit together and made our way towards the ops room, over on the right-hand side was a room that other units used to practice their personal skills and drills. We spent some time there practicing stacking up beside a building and most importantly how to break and enter without losing your men trying to gain entry. We used ladders and thought we were doing well, until the Special Forces came over and gave us some advice on moving faster, but still maintaining surprise with momentum. We took the advice on board and started to practice their way. It was effective.

Well, today being 11 July is in fact my father's birthday. I just hope and pray to God that OP MINIMISE does not come on. I know there in another battle group operation in full affect. Let's just hope it goes without friendly forces casualties. It took a while to get through, he had a lot of questions to ask me, but due to OPSEC, I couldn't answer him.

I wished him well, then we started talking about what the media had been saying. He mentioned that the American soldiers were taking a lot of casualties and that it was the top story every night on ITN NEWS. I could not go into any detail of what I have been doing. I did tell him that it was very hot and humid and it was difficult to manoeuvre across the ground and remain stealth (hidden from the enemy). Especially with all that weight we had to carry while on patrol, he was asking why we carried so much weight and why we didn't scale down for the patrols.

I explained that we needed the 3 litres of water, and batteries for radios and countermeasure equipment, then on top of that, the commanders had radios and rations. Then there was the fact that we wore helmets and body armour with plates in the front and back, then the ammunition we carried along with grenades and bombs for the 51 mm mortar.

Then there was our own kit, and most importantly the first-aid/ trauma kit, so when you take that into account, we couldn't really scale down. The Taliban knew this and took full advantage of it. During contacts they would hit us and move fast through the green zone, and we could never go in hot pursuit due to the weight we carried. I think my dad thought, 'Holy shit, son.' He was an ex-soldier himself, so he knew what we were going through. He was in his unit's recce platoon, so he must have been a switched-on soldier back in his day.

Today he just got his kicks out of watching what I did, and learning of all the things I was going through. I knew he was proud of me, but like all dads, they tend to not tell you to your face what they think. They use our mothers to relay the message.

We had a fastball thrown our way, a runner from the operations room went around the accommodation asking to get all commanders in the cookhouse for a brief, and we got everyone together and headed through the tented door. There was a white board with a diagram drawn on it, with red squares to simulate enemy out building. The map was a satellite map pined to another board, then there was a model that had been built using whatever scrap was available at the time. It looked rather good to be honest.

The brief began with apologies from the boss, he stated that this had just come in and that he was giving us a warning order for a future operation. He then told us that what we were about to see was classed as classified until the operation was over. He gave us a heads-up on what had developed from a previous operation.

He started by saying that Delta Force had been carrying out a task last night in the area north of Sangin. They had been tasked to sweep in and grab a high-value Al-Qaeda commander. But on approach, they came under heavy resistance. This had resulted in the Chinook being hit by machine gun fire. They had to make an emergency landing, the Special Forces then had to extract out of the area still under heavy fire from insurgents. They have asked that 3 Para take over that operation as they have jobs coming out their ears. After a long conversation to the commanding officer and brigade commander, I had been informed that we will carry out that operation.

'This is what I have so far, and does anyone here have any burning questions?' To be honest, you could have heard a pin drop. This was what we had wanted from the start.

Chapter 4

BATTLE PREPARATION

This was a chance to get out and soldier, the look on everyone's face said it all, if the Special Forces couldn't do it, what makes it that we can?

The truth was that we were a company group, we had three platoons, and the best thing was we were hungry for it. That's what made it that we could do it.

Over the next few days, intelligence was drip fed down to us, Ranger Platoon had been given target areas to clear. The ditches were 3 to 4 metres high, and it was very boggy on foot. The insurgents were in positions, which had three to four men in each. The overall number expected to be there was no more than fifteen fighters. The positions were well prepared and they were in fact dug in.

It sounded great yet a little scary. We just wanted to get on with it. News was starting to come in of friendly forces' casualties. Apparently two soldiers WIA, they had been hit from long range. It was assessed that the Taliban had good snipers, this was not good news.

Due to the amount of operations under way and combat outposts that had been set up to interdict Taliban movement, the re-supply into Sangin had now been pushed to the right slightly.

The plan was to conduct an air assault operation into Sangin. This was what was needed to re-supply a company group, and it was getting beyond a joke now. The operation would consist of A-Company and

B-Company pushing forward through the town and pushing the enemy back.

We would all be given Limit of Exploitation (LOE) phase lines, and these were places on the ground that we had to reach and secure, known as objectives. We would have four Apache gunships in the air stacked up for the whole entire operation. It was going to be the battle of all battles.

We spent the rest of that day going over what would be expected from us during the operation. Spence had each section take turns in room clearing at the specially built killing house. These were a few erected buildings on the approach to the operations room and were situated near the ranges.

At least we would go prepared for urban fighting if nothing else. The boss was starting to become the bringer of bad news. Every time he gave a brief, it started with the amount of casualties we had taken, and what outpost had taken a smashing from the Taliban. This time he stated that an emergency re-supply into Sangin had gone wrong.

The C-130 Hercules transporter that carried out the drop had gotten its coordinations all wrong. They had in fact dropped the under slung out the back far too late, and it had drifted out into a hotbed of insurgency. We had lost everything.

The morale of the troops in Sangin had dropped far too low. They were running on fumes, their rations were close to running out, the ammunition was dwindling away, and more importantly, their 81 mm mortar ammo was starting to run out.

This was a shock to the battle group. We had not prepared for such a loss, back in the UK the Defence Secretary had informed everyone that we would probably finish without a single shot being fired. How the hell could someone with his stature in parliament be so wrong, he became infamous within the military circle for such a bizarre comment?

We now had been given timings to adhere to; it was going to be a company lift, all troops to the HLS by 1300 hours. Two Chinooks would land, Ranger Platoon and OC TAC group along with snipers and machine guns would all get aboard the first Chinook, while 8 and 9 Platoon would all get on the second Chinook. We would fly into Bastion in order to start on battle preparation and conduct rehearsals.

The flight only took around twenty minutes. Looking out of the window I could see how much Bastion camp had grown already. It looked massive, the runway had been better structured now, and a NAAFI shop had been built close to the tented hospital. The troops based there were going to have an easy tour indeed, especially with fresh rations and Pizza Hut at their beck and call, or maybe I was just a little bit jealous of such surroundings. After all, I was going to do what most of the rear echelon wanted to do, and that was fight the enemy.

We landed on the runway. The tailgate dropped and we made our way off the aircraft to two straight lines. We were met by a few of our echelon troops that were based in Bastion. They took C-Company through the maze of tents to our new accommodation. We had been assigned to three tents, one for each platoon, and nearly forty cot beds in each one. This would afford us to let the attached arms in each platoon to start to mingle with the troops that they would be working with.

We each found a bed space and dropped our kit off. I got my American blanket out and began to make my bed, and I dropped my webbing on it and decided to go to the new NAAFI shop complex. A lot of the guys came with me, the only thing we needed to carry was our personal weapons, on arrival at the shop, and I just shook my head in disgust at how everyone was carrying on. There were a lot of people wearing tracksuit and jeans with T-shirts, not a single rifle to be seen, but everyone seemed to have a pistol strapped to their leg. Some with T-shirts saying 'Taliban hunting club' even though their beer belly wasn't quite covered by the T-shirt.

The looks of pure disgust etched across their faces when they had to look at us, we had not properly washed and our combats were rather coloured and worn. It got frustrating. Especially when a rather young second lieutenant told us to go and get washed before sitting down at the same table as him. This seemed to enrage the guys. I suppose as the commander I should have said, 'Yes, sir, will do, sir, three bags full, sir', but at that time I left it for the guys to sort out.

I just looked up and Davey was briefing him up. 'Don't you dare stand there in your Sainsbury's sport kit giving me a lecture of dress and grooming policy, you must have just left Sandhurst I take it, well, take yourself back there and learn how to engage with soldiers fresh off the battlefield.'

Davey had a way with words and I was not daft enough to cross him. He was from the country back in Northern Ireland. His dad had a lot of land and cattle. This had made Davey one of life's natural grafters, so when he got upset, he was a nightmare to control, saying that he was naturally a placid person and kept calm most of the time.

We sat there taking in the scenery. There were a lot of young female soldiers and nurses wearing trendy low-cut clothing also carrying pistols. We were starting to feel that this place had no idea of the reality of what was happening outside of Bastion camp. I sat there looking at Robbie, his ice cream had melted all over his hand and he was swearing like mad. It made us laugh, in fact Luke was laughing so loud that Robbie hit him in the face with the ice cream.

That made Robbie and everyone watching laugh at Luke. A girl thought we were a good bunch of guys and came across to have a chat with us. She turned out to be a combat medic technician (CMT) and was attached to C-Company for the operation. The chain of command did not want her going on the front line, but she was determined to do her bit. She thought Luke was a funny guy, he had her laughing her little head off at his jokes and tomfoolery.

We finished off our drinks and ice cream and made our way back to the tent. By this time some guys had begun to play volleyball, others were putting on baby oil, while some just lay on their beds,

I was one of those who just lay on my bed. Spence arrived across from the warrant officers and sergeants' tent with all his kit on, shortly followed by other senior NCOs. 'Right, fellas, get yer kit on for rehearsals.' The company had been given two Chinook helicopters for an hour. They would remain grounded while we practised our de-bussing drills. We each had time to stack up, get on the aircraft in reverse order, and make sure the quad bike was ready to go, when we got the green light to exit the aircraft.

It took about three attempts to get it right, the OC and CSM stood off to a flank watching us until he was happy. The last one was the best, GO GO GO, the quad bike drove off at speed into the distance. But not too far away so it didn't get protection. We then ran off the aircraft, keeping spacing between each other, we went left. The guys all lay down on their belt buckles and began to interlock the arcs of fire automatically. No one had to prompt them, the first section cover from 12 o'clock right through until 4 o'clock. Then second section from 4 right through until 8 o'clock, then finally third section 8 through until 12. Everyone was happy, the OC felt comfortable with the rehearsals.

We had a four-ton vehicle turn up at the tent. It was full of ammunition for the operation, the section 2 i/c plus one other from each section started to collect the ammunition. Spence was now in his element. This was his ball game, he had to account for every single round that we had, and he knew who was carrying what and how many they had. He was also a tactical expert, so he knew what weapon systems we needed for each specific job. He would explain that the GPMG needs to suppress the enemy, while a mouse hole charge would gain entry into a compound as the 51 mm mortar would put down smoke to provide a screen for the break in troops to cross open ground.

This was what we needed to know, as they say in the military that knowledge is power, and that's a true saying if you're in the infantry.

That night orders were given for the operation. It would be called OPERATION ATAL, it already sounded great, the battle plan was to have American troops on our right-hand flank providing protection, while the Canadian soldiers would be on our left flank doing the same job. It would be done in one clean lift. Five Chinook helicopters would lift the entire fighting force and drop them off right into known enemy territory. It would be unexpected by the Taliban and the sheer size of our force would have them on the back foot from the start.

We all boarded our specific Chinook helicopter. Destination was Sangin. It was going to be outstanding. I was apprehensive of the outcome, and the only thing that was always certain was if it went bad I would be home first.

After what seemed like ten minutes of pure radio checks, we lifted off as a complete fighting force. We were completely packed. It reminded me of sardines in a tin. I could see out of the window and the other Chinook helicopters. We were flying in a fighting formation very low, the Chinooks were weaving left and right, then we lifted up to about 1,500 feet. The warning came down the Chinook by word of mouth. Then we started to drop, ten-minute warning followed by five minutes, I could hear gunfire already. The door gunners on each Chinook were engaging targets. I could see green tracer rounds flying into the air, the sky was ablaze with tracer fire, it looked frightening.

We began to grit our teeth, then before any helicopter had landed, reports of casualties came across the net. The green tracer rounds had in fact came through the bottom of one of the Chinook helicopters. They had a casualty, nothing serious, just a gunshot wound to the shoulder. Our Chinook landed facing towards the Sangin wadi, the door gunner was suppressing a position. We all got up from our seats and started to try and get off the Chinook. It was taking incoming fire and we needed to get off quickly. We knew that we had to do exactly what we had practised back in Bastion. This time when the quad drove out the back of the aircraft it got bogged in, we had to now climb over Dean and all his ammunition. The drama was that the quad was carrying far too much weight and had stuck in the mud.

This was typical, they say that no plan survives contact, and in this instant, it sure as hell had not. We eventually got ourselves into a formation and began to space out. The boss called in the commanders and wanted to push on with the battle. We each identified our targets and began to push forward. The exchange in gunfire was unbelievable. The enemy fire was accurate and stopping us from getting a foothold.

Robbie started us off by suppressing positions that were pinning us down. This gave Davey the chance to move into a good position and get eyes on depth positions. This also gave my section the time to breathe properly and actually think of how to move across the open ground. Spence had pre-empted the strike by putting down smoke to mask our movement across the ground. The boss was manipulating us the way he wanted to good effect.

Assault, Suppress, Reserve. That's the way we moved through the green zone. It was working well. We stacked up at the side of the first compound. Ready, I said to O,Driscol, he nodded at me. Then with Luke giving suppressive fire, he threw the L109 grenade into the compound shouting, 'GRENADE', then BOOM. After only a few seconds, we each entered the compound. He went left and I went right, scanning everything that moved with the weapon aimed into likely threat locations. There was nothing there. I called for the remaining members of my section to enter the compound. They came straight in. 'Right, Speedy, where is not clear?' was the first thing Luke asked. I pointed to some of the outbuildings. He got the guys to pair up and each pair to clear the remaining positions.

We continued to do this for the next couple of hours. The other two sections had their chance. We started to rotate through the lead section. It also gave the reserve section some time to re-bomb their magazines and distribute the ammunition equally amongst the section.

The look on the face of Spence was priceless. He could now finally get rid of a lot of weight. He had been carrying 10% of the ammunition. Well, as much as his body could physically carry, and when we asked for a re-supply, he couldn't get it off quick enough, and who would blame him. He had been keeping us under control and tactically aware of who was where and what the remainder of the coy were. It was going well. The enemy fire was still fierce, other platoons had not gotten as far forward as us, but then again they were closer into the town, and had the stronghold to deal with.

After a few hours, the enemy momentum was dying away. We were still suppressing each position and now starting to assault them. The word that became etched in my head was in fact 'GRENADE', this would indicate that there was an explosion about to happen and we needed to take cover.

After we had taken our positions, we waited for the rest of the company to reach their own objectives. We had now reached ours. All we had to do now was interlock arcs and get sentries on. The fire fight that 8 Platoon was involved in seemed to last forever, in fact the OC was starting to get annoyed with the whole situation. He got the Forward Air Controller (FAC) to call in fast jets. They were already in the air stacked up, the noise they made when flying low nearly blew my eardrums open. There was a 'whooooosh' shortly followed by a massive cloud of smoke in the shape of a mushroom, then a colossal explosion that shook the ground.

There were a further three more J-DAM bombs into key positions, then the radio messages were coming in. All three platoons gave their code word across the net, and it was easy to tell which one was ours.

This meant that we had reached our objectives. We then took it in turn to extract into Sangin DC. There were still other call signs in contact right across Sangin. Apache gunships were engaging with hellfire missiles. It sounded like and looked like a World War 2 movie. It was the most surreal thing I have ever seen.

Once the other two platoons had safely made it into Sangin DC, we could relax slightly, even knowing that other call signs were still in contact, with our fast air up there and other assets, they would be fine. We then got told to move to specific areas within Sangin camp. We were in fact to bunch up, so that was a good call from Spence, he was always thinking tactically.

One of our soldiers, Shankill, was starting to feel shaken up. We could see he was not coping too well, but there was nothing we could do at this moment in time, apart from keep an eye on him. That night we had only one platoon stag on. It gave the guys maximum rest and time to recharge their batteries. The same was happening with the other two platoons, and by God did we need it.

The next day after having a fantastic sleep, the boss spoke with all three commanders. We were to leave camp at midday and conduct a patrol into Sangin town and assess the atmospherics amongst the people. I said straight away, 'You're taking the complete piss, sir, we have just dropped three J-DAM bombs onto their village, we have destroyed the complete town by use of air strikes, and now you want us to go and find out if they are in good spirits.' He just looked at me and with sarcasm stated, 'It's not my bloody idea, Speedy.'

It had in fact came from the JOC back in Camp Bastion. They were worried that the hearts and minds campaign was now completely destroyed. It had been, and it was going to take years to rebuild what we had done. We didn't plan to do this, the Taliban had brought this on themselves, British soldiers don't just fire a weapon at you without justification, there had to be reason.

The patrol into Sangin had us all on edge. We left through the pipe range. This was an area that was overlooked by a Sanger, and during a contact, it was like a range. You just aimed up its narrow road and insurgents fell like figure 11 targets, not a great place to be caught out.

The town was like a ghost town, every part of it had holes and what remained of the previous battle, in certain areas, and we could see empty casings, from where Taliban had taken up positions to engage us. This was very rare to find, as the Taliban are actually very good tactically. It could have been what was known as a 10 bob Taliban that had left the empty casings there. They were locals who just fired at you for a few quid in their pocket, not very professional at all.

We returned after the patrol and back briefed the OC on what looked like a town ready for the scrap heap. He was not happy at all, that was not his intention, he was trying to build a rapport with the locals. But every time he thought he was getting somewhere, he would have his base attacked and this was not some burst of gunfire from a hidden location. It was from four or maybe five positions at the same time.

Still mounting patrols from Sangin DC, it feels a little weird now that Sangin D.C is now called the platoon house, every location has now got a platoon house, and this name was in fact started by our platoon. We have added to the history now, but I'm sure everyone will claim they started it. However we were in fact the first troops to set foot in Sangin, so it will remain our claim to fame.

This patrol we were going on was to secure the north-east of the flyover and interdict enemy forces movement. We had to remain on task until all three convoys pass through our location, and we headed out towards the pipe range again. We had over watch from the Sangers. This made it easier, the road was falling apart there, the shops were still not open in the bazaar, but that's to be expected. We made our way across the narrow streets keeping one foot on the ground at all times. Each section was moving perfectly across the ground, we had this down to a fine art. Spence hardly had to say a thing anymore. He knew that we were top of our game, and if we did start to make mistakes, he was there to guide us.

After only a few hours, the convoy slowly passed through our location. We moved a few guys out into the open in order that the drivers and commanders could see us. This also gave them a warm and fuzzy feeling knowing that we were there as protection. They passed waving at our call sign. We remained there for a further thirty minutes, and this was what we call a soak period, just in case they were either being followed or in case they got attacked.

On the way back to the DC, we used a different approach, so as to not set patterns. This would keep any would-be attacker or ambush site on their toes. They would have to get up rather early if they wanted to catch this platoon out. When we got back in, the boss was summoned to the ops room. The OC briefed him that we were getting heli-lifted out and back to Gereshk. The manpower there was being dwindled away somehow, anyway we would be back soon.

The heli came into collect us was firing flares out of the back. The Sangers in the DC were again in contact. It was starting to become the norm; we lifted off with the door gunner firing into enemy positions.

It wasn't long before we landed in Gereshk. During the short flight of only thirty minutes, I managed to get some rest. This was all our bodies were used to and now it was what we needed. Once off the heli, we headed to our old accommodation. It was very dusty, my bed was covered in sand, where my spare combats hung was now dirty. This was not good, especially with my ever-growing OCD. I needed to open the back of the tent and grab a brush. I tasked everyone within the section to get on with a job, and the sooner we had cleaned and sorted out our living area, the sooner we could relax.

The boss came into our tent for a quick chat. We gave him a cold drink from our little fridge. As soon as we both opened the can, I could see Luke looking at us. He smiled and said, 'Speedy, I forgot we had a fridge.' The boss laughed.

The boss wanted to let us know that we were doing a great job. He was proud of us, he was doing a good job too, and we just never told him to his face. I think he knew now that we were his Jack Russells. All he had to do was point us in the right direction and remove the lead, we would destroy anything that he wanted now. He had earned the respect of the whole platoon along with Spence, and rightly so.

We would find ourselves again on the dreaded guard. It was an easy task, just long hours for the guys. Once we had come off duty, it would be some rest followed by weapon zeroing. If you were zeroed already, then you would go around our section and get the clothing sizes. All three commanders within the platoon already had their sections sizes, so that was a case of trying to get fresh combats for each guy, or at least get some exchanges carried out. It was like shopping at Next. We all liked to get new things, it made us feel good.

We even got to carry out some medical training. The platoon CMT would get the platoon's team medics and practice them on tourniquet fitting and IV drip training. It put the guys' minds at rest knowing they had been refreshed in it. It also gave a warm and fuzzy feeling to the platoon sergeant.

Word came across from the Sanger that they could see tracer rounds being fired in the town of Gereshk. The ops room informed us that the ANP were in a contact with the Taliban. The Taliban had actually walked into town dressed in ANP uniforms. They opened fire into the ANP station. This would become a normal way for the Taliban to operate, and they were very cowardly.

Another day being given tasks that did not make sense, this time it was to go and retrieve another UAV that had come down on the outskirts of Gereshk. Again the locals had stolen it. This was becoming very common, and I think once they worked out that they could possibly booby-trap it, we would stop collecting them.

We spent the remainder of the day on the range in Gereshk. We needed to practice our contact drills and re-zero. Spence had the guys including me fire pistols at figure 11 targets. He would shout, 'Targets up.' We then turned left fired two rounds standing followed by two rounds kneeling. This would go on until he and the commanders were satisfied that we had achieved a good standard.

We expended a lot of ammunition on the range that day, so as expected the remainder of the day was spent trying to get the carbon off the pistols and our own personal weapons. It took a couple of hours to clean all weapons 100%. After all, this was going to save my life, so I wanted it spotless.

Due to the threat constantly lifting, we had to start putting two of the guys up in the sniper tower. Snipers were an asset to the company, but were limited, so we helped them in the tower, even if it was only to spot at least we were helping.

Medical training was the big thing in camp. Messages were coming in of soldiers using the morphine pens upside down and injecting themselves instead of the casualties. It made us check our drills and confirm that we knew the right end to inject. This was understandable why soldiers were getting it wrong, especially under such amount of pressure having to apply dressings to not only someone in your section, but also your best mate would have your nerves wrecked.

The date was 23 July and we were well over halfway through this tour. I hadn't really showed to myself what I could do under pressure. I knew that I wanted a challenge, but a little apprehensive on what it would entail. I suppose the main thing was finishing in one piece. Let's hope that remains.

Later on that day, news came in that Gereshk was under attack. I thought to myself, was this idiot for real? We had been hearing a contact go on for the last twenty minutes. Now someone had been tasked to come and inform the platoon that there was gunfire in the town. Either you wanted us to stand to, or just went away. It's Afghanistan, for Christ's sake, they live a weird life full of religion. Religion brings war and hate, everyone knew that, especially me. I had grown up in Belfast and had lived amongst people who had pure hatred towards Catholics and others I knew who hated Protestants. That country was just as bad to be honest.

There were two massive explosions that rocked the town of Gereshk. Everyone in camp heard it, in fact some of the troops were now going into the unmanned Sangers to get a better look at the town. The ops room had now tasked an A-10 bomber to assist the ANA. It flew over our camp within ten minutes. It looked like a cross in the sky. It began engaging specific targets, and then an Apache fired its cannon into other targets. Within thirty minutes, the gunfire stopped.

Shortly after that, the ANA arrived at our gates with guns waving in the air. They looked extremely proud of themselves, then again I'm not surprised, they had after all brought with them two Taliban fighters. They were blindfolded and plastic-cuffed to the rear. We had to set up a makeshift holding area for them. We couldn't leave the security up to the ANA, they were dodgy most of the time.

I spent the rest of that day getting ready for Rest and Recuperation (R&R). I couldn't wait to have a proper sleep in a good bed. I also felt apprehensive about leaving my men, just in case I missed out in something. That was the feeling of most of the troops—'what if'. I got on the next helicopter into Bastion camp, and it looked even bigger this time. The infrastructure had grown somewhat to what I could remember. We were going to be here for a long time, it was obvious.

Once the heli had landed, I made my way across the HLS with a couple of troops from our sister platoon. The CQMS had sent a vehicle to collect us. He was asking how we were and if the guys back at camp need anything sent up. To be honest we didn't need anything. He explained that we needed to hand in our ammunition and medical kit along with weapon. We knew that anyway, once we had time to find a bed space, we would begin in de-kitting.

We began to unwind a bit. This was the most exciting tour that we each had ever done and it was far from over. R&R was well and truly needed, but I could tell that none of us really wanted to go. We each were given clear plastic bags to place our kit into and made our way over to the ISO containers. This was an area near the QMs tented office and where the Third Battalion, the Parachute Regiment, had their flag flying high across camp, and I hate to say it, the only place in camp where there was no bullshit, something that the Irish Rangers were well and truly used to.

I was surprised how quickly I was able to just relax. The paratroopers didn't believe in giving someone hassle who had just returned from the battlefield, they made them feel welcome and left you alone to sort your own head out. It was just what was needed, it gave me time to reflect a lot on what my priorities actually were, things that I had thought were of value in my life had now become just a nicety instead of a necessity.

I put my desert shorts on, with my company T-shirt, and walked up to the NAAFI for a relaxing sit down with a nice cup of fresh coffee. It was surreal to be sitting down with no threat and with no weapon system. I had now handed all my kit in and was waiting for my flight out of here to Kabul, which would be the first leg of my journey home.

The rest of the day was spent sitting with Rupert. He was not an officer, in fact he was a lance corporal (L/Cpl) and from 8 Platoon. He was good craic and was just as happy to be chilling outside the NAAFI. We had to return to the tent for a brief just before evening meal. We were given our flight number and information on welfare issues, and as soon as the brief was over, we both grabbed our chequebooks after heading across to the admin office for a few dollars.

I wrote my cheque out to the command cashier and we proceeded to the ever-growing queue that was outside the cookhouse tent. It only took ten minutes to get inside; everyone had to wash their hands before entering the tent. Once inside the selection of fresh hot food was out of this world. Well, from eating rations to this, anything would go down well. The food was amazing. I had roast lamb and all the trimmings. It looked like a Sunday dinner that my mother would prepare for us at home.

I was not going to leave a single piece on the plate. I decided to have cheese and biscuits to wash it down, and I looked around the tent and could see the usual pistol wearing lot. Guys and girls who were dressed like John J. Rambo, probably couldn't even fire straight, but that was not my drama, I was going home in the morning.

We spent the remainder of the night sitting outside the NAAFI. I even bought a pizza. I know I wasn't hungry, but the thought of not having one made me panic-buy one anyway. After having an eyeful of some nice-looking women, we made our way back to the tent. We left the radio on all night and drifted off to sleep listening to BFBS radio. After what only seemed like a short period, it was the next morning already. We put on fresh combats and headed to the cookhouse for breakfast. It was good to get a proper fried breakfast at last.

We had to wait for about an hour before going through the RAF Movement Control Checkpoint (MCCP). This was where we had to get checked to make sure we did not take anything out of theatre that would be of danger to the aircraft or in fact the passengers. They would scan all our bags for metal.

Then there was the odd jobs worth that would make sure that you didn't take more than two hundred cigarettes out of theatre. They would get confiscated and thrown into a massive container-like bin, which already had over 10,000 boxes piled up.

We sat around for a short period then walked up the steps onto a C-130 aircraft. I sat beside Rupert, we were a little excited about what we were going to do on leave, and he had plans of drinking and partying. I just wanted to put my feet up at home and try to relax. I'm sure it wasn't going to happen, but wishful thinking on my part.

Shortly after boarding the aircraft, we heard the announcement by the captain. He welcomed us all aboard and explained the flight time into Kabul and told us to try and relax. We then were told to put body armour and helmet on for the take-off. This was now standard practice in theatre, it was also the time when you could spot the

Special Forces soldiers. They had different Kevlar helmets compared to the green troops and stuck out like sore thumbs, but then again they were in a safe environment.

We didn't stay awake long. As soon as we had lifted off into the air, I had fallen asleep. When I awoke, I could see everyone else had already taken their helmets and body armour off. I joined in but for no reason. As the minute I took it off, I was made to put it back on, we were coming into Kabul, and again it was now best practice, we landed and began to taxi up the runway, until we came to a sudden stop.

After what seemed like a few minutes, we were allowed to leave the aircraft. There were a few buses waiting at the foot of the steps. The first bus was full up so we ended up on the second bus. We got driven to area were we had to wait for the arrival of our baggage. The wait seemed longer than the flight, then the baggage turned up. It was now 0200 hours in Kabul. Everyone looked tired or just fed up. Once the bags were collected, we had transport to take us to a massive tent, where we spent the rest of that night. Inside the tent there must have been two hundred camp beds, a few fridges that had cold bottles of water inside them, along with a massive map of the camp, starting with YOU ARE HERE and an arrow, just in case you were indeed thick.

It had the cookhouse location and numerous shop and phone locations. This was great, however I wanted to know where the toilets/showers and internet were all situated.

We both picked a bed and went on a little recce patrol to identify these key areas. It must have taken us an hour. But we had located a few bars and restaurants that were packed with people in smart civilian dress. I could not see for sure if they had alcohol, but it sure looked like it from a distance.

We had stumbled onto a little gold mine, this was a village inside camp, it surely wasn't the Afghanistan that we had just come from, and it was from our perspective a non-combat zone. This is where the countries that want to be in NATO, sent their soldiers to work just to say that they had done their part, as a logistic role, like the Swedish or the Italians. I even noticed soldiers from Holland sitting out eating nice meals. I felt sorry for them, and they probably didn't even know where Sangin DC was.

We found the internet suite and sent a few emails home, but not compromising OPSEC, that was a big NO-NO. Once finished and back in the tent, it was shower and then bed, the next day would be very long indeed, and we would need rest for the journey.

We all were awake from 0500 hours. It must have been our body clocks' natural time to wake up. After having a quick wash and shave, it was breakfast time, and our last breakfast in Afghanistan before I had an Ulster fry up. The remainder of the morning was going over my obsessive cleaning disorder (OCD) and it was packing followed by un-packing, where was my passport and wallet. Did I have my cash card handy, and the biggest worry was did I remember my PIN, how the hell was I going to get cash out of the bank? I'm sure my father would understand when I asked him for twenty pounds until I got to the bank.

The transport turned up shortly after 0700 hours. We climbed aboard the bus and were driven the short distance to the runway. The aircraft looked massive, and its windows were all lit up by the light inside. With a massive RAF logo on the side, this Tri-Star would be taking me home. I was now getting more and more excited. Rupert was in good spirits as well, I thought that the sooner I fell asleep, the sooner I would be at RAF Brize Norton in Oxford.

The flight was packed, the thought of having a spare seat to spread out on was never an option. We did however get given a tin of beer each. This was from a fund that had been put together by the *Sun* newspaper called 'BEER FOF THE BOYS'. The people back home were on our side. They had been following our stories of heroism on the battlefield and wanted to give their support in whatever means they could, and to be honest, it was very much appreciated.

The flight didn't even have a screen to watch a movie. This was where the RAF had let themselves down. Why the hell in 2006 did they not have a television screen? The civilian flights had them. Well, anyway, I just listened to music then fell asleep. I was woken up periodically for meals, which at the time did not make me very happy. Why didn't they just leave me alone? I was actually thinking about the troops back in Afghanistan and what they would be up to, deep down I was praying that I didn't miss anything big.

After a whistle stop at RAF Akrotiri in Cyprus in order to re-fuel, we were back in the air and heading for England. It felt like the longest journey ever, I just wanted to get off the plane now, the smell of peoples' feet was starting to become overpowering.

We landed at Brize Norton a few hours later. It was bloody cold, and the ground was wet. I thought that the RAF standing waiting for our plane to come to a halt looked completely weird. They were wearing Combat '95s, I hadn't seen green kit for some time now, and it did not look right.

They started to unload the baggage, while we all got off and headed for the terminal. It was wet and windy, just what we had been expecting. Even now we were wet, it was great to be back on British soil. All we had to do now was wait for the baggage and be on our way, because I had onward travel to Northern Ireland to do. I had to go to an area that had been set aside for helmets and body armour and that was just as well, because they would have charged me a small fortune because of the weight.

I made my way outside the terminal and climbed aboard the bus. He was taking me onto Gatwick airport for the final leg of my journey. After only a dozen guys had sat down, he began to move off. I think he was in a hurry because the speed he left the terminal in was pretty damn fast. I was still tired, I think my body clock was just messed up, and also because I was excited a bit to be going home.

Once we drove into Gatwick, the rain had in fact stopped. While approaching the checkout, I was looking at the girl. She had no idea that two days ago I was firing a weapon into someone, no one knew I had in fact killed a man. Well, it was a joint effort, but they all still count. I checked in but kept my hand luggage nearby. I then went to the bar and ordered a pint of Carlsberg, it tasted weird, I suppose because I hadn't drunk beer in a while. I was thinking, this tastes rubbish.

It didn't stop me from drinking it though. I only had two pints and now I felt drunk, I decided to drink some water to try and feel better. To be honest I didn't actually care, I just hoped that they would let me on the plane, which they did.

Only after I had walked the 20 kilometres of the airport to the farthest place possible to board the aircraft, well, it felt like 20 kilometres anyway, that was everyone from Northern Ireland who might be in a terrorist organisation, if they blow up, the airport would not be wrecked.

The plane was an Easy-Jet one. The crew all had orange skin and bleached hair. They actually looked okay. I think they had taken their personal tan a little bit too far. As long as they got me into George Best airport in Belfast, I didn't really care what they wore, my parents would be waiting there to greet me, my mum would probably cry and my dad would just shake my hand.

I was right. On making my way with the trolley, I could see my parents eagerly peering around the corner trying to catch a glimpse of their son. They would be in for a shock, and I had lost over 2 stone since they had last seen me. But I was the fittest that I had ever been, and I was hoping it would remain that way. On the way back to the house, I was being told that Belfast had changed a lot. New buildings were going up every day and the town was in fact thriving with shoppers. I couldn't wait to spend some of my hard-earned cash on new clothes and treat myself. I would probably buy a new watch. I loved collecting watches, they looked great.

Driving up the Hollywood road was weird, people just going about their day. It took a few days to adjust into a routine, but I couldn't really settle. As expected once we pulled into the driveway, the garden was blooming in full colour. They smelt wonderful compared to what I was used to.

We got inside the door and the first thing my mother did was give me a big cuddle. They had been following every single headline that was on the news. My dad had taped all the coverage of Afghanistan, and my mother was living through the whole operation from the living room. In fact my parents knew more about the battle than me, then I was shown six different scrapbooks that my dad had put together. This just proved to me again that he really did care, he was proud as hell that I was going through this.

I could also tell that this was something that he would have loved to do when he was still serving, that was the same as a lot of ex-Forces, they were a little bit envious of what we were achieving out in Helmand, but different eras bring different challenges.

I spent the next few days pinned to the sofa, either watching footage that my parents had taped or going through scrapbooks that my father had put together. I found that it kept me thinking about the platoon, and by doing this I was not missing out on anything, as in my head I was still there.

I managed to peal myself off the sofa and visit my sister and her family. Their house was in Ballybeen Estate, the place where I had grown up. I actually loved the time that I had spent there, the people were fantastic and friendly. I still had a lot of friends living there, only problem was that each year I lived abroad the further I drifted apart from them.

My brother-in-law Craig was a decent guy, he would spend about an hour letting everyone say hello and reminisce about the old days. Then BANG, he would rub his hands and say, right, Helen me and your brother are heading to the pub for a wee beer.

It would be good to get out and let my hair down so to speak. We would walk down the road chatting about Afghanistan and Liverpool football club, and how they were playing rubbish.

Once in the pub, he would buy the first round of drinks. Some of the guys would stare at me and come over to acknowledge that I was very gaunt looking with pink skin. I would explain that I have just flown in from Afghanistan that would be me having my beers bought for me for the remainder of the night. They treated me with respect, they were a very loyal bunch, even the manager of the Moat pub was a decent guy, the Crown of Cavey and Mickey added to the atmosphere, they were good-enough guys to drink with. I actually enjoyed standing there and listening to Mickey and Craig arguing over what rubbish Man UTD and Liverpool were playing at the time.

At this point I would step outside and phone my parents to tell them I would not be late and that I was okay. They would be a little bit worried of my whereabouts but that was to be expected as all parents worry.

I would stay for a few more pints, then order a taxi home. I would stop at the Belmont road and buy a Chinese take-away, one for me and one for my dad, he always said no. But once I had left it in the kitchen for long enough, he would make a sigh then say, well, I might as well, it saves it from going to waste. I always had a laugh inside. It was like clockwork.

I spent the next few days going shopping with my mother, helping her with the groceries, and being introduced to people that would bump into her while out shopping. It was fun actually. My dad would call me from upstairs and tell me that one soldier had been killed in Afghanistan.

This news would always have me on edge, hoping that it wasn't someone that I knew. I enjoyed spending nine days with my parents, it was just what I had needed, and having my feet grounded for a few days had been fantastic. But I now had to leave, I was flying back to England, I wanted to spend my last forty-eight hours with my brother. We got on very well. He had served with me for eight years in the Royal Irish Regiment and had completed many operations. He had been an NCO in the special Close Observation Platoon (COP) and had been in recce platoon when we had invaded Iraq during the Gulf War. He then went on to try Special Forces selection, but had come off it after a short period of time. He had met his wife back then and the prospect of going back to battalion life and all the bullshit that comes with it. He had decided to leave and become a bricklayer instead, what a 100% change in career that he had done.

He had in fact done rather well out of it. His house was fantastic, he had managed to do most of the work himself, including the fitting of bathroom suite and the plumbing. He was at the airport waiting for me to pick up. We spoke about a lot of things, though he never once did mention about who I had killed, that was one thing that soldiers do not ask soldiers. We tend to block it all away somewhere in our heads, no wonder we all had traumatic head injuries, there was a lot of stuff flying around in my head.

I was staying with him, so he had me sleep in the spare room. Once settled in he gave me a beer, we had a chat about Afghanistan and how the next few days would work out. He was due to be married to Liz. So most of my family had in fact travelled to Whitstable, my sister and her family were staying in a house that they had rented out for the duration of the wedding. This meant for the first time in a long time, I actually had all my family in the one place.

With the wedding fast approaching, there were people from old who had made the journey across to Whitstable, the Macintosh family that had grown up with ours. Then there was Brenda, who had been through a lot with my mother, especially when her brother was taken hostage in Beirut in the '80s, and my Aunt Pat from Scotland along with my uncles from Hull. It was great to see everyone, the only drama I was having was that in my head I wasn't truly there.

The wedding was a fantastic day. Everyone had come together, the meal was not what I had expected especially when my aunt began to choke and slide down her chair, and everyone was stunned. What happened next was the funniest thing that I had ever seen. Someone went across and began to give her water, then someone else came across and insisted he was a lifeguard and began to intervene. Then someone else stated he worked on the boats and knew first aid. This made me laugh. I remember saying at the table that the next guy across worked for slumber land and was going to put her into a recovery position.

We arranged to go out for a pint with our old chum Willy Russell; he was an ex–Irish Ranger and had served with us back in the day, he had since transferred to the Royal Scots and was a corporal. Actually a great guy to have on your side, very funny to be around, but could turn nasty very easily, that was how our Willy rolled, as he used to say.

We went into a few select pubs in the town of Whitstable. It was a lovely little town near the coast and on good clear days you could spot Frances coastline. We chatted about the old days and what I was up to in Afghanistan. The news came on and the headlines were '1British Soldier killed in Afghan Ambush'. I was watching to see who it was, praying that I didn't know him. It was a photograph of Capt. Alex Ieda. He had been killed two days previous, but he was now being named, then on the television network showed his picture, it had me in shock.

I had been on previous patrols with this officer. He was a good guy, and he had also taken part in the Ranger Platoon contact into Zumbelay. This was the first time I had in fact known one of the guys that had been killed, it was the start of things bad to come.

Willy and my bro just looked at me with the look of shock. 'Did you know him?' Willy said. I explained that he was attached to my platoon for a few patrols. We raised a glass to him and tried our best to enjoy the rest of the night. The truth was we couldn't. We had a few more pints and went on our way. I went to my brother's house and grabbed a bite to eat. After another beer, he went to bed. I just lay there wondering how my platoon was in fact getting on.

The next day my brother drove me all the way to RAF Brize Norton. He volunteered to do it, I would have been happy to get the bus from London, but I suppose this was his way of saying goodbye. We both knew I would be coming back, but I know he would not have been able to forgive himself by not driving me if I was to be killed in theatre. We had along chat about plans after I got back, what my next step would be and how he and Elizabeth (Liz)wanted to have children. It all sounded rather good. After less than three hours, we had in fact got to the RAF camp. He drove me right to the terminal, then helped me to get the bags out. He shook my hand then gave me a hug. I told him I would ring first chance that I got. I turned to walk into the rotating doors, as he climbed back inside his car. When I looked back, he had already driven off.

I'm sure to this day he probably had doubts of me returning without a scratch, but that's what family do—they hope for the best but are also realistic.

The departure lounge was full of troops returning from R&R. There were also a few concerns etched on the faces of officers who had just found out that some of their soldiers had refused to return and were now AWOL. Some soldiers were a little scared of what the outcome would be. Others had some close calls and were not willing to risk it again.

We had to wait for about an hour before we boarded the aircraft. This gave me enough time to go and collect my helmet and body armour. Once aboard I had to try and find somewhere big enough to put my helmet and body armour as most of the overhead lockers were filled already. I looked down the aircraft to see if there was any spare seats and was taken back a bit at the emergency gas canisters and hospital beds there were, intravenous drips hanging over the beds. Along with two nurses who sat there, they would be used to bring injured soldiers back to the UK. The flight was going to be long again. It was as if we were in a time warp, we couldn't help or do anything until we had our kit issued back, and that would not be for another two days.

Again we had to stop off in Cyprus to re-fuel, this time it took two hours, just enough time to call my parents and let them know I was okay. We spoke about what my dad was up to, he had in fact began yet another diet. He blamed me for him gaining a few pounds. Apparently the Chinese food that I kept buying had started to show on him. Well, that's what he said, I didn't remember putting a gun to his head and forcing him to eat it.

After the short delay, we were all called back to the aircraft. We walked the short distance up the steps and back into our seats, from here it was another four hours into Kabul. The rumour was that we might in fact fly into Bastion, they had been working on a new runway, so anything was possible.

We managed to get some sleep. I was only woken up the once and that was for a meal, so I was very well relaxed. The flight then started to come into Afghan airspace, then we were again briefed. 'You're about to descend into Kabul. I ask all passengers to return to their seats, put on helmets and body armour, and fasten your seatbelts, thank you.' That was all we needed to know, windows again had to be closed along with all the cabin lights going out, it was a very daunting time.

We gave the usual sudden drop in aircraft drills, this was to ward off any possible surface to air missiles (SAM) attacks that could be launched. The aircraft gave the usual bump when it had landed safely on the runway. After taxiing for almost eleven minutes, we came to a stop.

I could feel the difference in temperature straight away, and with the amount of passengers on the aircraft, I was beginning to sweat. I just wanted off, the door opened and everyone was already standing up grabbing their daysacks and belongings from the overhead lockers.

I made my way to the door only to be given a bottle of water by a nice-looking RAF girl; she smiled and wished us a safe tour. That was nice, I thought as I made my way down the aircraft steps. I was now starting to get the paranoid head on. I watched everyone with pure suspect.

This was what this place had done to me. I was a paranoid wreck, but deep down inside I was loving this feeling. It wasn't until now I had felt like a real soldier. All those years I had served before was wasted time. It had been building up until now, and the only thing on my mind right now was how were my section getting on, I hoped the platoon were okay.

The transport took us all to yet another departure lounge, where we waited to be flown into Bastion, this time it would be by Hercules C-130, and it would take an hour. This may seem a little extreme instead of using a Chinook, but at the time all Chinooks were out on the battlefield. And if they were in Bastion, then they were being repaired from bullet holes that they had taken while trying to land with troops, drop supplies, or even collect wounded soldiers off the battlefield. It was great to see this happen as it lifted the morale of the troops, knowing that the pilots would fly in no matter what the threat was.

On coming into Bastion, the camp had doubled in size, its perimeter was almost 5 miles now. A lot of it was in darkness, and the electricity generators were working overtime just trying to light up the perimeter fence and areas of possible attack. You could now make out where each unit was situated due to massive regimental flags dotted around the base. The Danish had their own camp with flag flying; the Estonians also, at the hospital, had the star-spangled banner (American) flag flying high.

The aircraft came to a stop very suddenly. I think this was down to the runway not being that long, however it had worked so I can't complain, and we stood up and walked off the back of the Hercules. There slightly off to a flank waiting was a member of C-Coy 3 Para's CQMS staff, and it was glad to see us. He gave us a little bit of a back brief of what each company had been up to and explained that the battalion had taken quite a few casualties.

This was very frustrating, the people back home were in fact only hearing about soldiers killed in action (KIA), they did not know the extent of the fighting. For every five soldiers that were being killed, we were in fact losing twenty more to wounds.

Statistically this was shocking, but in Whitehall where all the movers and shakers worked, this was acceptable, this would always be the case in British politics, they would make the decisions and the soldiers would pay the sacrifice. After a ten-second acknowledgement on the news, they would spend a further two minutes talking about how a member of Parliament had claimed £500 for having his pond cleaned out. I felt no one really cared. He dropped me off at the rear echelon tent. I looked around for some clear direction only to be told that my platoon was on Immediate Response Team (IRT). I thought great they are only 200 metres from where I was. I then thought why again, this was a terrible task to get.

I walked across to be greeted by Luke and the rest of the guys. They started to tell me about the last two pick-ups that they had been called out to, there had been a KIA and three WIA paratroopers. It brought reality straight back to you, my R&R was now completely out of my head.

Chapter 5
INCIDENT RESPONSE TEAM

I had been put straight onto standby. I had to stay within shouting distance of the accommodation. There was also a location board that the guys had made and a runner sitting in the JOC. He would come running straight out and get the guys ready, they would jump into the vehicles and drive to the back of the Chinook. By the time we had all gotten on, the Chinook was ready to deploy.

The crew would have briefed us on where we were flying to and what the situation was. Most of the time we just ran off the aircraft and provided protection for the casualty extraction; sometimes depending on the ferocity of the attack, we helped carry the troops back onto the Chinook.

My first job back was to fly into Musa Quala; this was a hot bed of insurgency. It was just as bad as Sangin, if not worse. The troops there were in fact Royal Irish. They had volunteered to come out to Afghanistan. They had heard that we were doing proper soldier things, and as soon as the casualties started mounting up, the manpower began to dwindle.

These guys were high-calibre soldiers. I knew a lot of them from battalion, I just didn't want to have to collect them, let alone put them into body bags.

We flew over Musa Quala. We could see the tracer rounds being fired, the door gunner began to engage depth positions, the Sangers in the small camp were all in contact. It wasn't a good sight to see, the guys were very much in the thick of it, it looked scary from the Chinook. We got off and began to run forward.

I do not know how they had managed to get outside their camp, but they had two casualties on stretchers, the look etched across their faces was that of pure panic. We helped with the stretchers; it seemed only seconds that we were on the ground before we lifted off.

Once the Chinook was off the ground, we began to weave in and out of the wadi, until all of a sudden we lifted straight up. We were now about 2,000 feet off the ground. I could see the doctors and surgeons along with nurses working away on the two casualties. One had been shot by a sniper right in the head, while the other had been shot through the ear.

This was a commander who had been briefing his sentry on the arcs of fire. They had been in the Sanger when they were fired upon by a sniper, and they turned out to be Ally McKinney and Ranger Armstrong.

This was a blow to the Royal Irish Regiment and all the guys on the IRT along with a drop in morale back in Musa Quala. I'm sure with the amount of incoming, what a welcome back to theatre.

The next day could not be as bad. No matter what we did, it could never get that bad. We sat around most of the day playing with a long piece of metal. For some reason, we all took it in turns to see how far we could throw it like a javelin, it wasn't long before some sergeant came out wanting to know who was in charge. I told him that I was and continued to throw this metal bar, so he asked us if we would stop. I told him no, we were playing, at that time I felt like I could easily have killed him, he soon went away.

Ralf ran over to the tent saying stand to, the IRT had been tasked; we quickly got our belt kit on and made our way to the Chinook again. Once we were in the air, we were told that it was the Estonians that had been in contact, and it was going to be a Hot Landing Zone (HLZ). With a deep sigh, I prepared myself once again. Coming into the HLZ, the door gunner opened fire, another battlefield going absolutely crazy, green and red tracer everywhere.

The first casualty walked on and sat down beside me, the other one was on the stretcher and not breathing. I looked at the Estonian soldier beside me. I would never forget the look on his face, he looked tired and confused, his face covered in dirt.

I could see blood seeping out of his combat top. I asked him to lift his top up, but due to the language barrier, he just stared straight through me. I started to have a closer look at him, he had some bullet wounds in his arms and legs, but due to the amount of adrenalin being pumped through him, he didn't either know or care. He was given morphine and the CMT on the aircraft began to strap him up.

This IRT task was really not for the faint-hearted. I couldn't wait to hand this over to the next platoon. The news coming in was that of one soldier from the household cavalry regiment (HCR) had been killed as well as one other soldier from the Royal Horse Artillery (RHA). He too had been killed in Sangin DC. This was another sad day for the guys. No matter what regiment you were in, you all felt the pain every time someone was killed. We all in turn had a minute to reflect.

Now been relieved by 9 Platoon, they don't want to do IRT either, I don't think anyone does really. The IRT couldn't operate without us though, and it was a vitally important task, so we had to do it.

We arrived back into Fob Price (Gereshk). The atmosphere was that of excitement, the threat had gone up again due to the amount of Taliban activity in the town, and due to the ANP being killed by Close Quarter Assassination (CQA), it was more dangerous than ever before.

It wasn't long after arriving back at camp that we found ourselves again going over some trauma training in order to blow away any cobwebs. The biggest threat to the platoon was going to be complacency. We did not want to be caught out. Spence entered our tent with the news that the OC wanted every man to go onto the range. He wanted to watch us go through section attack drills. The news was meet with a little anger, why the hell were we doing this. Spence and the boss were not ones for bullshit, so there must be a reason behind it. We waited to be called forward. Spence was doing our range safety along with a few of the paratrooper NCOs. My section began to space out across the range. The word of command came across as 'WATCH AND SHOOT, WATCH AND SHOOT'. We began to advance forward. I was constantly talking to Luke, we moved about 20 metres, then 'CONTACT FORWARD,' I shouted out, a few initial rounds at the target, then onto the belt buckle. 'Delta fire team, give covering fire. Charlie, prepare to move 'MOVE'. We checked our pockets and pouches, got up, and zigzagged forward 10 metres, then back down, once engaging the target area. Delta carried out the same drill, before darting forward 20 metres. They had to get past us before going firm.

We approached the bunker position. Delta were now suppressing the depth position. I had placed down a point of fire and moved forward with Stewarty. On the approach I told him to get the grenade ready. He took off the safety clip and looked at me. His magazine was fresh on. He was like a Jack Russell ready to be let off his leash. I gave the nod, he leaned forward and launched the grenade at the target, shouting, 'GRENADE', he then got up and began to fire automatic fire into the bunker.

There was a slight problem, his weapon only fired two to three rounds, and he shouted, 'STOPPAGE!' I moved over the top of him and began to fire automatic fire into the bunker. 'POSITION CLEAR,' I shouted at the top of my voice as I moved forward onto my belt buckle. I then gave the order to regroup. I started to shout out, 'ARC, Luke, your fire-team cover from 12 around until 4', then I heard the words of command, 'STOP, everyone stand up, keep your weapon pointed down the range. UNLOAD, safety show clear.' I could see the look of delight on Spence's face. We hadn't let ourselves down or him.

After a de-brief from the safety staff and the OC, we left the range on a high and began to make our way back to the tent. Spence wanted the whole platoon in my tent for a brief. Weapons were to be given a 100% clean and the section commanders were to check them.

He arrived over a short time later, with him was the boss. 'Right, fellas, close in.' The boss gave us a quick sit rep on the situation that was unfolding at Musa Quala. It did not sound great, they were surrounded by the Taliban and finding it hard to get resupplied. They had taken numerous casualties now and IRT could not get there, the air threat was through the roof. Two Chinooks had been hit trying to get in and lift casualties, so it remained a no-fly zone.

To be honest I didn't think anyone in the platoon was the least surprised. We knew that the Royal Irish platoon would be putting up the fight of their lives. They had now been known as Easy company throughout the JOC, it had been adopted by them from the series BAND OF BROTHERS about a company group that was ferociously attacked day and night by the enemy, in the end the only thing that they had that could not be broken was their morale.

Another brief started by the news of two WIA soldiers in Musa Quala and one WIA at Sangin. The casualties were now into the thirties, while it's double figures with soldiers KIA. It seemed like nowhere outside of Camp Bastion was safe, even the convoys were getting ambushed shortly after leaving camp. Sometimes when I had a few minutes to myself I sit down and wonder what the hell we were actually there for.

Today 16 August we got warned off for a brigade operation, the battle group needed morale lifted massively before it went completely. It seemed like no matter how many Taliban get killed, they seemed to come back twice as strong, whereas we were limited in our numbers, and when we got briefed only to find out that Sangin, Musa Quala, and Nowzad, all being attacked at the same time and that left Gereshk with no air cover, it made it all sound a little half cocked.

Today started off with all commanders doing kit checks. We also carried out a 100% serial number check. This was just one of my many things to do, I needed to hand into Spence a copy of all kits held by my section. He already had his own list, but this way it was confirmation that I was carrying out my checks as well as the other two commanders.

Spence told all three commanders to go and grab claymores. We were to start giving lessons on how to assemble them. He wanted every man in the platoon to be able to erect one in a split second. He wanted us to be able to bank them as well, this was where more than one was placed out while the wires all came to one place. It looked like a small green calculator.

We now had situation reports coming in that the Taliban are quite close to our camp. The Sangers were putting up illume in order to pinpoint them. I could now hear the Sangers engaging enemy outside of Fob Price, for god's sake, don't tell me we were going to be attacked, this camp was not that great, apart from all the special forces that lived here, it would be easily taken over.

The Sanger had reported firing fifty rounds of 7.62 mm; I
suppose that's nothing in the grand scale of things, if anything it
kept the Taliban at bay for another night. The daily down report had
just reported of a four-hour contact at Sangin DC. They had two
WIA, and reports of nearly fifty Taliban had been killed or seriously
wounded. Morale in camp had now slightly lifted amongst the troops.

Musa Quala had Chinese rocket fired at the front gate of their
base, resulting in one Danish soldier WIA and the gates needed
repairing. I'm sure that task was envied by everyone up there.

Sangin valley now being mortared by the Taliban, another one
soldier KIA and two WIA, the Taliban were getting more and more
daring. They tried to assault a platoon, both sides received a bloody
nose. It just went to show that they were not scared to take on big
numbers. Well today was our last day preparing for this brigade
operation, as tomorrow we move out for what was being billed by the
guys as a great opportunity for some trigger action. I would wait out to
see if that's true.

Every commander's main effort at this stage was to bring all his
men back in one piece. I just wanted to be one of them.

Today was the day for what was called OPERATION ATOMY.
We are all flying into a drop-off point at Musa Quala. By the time we
get there, the DZ would already be secured by the Pathfinders. They
left yesterday and slowly made their way across the ground trying to
not only avoid the Taliban, but the many minefields that lay dotted all
over the ground by the ten-year Afghan-Russian war.

The amount of firepower that we had on offer during the
operation was colossal; we had fixed wing fast jets, 81 mm mortars
along with 51 mm mortars, four Apache gunships stacked up, an
A-1O gunship. HCR had scimitars in the wadi. Snipers were in covert
positions and we had pre-fire going in, and this was just to get the
Danish soldiers out of camp.

When flying into our drop-off point, I again managed to look
out the window in the Chinook. I could see three other Chinooks
all doing the same thing; we landed in open ground and began to
spread out.

News came across the radio that there were 2-300 Anti-Coalition
Militia (ACM). This would be a massive force to take on. They were

carrying AK-47 and AK-74 assault rifles. These weapon systems in some areas were a lot better than our own SA-80 rifles. They also had sniper rifles and rocket-propelled grenades (RPG), the Wombat rocket would be deadly, the most terrifying weapon that most of us had grown to fear was the mortar. This would prove to be deadly, they had now practised firing it and now they were accurate.

Looking from left to right, I could now see the mass of friendly soldiers all moving across the dead ground and into whatever cover was available. I could hear the *whooooosh* followed by large explosions in the distance, the Apache gunships had begun engaging positions, this was followed by RPGs being fired into the air, then automatic gunfire from every angle was now being fired at the troops to my left and right, and into the compound with friendly forces.

The noise became deafening, there were strike marks and sparks coming from all surfaces' metal that the bullets were ricocheting from. I could hear screaming from other platoons as they had come face-to-face with the Taliban.

The boss began to scream down the radio. 'Speedy, take your section and clear that compound.' I acknowledged the boss and began to move across the ground. Luke was watching my fire team move into position before he would get up, thus keeping one foot on the ground at all times, tactics used by British forces. It worked and proved to give us maximum weapon systems accurately facing the enemy at any one time.

We made our way there by leap-frogging each other towards the compound. Grenades were now prepared for entry, Luke then shouted and fired his 40 mm grenade launcher towards an enemy fighter. I could see he had had a direct hit, below the waist on the enemy fighter had just disappeared. From what I could see, the legs had been blown off and the remaining parts of the body had been blown back into the compound.

The smell was sickening, we were now all on edge and prepared for a fight. With the automatic fire coming from across the wadi, and fast jets now dropping bombs onto targets, it was becoming surreal very quick, with the other two sections now providing over watch for us, we had at least got cover from enemy forces that could want to follow us.

It felt better now, we began to line up against the wall, grenades now all prepared, fresh magazines all on the weapons, every second man had turned his change lever on his weapon to automatic, this allowing us all to change magazines at different times, then a radio message from me to the boss. 'Boss, it's Speedy, going it 10.' 'Roger, Speedy,' the reply came—5, 4, 3, 2, 1, 'GRENADE!' . . . BOOM! The compound filled with dirt and dust, then *crack crack dud dud*, we were taking incoming fire. O,Driscol began to fire automatic into one of the rooms.

The guys were now coming through the entry point two at a time. They had now paired up and were beginning to clear the rest of the rooms. I was keeping the boss informed of everything we were doing. I could see the blood trails where we had killed or wounded the Taliban, before we had gained entry into the compound.

The Taliban had clearly extracted their men from the area. After twenty minutes and using all twelve of the L109 grenades, we then used phosphorous grenades to provide a screen so we could extract safely to our over watch position.

The boss was happy with our work. I turned to look at the compound and was pleased with the outcome. The walls of the compound were black, while flames came from the roofs of each room. We walked past Spence. I looked at him and all he could say was, 'That's how you fucking clear a compound', then he winked at me. I felt great, the troops all had a warm feeling of satisfaction of a job well done.

We moved through the rest of the platoon and into an irrigation ditch. It wasn't a great place to carry out administration, but it provided good cover from fire. It also looked right across the wadi and into the town of Musa Quala. The only drama we had was that it was full of stale water and at least 3 feet deep. When I got in, it was up to my chest. I put myself in the centre of the section to give me more control over the troops.

I could see that most of the guys had embraced the fact that they were going to get wet apart from Luke. He was trying to lie on top of the ladders that he had placed across the ditch. He didn't like to get wet, even the paratrooper MFC that was attached to the platoon was laughing at Luke, then the ladder slipped and he was head to foot covered in water, now that served him right.

We could see the enemy gunfire was very constant and sporadic. The noise was deafening and all we (was it constant or sporadic?) could do was observe. The main reason that we had been placed there was to give cover and over watch the target area from a flank position. If any fleeing enemy came our way under Rules of Engagement (ROE) 429A, which was war fighting, we could kill any fleeing enemy forces.

Every ten or fifteen minutes there were fast jets flying at 100 feet. They would nearly blow our eardrums, then a mushroom cloud would appear over the town followed shortly by a massive BOOM. It looked surreal and was always followed by a cheer from the lads.

After a few hours and thousands of bullets exchanged with the Taliban, we could see the Danish soldiers emerging from the town and beginning to hand-rail the wadi during their extraction.

This was shortly followed by two Apache helicopters that had to escort the Danish most of the way out of Musa Quala town. Once the enemy fire began to fade away, we started to move backwards into an area that had been secured for us. We started to pair up and took up arcs of fire so the enemy couldn't infiltrate our location. It was nearly one kilometre from the enemy location and gave good cover.

Once the platoon sergeants had reported into the CSM that all men had been accounted for, we began to move into two lines (chalks). This would make it a lot easier when the Chinooks came in, they would land and we would run in to the back of them already in two lines.

This all sounded great, but as soon as the Chinooks actually landed, the amount of sand and dust thrown into the air was too much. We couldn't see a thing and that was with goggles on. We had to hold on to each other and keep our heads down while moving forward. I could taste the dust-like sand in my mouth. Most of the guys were gasping for some air. I just placed the straw of my camel-back in my mouth and took a few gulps of water to kill the taste.

With the sweat running down the back of our necks, the carbon that was now ingrained on our hands and combats and the look of thank God that went well across our faces, you could now see the smiles begin to appear on some of the guys' faces.

I looked up at the door gunner, he was wearing fresh combats, he also had short hair, he looked like he had just arrived in theatre, he didn't know what to say to us, he just began to hand out bottles of water, and to be honest, that's all we wanted.

The word came down the Chinook from the pilots that we were being dropped off at Bastion camp. Everyone was happy with that, it meant that we could get a lot of administration carried out, maybe grab a shower and a haircut, followed by a pizza. I had to get that out of my head for the time being, the first thing I wanted my guys to do was to clean their weapons followed by battery re-supply for radios and countermeasure kit. Obviously we would need rations and more water, so between the three section commanders, we equally tasked enough men to complete each task.

We spent the next few days getting briefed on an air assault mission that was to take place in the town of Sangin; this was met with shock, nervousness, and a little bit of let's just get the job done. We all had doubt in the back of our minds.

Sangin had become the most dangerous place in the whole of Afghanistan, up until now there had been seventeen casualties in the battle group and four had been killed in Sangin alone. It was going to be a test of soldiering ability by every single man. There was certainly no room for passengers.

The intelligence would be drip fed to our platoon every single morning and evening. I knew that Spence and the boss felt it would be the first loss within the platoon. It was etched across their faces. I did not have the heart to tell them that I knew what they were thinking, it's not exactly something that you bring up in a conversation.

I just looked around at my section and started to imagine what it would be like without each of them. I knew it's not what should happen, but it's realistic to believe that one would probably leave us before the end of the tour; it could very easily be me.

Today, 25 August 2006, we began the day with OP MINIMISE in place—yes, another one had been killed within the battle group and another two casualties. It's not good news, the morale started to fall yet again. It began to play mind games amongst the troops, we needed a good news story and we probably needed it fast, especially with this operation into Sangin only twenty-four to forty-eight hours away.

The brief began today by explaining that Sangin was, as we speak, in a battle with the Taliban, four Sangers were all fighting at the same time, the enemy strength was still unknown, but believed to be 300–400, they were at times surrounding the patrol base and attacking every Sanger at the same time. This would lead to total confusion within the camp as to where to strengthen and where was in fact vulnerable.

News kept coming over the next twelve hours that the Taliban had grown strong again in Sangin. We needed to go and go soon. Morale within A-Company 3 Para was beginning to subside, the soldiers had been fighting day and night, re-supplies had fallen short of the camp, and the guys were fatigued.

Now battle-hardened and able to take on anything, they still needed rest. Some hadn't slept properly now for weeks, the Taliban had ambushed them on several occasions. They had killed dozens of Taliban fighters, yet they seemed to not weaken them.

The officer commanding the company was now losing patience with the brigade commander and in fact his own commanding officer. They had just sent a platoon out on patrol and yet again it was ambushed, one of the section commanders moved away from the remainder of the platoon along with his section. It was only 300 metres to the north of Sangin DC, but with the cornfields in full growth and the way the ground lay, it was impossible to see the section as they advanced.

In one daring move, he had to make a decision. His section had been split into fire teams, with his platoon commander trying to get a message to him that the Taliban forces were extremely strong; there was automatic fire that was the message that got passed to the rest of our company.

The soldier involved in this complex ambush carried out by the Taliban was in fact Corporal Brian Budd. He was from the elite pathfinder unit and now a commander within the elite Parachute Regiment, and he would later be awarded a Victoria Cross for outstanding leadership and bravery in the face of the enemy.

We were given more maps than we could carry. The commanders amongst us moved off to a quiet area of the tent and began to mark up the northings and eastings on the map.

I sat in the tent and began to see the difference in Sangin, it was a war zone now, compared to when we first entered the town, the platoon house was now reinforced so much it looked like it might collapse in on itself. The town was now known as a no-go area, the Taliban had in fact taken over the town and they dictated the movement within it.

The boss told us that he didn't want to interfere with the sections drills; however, there were a few things that he wanted us to rehearse and that was using ladders and getting over walls with kit on.

The thought of fighting an enemy force in their own backyard was a little daunting especially in the heat and humidity that waited for us. I sat the guys around and explained what would be asked from them. They looked anxious and rightly so, I was secretly looking forward to what would be the icing on the cake as far as soldiering terms. This would either make me or completely break me.

Before the end of the day, I also took the guys away from prying eyes and rehearsed break contact drills. I wanted to make sure that we were slick; I didn't want any mishaps when the time actually came.

Today I got bad news, well, I suppose it's bad. B-Company was down a section commander, they needed someone to fill the gap. Spence wanted me to go, he looked at the other guys and explained that Davey was his choice as the platoon sergeant, if he had to go anywhere, Getty was newly promoted and he would not send him. 'Robbie is needed in the platoon, so, Speedy, it's you, mate.'

To be honest after only a few minutes I was looking forward to the challenge. Every one of us was capable of doing it; all four of us corporals were good tactically and wouldn't let the platoon down.

Then I got some good news from Spence. 'Speedy, pick eight guys from the platoon and take them with you.' I was very happy with that. I picked a great bunch. I wanted Tam, Zac, Ralf, Mac, O,Driscol, Devine, and Luke. This was a strong section, some were already in my section, while others I wanted for their sheer strength and firepower.

The look on the rangers' faces when I explained that we were now part of 8 Platoon C-COY but attached to B-Company was priceless. We received a set of orders for the operation. I listened intently, but this wouldn't matter to me, my orders were part of B-Company, and our objectives would be different, but listening to C-Company would at least help me build a picture of where everyone would be on the day.

It sounded like a lot of trouble for each company. There were known Command Wire-Improvised Explosive Devices (CWIED) placed out by the Taliban in order that one of soldiers would walk into it, the command wire lengths were reported to be between 5 and 10 metres. That did not give the enemy much room to escape if it didn't detonate, so the enemy strength would be at least section strength around the trigger man. It sounded like it wasn't going to be easy.

Our report lines would be called ARNHEM and BRUNEVAL. Well, we were part of the parachute battle group, so it made perfectly sense to name the report lines after famous battles where the paratroopers had fought bravely in the past.

B-Company orders went on forever. Everything had to be just perfect, one step wrong and we could very easily lose soldiers. This needed to be rehearsed, the preliminaries were alone nearly thirty minutes, moon state, weather forecast for the next seven days, what the ambient light would be like if the battle went on through the night, the heat between 40-50 degrees Centigrade would make it a testing time for everyone.

Situation enemy forces, this took some while to get across to the troops. The enemy was in a strong position. Sangin was their home and they didn't want us there, the only drama was the paratroopers had a different idea, they were going to take Sangin no matter what.

With my section attached to 8 Platoon in B-Company, it was going to be everything we had trained for rolled into one operation. Our given objective was to reach and secure the old National Directive Security (NDS) building. This was some distance from our DZ, we would have to get across the Sangin wadi to reach there, and with it being open ground, it would take a lot of suppressive fire in order for us to get across in one piece.

As for the other objectives within the company, they were the Chinese restaurant, that was 4 Platoon's objective, it wasn't really a Chinese eatery, the shape of the building just reminded all of us of what a Chinese restaurant looked like, while 5 Platoon was given their line of exploitation (LOE). It was the farthest north compound before you get into the green zone, it sounded easy, but with the amount of enemy forces in the area, this was going to be the hardest thing either of us had ever done.

We all stood in chalks just off the HLS in Bastion, to my left and right were row after row of paratroopers just staring into space. They all had the same look of frustration, they just wanted to go and get the job done.

I didn't speak a lot either, just the usual chit-chat, everyone ready, weapons all prepped, then I started going through the usual stuff that commanders do in their heads, depending on which way he lands the Chinook, will depend on which way the threat is coming from.

We went off and peeled left. 'Mmmmm, forget it, let's just wait and see', then the word came across from the JOC, fifteen minutes. Everyone began to do final checks to their section and their kit. I gave a radio check to the other call signs within my platoon, all good, I was happy.

Then what looked like a scene from *Apocalypse Now* came four Chinook helicopters, they all landed at the same time, the down draft was unbelievable, and we nearly got blown off our feet, it was just the amount of weight that we were all carrying that kept us upright.

We moved forward wearing goggles. My section all had their weapons wrapped in bin-bags to prevent dust and dirt being blown onto the weapon, especially after we had oiled them for battle. We couldn't afford any stoppages at vital times throughout the battle, and it would mean life or death.

It wasn't long before all choppers were loaded up; we sat there on the HLS for the intelligence to filter down from the head sheds that in the Joint Operations room (JOC), this usually took some time to get down to the troops that were waiting to be given orders, due to a lot of working parts and report lines and restricted firing lines, it all had to be closely monitored and maintained.

As soon as everyone who was playing a part had given their brief to the battle group captain, the information was very quickly disseminated to the Chinook pilots. The rotors began to fire up and we were quickly back into our chalks waiting for the word to board the heli, then one at a time we lifted off into the sky. It was a very nervous yet exciting time, not knowing what was waiting at the HLS. I felt my guts began to churn at this moment, I also noticed that no one was talking again. We just wanted to kill the Taliban and not be killed ourselves.

We would find out very soon if they were a match for our superior firepower. Let's hope they were not.

Chapter 6

BATTLE FOR SANGIN

The look on everyone's face told a story, they were ready for whatever was going to be thrown at them. I was nervous, this was the first time since the Second World War that a commander from my regiment had been in this situation. I was the first to do it, and I didn't want to let my unit down, more importantly I didn't want to let my section down, and they didn't want to let anyone down.

Once in the air I just watched as Bastion drifted off into the distance. We were all crammed in like sardines again, this was becoming a regular occurrence, but what the hell, this was war. At one stage I couldn't feel my legs as someone else was resting their backpack with ammunition on them, there was no point in complaining as everyone was in the same position, you just had to grin and bear it.

I was starting to feel on edge. We were now only ten minutes out. It was passed through the Chinook by word of mouth, then I could feel the person behind me get to his feet. He put his hand out for me to grab and scramble to my feet. Within only a couple of minutes, everyone was standing up and staring out the back of the Chinook.

Then the words came down the Chinook five minutes to target. Now I still didn't know what I was thinking, but I began to check my ammunition state. I had it written down on a piece of plastic, and it was in permanent black pen. I'm sure others were doing pointless things at that time, it helped the time tick away for me.

Then, three minutes to target, you could hear some guys swearing and shouting, 'Let's fucking go', get some Taliban. Everyone was now fully pumped with adrenalin, they wanted battle and wanted off the Chinook ASAP.

Then the door gunners began to engage targets in the near distance, the Taliban gave as good as they got, the red and green streaks of colour were everywhere, explosions from bombs being dropped by the RAF and Apache gunships firing into enemy position it was surreal. We landed under heavy enemy fire. I ran off the Chinook and immediately went left into line with the other sections.

Then I heard the boss shout for covering fire. We were in the open and needed to move away from this area, the Chinooks were screaming out for us to hurry up. They were attracting much fire, the Taliban would have loved to shoot one down, and we couldn't let this happen. Without them we would be stuck with no ground troop support. Mortar fire began to go into depth positions. This enabled us to move forward undetected for about 50 metres. We had now moved safely to the front of Sangin DC, we had moved north-east up the wadi.

C-Company at this stage had moved off the HLS and began to go south-east from the DC and had already started to secure buildings along the 611 highway. This was to allow a convoy to pass through unchallenged by the Taliban and re-supply the troops with water, food, and most importantly, ammunition.

The convoy had safely reached FOB Robinson, and was now approaching Sangin; we now were all spaced out quite well and began to move across the wadi. I could see friendly forces to my half left in the distance, approximately 70–100 metres away. We moved off the hard standing and onto the grass area just on the edge of the green zone, then in micro seconds it began.

Whoooooooooooosh . . . BOOM . . . BOOM . . . BOOM! *Dud Dud, Dud Dud Dud,* there were bullets bouncing off the ground inches in front of us, we had to take cover, everyone was screaming for some sort of target indication, reference points, just give us something.

Then I heard that C-Company was in a massive contact with the Taliban. I looked over at the platoon sergeant, he was just as in shock as me, we had been caught out, even knowing that we had expected it, we didn't expect that much resistance.

The Taliban were relentless in their attack, then RPGs began to fly past our heads. We couldn't stand up for fear of being hit, we all started to extract back into cover. I informed the rest of my section that when they hear the rate of fire being lifted by the other two sections, they were to move back as a fire team, they understood loud and clear.

They couldn't get off their belt buckles, the rate of fire coming from the Taliban was actually quite scary. I didn't know they had such awesome firepower, I then spotted a weapon system being fired from what can only be described as a port hole, they were just sticking their weapons through and hoping that a stray bullet would in fact hit one of us, but when you have a building with numerous holes in it, you are going to hit someone sometime.

We managed to get everyone in the platoon safely extracted out of the killing area, and into some sort of cover. By hand railing the compounds with the rifle firmly placed to the front, my safety catch was off and I was ready to kill, with rage tattooed across my face at the near-death situation that had just occurred. I was fuming with anger, we got about a further 50 metres north-east and began to spread out again, this time we had a condor moment.

The boss was now working out where the other platoons were in relation to ours. The officer commanding came through our platoon and now wanted us to clear a building so he could get onto the roof, my section was looking at me for instruction. I moved forward and tried to look around the building, then automatic fire came straight at me, it passed and hit the wall behind where I was standing.

Jesus Christ, that was close, I said, then more fire directed straight at us. I told O,Driscol to try and see what was around the other side of the building, but he had the same problem, by this stage my section was all stuck behind a compound wall, the OC screaming down for us to take control of the situation. To be honest for the first time in my career I was lost for words, sweat trickling down my face and back I had to make a decision and fast.

I stood back from the wall and noticed square concrete pillars. They were 2 foot thick and evenly spaced out, it was nearly 10 metres between each one. I made a command decision, I wanted someone to run out as fast as they could and then stand behind one perfectly still, it would take someone with a lot of balls, guts, and courage. The guys knew I had a plan, I looked at Ralf, he nearly cried back at me, but he didn't, he found some inner courage. I explained my plan to him then told O,Driscol that as soon as Ralf was taking incoming fire, that he and Zac were to engage the enemy position. I let Ralf have a few minutes to get his adrenalin pumping much faster, then he said, 'Right, Speedy, I'm ready.'

In an instant we all got ready. GO! Ralf ran as fast as he could, the Taliban began to engage him. I could see the bullet's sparks following behind him, then my section got into a position and began to fire. I took the safety clip off the grenade and threw it at the position. GRENADE! BOOM! shortly followed up by a burst into the Taliban position. We had done it, only one drama now, poor old Ralf was standing behind a concrete pillar shitting himself.

I got the section to move into a position that afforded us good arcs of fire and cover from enemy fire, we had achieved something special that day, and Ralf had proved to be the bravest by far, from that day onward I would always hold Ralf in high regard.

Finally we were starting to get a foothold on this one-sided situation. The attack was relentless, it just seemed that it wouldn't end, the OC would call in fast jets and drop a joint direct munitions (JDAM) right on top of the target, then within minutes they would engage us from the same position. They must have had a tunnel system, but we never seemed to find one.

I could see that 4 Platoon was pinned down by sporadic enemy fire. This was not good news, 5 Platoon then got tasked to suppress enemy positions to the north-east of 4 Platoon. It may have been very confusing to control at a higher level, but for me and my section, we actually knew where the whole company was but not exactly each call sign's position.

The enemy fire seemed to get stronger for a few minutes, then I heard mortars hitting the compounds in the far distance shortly followed by a massive rate of fire, then word came across from the cornfield opposite us, 'MAN DOWN, MAN DOWN!' Morale seemed to drop slightly, everyone was listening in for his zap number and call sign to come across the radio. It was the 5 Platoon sergeant who had been hit, he had been shot in the neck and dropped to the ground immediately, they were finding it hard to extract him off the battlefield due to the amount of enemy fire.

The OC began shouting down from the rooftop. 'Get me a section together and get that casualty back here!' It was easier said than done, it would be suicide to just run out into the open, we would need heavy fire going into likely enemy positions and loads of smoke to cover our movement.

We managed to get guys and they made their way across yet more open ground to extract the casualty, then more enemy fire began to strike the ground in front of them. This was a bloody joke, now we needed to get them guys out of the open. I could hear the OC swearing his head off, then again a fast jet appeared and dropped a massive bomb, but this time it was accompanied by a B1 Bomber, I could hear the Household Cavalry coming up the wadi in their vehicles. I moved out into the open and beckoned them to come to our position, I think they had already been tasked by the boss to come to where we were anyway.

By the time they had brought their vehicle to where my section was situated, a 3 Para medic was driving a quad bike towards me, on the back was the platoon sergeant on a stretcher, the quad was flanked by four other paratroopers acting as protection, the OC by this stage had come down off the roof to meet the casualty. I remember seeing the casualty raise his hand in the air and give the thumbs-up to the OC. When speaking to him, today, he states that he cannot remember doing it. He blames the morphine for his actions, but it just shows the temperament of the paratrooper, always fighting until the end.

With the casualty now safely into the back of a scimitar vehicle, we could now begin to sort our men out, ammunition states and all the usual service support briefs began to take place, my section had now fully secured the area and had linked up with the other sections. The sheer relief of everything was overwhelming at times, now we had to do the same again to get back into Sangin DC.

It was never ending, after fighting for our lives to get to where we were, we now had to extract and get back into the FOB. It wasn't long before word got passed down the chain that we had failed to reach our objectives, this was as far as the OC had decided to push forward to, he himself had made the decision that this was our new LOE. To be honest I think we were all well chuffed.

The convoy had now safely reached its destination. We began to move back up the wadi towards Sangin DC, this time we moved platoon at a time, with Apaches hovering about the troops. It gave us a warm fuzzy feeling, what a crazy day it had been, I moved back thinking about the injured guy on the stretcher with his thumb in the air, and where he would be right now.

This was proper war what we had all joined up for; I just didn't think it would be so intense for so long. I wasn't complaining though, as long as I could get my section to the end of this tour without losing anyone, I would have done my job.

When entering the DC, I could see troops spread out all over the place, there were scimitars sitting up on ramps facing up the wadi, guns being manned every 5 metres along the hesco wall. We quickly moved into cover along the wall. Well, when I say cover, we actually sat along a hesco wall waiting direction from the boss. The OC and Pl commanders went to the headquarters for a set of quick battle orders.

A-Company was very quickly to hand over the Sangers to C-Company, they had suffered a lot of casualties and had a few good men killed in action, the handover was non-existent, but that's how it is, especially when you are in contact, it's just a case of pointing out reference points along with arcs and firing at the enemy. Everything else can be learnt over the next few days.

The Chinooks both landed at the same time, there was a lot of fire from the fire support group into what was now known as wombat wood. With all Sangers now engaging enemy positions, the Chinooks both lifted off into the sky, both door gunners were firing their general purpose machine guns into Taliban firing points, they were finally gone from this hell hole.

The boss was away for about thirty minutes, just enough time for all of us to have a complete ammo state. The platoon sergeant then told me that I could return to my own platoon. I got the guys together and walked for about 100 metres until I found my platoon, starting to set up camp in the Orchard area of Sangin DC.

It looked very quiet and the trees were in full blossom, pomegranate fruit was growing from them, and they were delicious, what more could you ask for, especially after a long day in that heat. It tasted like heaven. I quickly found a space between two of the guys and began to set my Bergan down with my webbing on top of it.

The guys had started to put up their mosquito nets and hang their towels off them. Dougal had his famous Celtic football club towel on show for everyone to see. This was mainly to wind up the ranger fans amongst the platoon. Spence called for the commanders and got us to walk around the DC to identify each position. We needed to know where the arcs of fire overlapped from each Sanger and especially the quickest route to the medical building, casualty evacuation was still fresh on everyone's mind and this needed to be rehearsed.

We quickly began a love and hate relationship with Sangin, the facilities we had were basic, if in fact any at all, the Helmand river flows very fast and it passed through the middle of our camp, it was quite something, a rope was tied on tightly and thrown across the other side and again tied on tight, this was in case the soldiers got lifted up and taken by the strong current, they would grab the rope to stop themselves being taken downstream.

If anything it was peace of mind for us, everywhere we moved in the DC, it was with helmet and body armour with weapon made ready. The sections' second in command all began to draw up stag lists, we made the decision with Spence to break the sections down into fire teams, this would enable us to cover all the Sanger positions, and with two hours on and six off during the day would be pretty chilled out, we would be able to get lots of rest, at night it would be three hours on and again three hours off. Everyone seemed happy with the rotation,.

The other two platoons were getting to grips with their rotation, 9 Platoon was going onto patrols and would learn very quickly that it was a nightmare to conduct anything outside of our FOB, 7 Platoon would be going onto QRF, they would react to any problems that we had outside, mainly with casualty extraction and re-supply, what we quickly learnt was that the QRF would get all the CQMS tasks, like help unload the choppers or collect the rations, clean out ISO containers, and so on.

The QRF would also get the task of cleaning out the toilets. This would be a two-man job, they would move the rusted oil drum from below the manmade wooden toilet, then pour diesel onto it, one of the guys would then light the diesel, this would make the human excrement catch fire, it smelt terrible, but after a while, you got used to the smell.

I was actually on sentry when I heard a lot of laughter coming from the toilet area. Two of the paratroopers from 8 Platoon were trying to burn the excrement with a lighter, but every time they leaned into the oil drum, the smell put them off, then eventually it caught fire, then they began to stir it with a branch, I don't know why they did this, but within seconds, the ISO container that had all the ammunition in began to go up in flames.

They had started to use the stick to flick burnt excrement at each other, they were laughing their heads off until they realised that the ISO was covered in burning excrement. The CSM was not impressed, let's just say those two paratroopers received a few more dirty jobs after that incident.

For the next couple of days we received continuous attacks onto the DC, it was relentless. At one stage I thought, someone's got to run out of ammunition soon, whether it was the Taliban or us, but I knew we couldn't keep this up. It happened like clockwork, first light they would hit us with mortar fire, this would land just outside the front of the DC in the wadi, at the same time the front gate would be attacked with automatic fire and RPGs, followed by Sanger 4 being fired upon, this was a terrible Sanger to have, it was vulnerable and easy to hit from a building that sat only 100 metres away.

At night time I would look out from my position into the town, and I would hear the speaker system giving a call to prayer across Sangin. We knew we had approximately thirty minutes to forty-five minutes to sort ourselves out. It gave us all time to have a hot meal or just relax for a while, all the Taliban were praying in the mosques across the town, that was one of the places that we would not hit or destroy. After all we are British soldiers and we abide by the law, that's what sets us apart from the enemy, however there were some testing times when I thought why not just blow them up, they were full of Taliban, for Christ's sake. Discipline was the key, in saying that had

I been given the order, I would not have hesitated to drop a bomb in order to save life, and when I say life, I mean my fellow soldiers, Irish rangers or paratroopers, out on Herrick 4 we were together through thick and thin.

Well, just as I had expected, another night approached and it's 5 p.m. Afghan time, and the call to prayer had stopped. Wait, Whooooosh! Yes, we were in contact, an RPG had landed in front of Sanger 4. The guys were engaging enemy from that building, now Sanger 1, 2, 3, and 5 were all in contact with the enemy.

I could hear the .50 Cal from the top of the FSG building now engaging Taliban in wombat wood, another surreal battle. I could see green and red tracer rounds flying in every direction, the worst thing about this was the fact that I'm used to it now, it's second nature.

Browner and Dougal had come up to the sentry position just to fire the GPMG into the enemy. That's one thing I could say about every man in the platoon, at first we all didn't know how we would react in the situation we find ourselves faced with every day, but I'm proud to have served with every man, they are warriors, they can't seem to get enough of the enemy.

Everyone wanted to kill the Taliban, not a single man had let the great name of the Royal Irish Regiment down, they should all be proud.

That night was spent re-bombing our magazines and plotting grids for future DFs, the mortars would be informed of firing points and would now be able to drop bombs on the Taliban, if they attack from the same place.

Being a corporal back at unit, there are a lot of perks, one being sentry. Out here in theatre every man mucked in and did their part. It helped the platoon to gel better and show the troops that we are a team.

The nights seemed to drag by, especially when you were on duty. I swear I used to come off sentry with sore eyes, we would spend the whole night scanning areas of enemy activity. If something caught your eye, then the operations room were informed.

The FSG tower would put their gun onto it, and a flare would be fired up to light up the area. Most of the time it was nothing, but when it was Taliban, the guns would open up and destroy the enemy.

The next morning was spent, rotating through the sentry position, two hours on four hours off, it gave us all a chance to wash our combats in the river. We would put on fresh combats from our Bergans, they would make us all feel good, and with the heat, the wet combats would be dry in an hour.

Spence didn't like the fact that the orchard area started to look like a Chinese laundry. We had green string tied from tree to tree, there were washing lines everywhere, even though our admin was good, it made us look like it wasn't.

The engineers came across from the other side of the FOB and began to make us a shell scrape. They used the digger and prepared a bunker for the platoon, then they moved across to Sanger 2 and made another bunker. These would be used by the platoon if we were attacked, at least we now had something close to our living areas, when we get attacked if not on sentry we would all get into these bunkers for safety.

They were well put together by the engineers; the engineers attached to the company would get bored after a while, especially when they worked right through the night on most days.

I would find they would come to the orders groups at night, wanting to go out on patrol just to get a rest. This made me laugh, they actually wanted to go out into enemy territory where they could be killed just to get a rest from building in camp. Well, they were an asset, especially with the explosives, and when they came with our platoon, they got to use them.

Another day comes to an end in Sangin DC, but like no other place in Helmand, it's about to go live with gunfire at 0459 hours, we had one minute to prepare ourselves, it was laughable but serious, then on the button, we had enemy fire onto every Sanger, two more Sangers than last night, they must be upping their game.

The sky looked amazing, red and green tracers coming from every angle, RPG being fired at the front gate from across the wadi, mortar fire coming from wombat wood. We were hitting them just as hard, a Javelin missile has just been fired from the roof; it has a direct hit onto a vehicle carrying Taliban across the bridge.

Our mortars were getting a lot of bombs down into Taliban positions, the engineers had just climbed up into our Sanger with two more GPMGs. They were helping out, the guys were changing belts on the guns, another 200 bullets, we had to slow down the rate of fire.

The barrels were beginning to overheat, they don't teach you this at the skill at arms wing, when you are in war and you have your spare barrel already used and it's cooling down, what do you do. If you are in a contact with the enemy for another four hours, you need to keep engaging him or you will be killed.

It was now nearly nine o'clock, this had lasted just under four hours. Every few minutes they kept firing at the camp, but it's just sporadic fire, nothing serious. Because it was now dark, we could get the guys on sentry rotated into the bottom of the building and get some food cooked up for them.

I got down from the Sanger to see that the guys had managed to make a seating area out of bits of wood and scrap that they have found lying around camp. It looked very relaxed, just what we needed. Having just got out my hexi-burner, I could see the engineers were right next to us, which was handy in case we needed to build anything. Just when I was beginning to drift off asleep, I got rudely awoken by one of the guys. 'Speedy, the boss wants all commanders.' I never questioned the boss when he had us woken up, it was always for a reason.

He had just received a brief from the OC and was now back briefing us, another not-so-good day for the battle group. Musa Quala had one of the guys KIA and another guy WIA. It looked like they were under a lot of pressure up there. We all knew the Royal Irish had two platoons up there, and by looking at the commanders that they had there, they couldn't ask for better leadership.

I cannot ever say what they were going through, but from what we had heard and the messages being passed to us from the JOC, it was the worst ever situation imaginable, they were taking casualties, they were fighting for their lives.

Helicopter support was available only at certain times, the United Kingdom Special Forces (UKSF) took priority with the air support. Orders came down from the top to make it a no-go area for helicopters, it was too dangerous, the threat for a Chinook to be shot down went through the roof.

I could see that 9 Platoon was all getting their kit on, they were trying to look relaxed but I could tell from their body language that they don't like this task. Spence had just shouted up that he wanted the Sangers doubled up with manpower. This looked like it's because 9 Platoon was about to go out on a patrol. From where I was standing, I could see the sections spreading out into whatever cover was available. The commanders were sending radio checks across the net to zero and each other, the countermeasure kit was checked for the right tones and lights.

Then I spotted the guys moving down the pipe range and onto the main road, so far so good, like professional soldiers they scanned their sights with slow motion, every man looking in alternative arcs, it looked good from this Sanger.

Then as soon as the point man moved across the street, he was hit by a wave of gunfire. I could see him run back into cover firing in the direction of the enemy, from nowhere an RPG got fired across the front of him, followed by small arms fire, the lights in street just all went out at the same time. It now looked bad.

We had to use our night-vision goggles to spot our own friendly forces, the mortar platoon guys have pre-empted this and they had fired 81 mm illume into the area, I could see the platoon trying to get out of the killing area, then I heard the OC telling them to extract back to the DC, another typical night in Sangin.

Chapter 7

BLOODIEST EVER DAY

Today we got word from the boss that the Royal Irish in Musa Quala had one of their guys killed and another one seriously wounded. It had been a complex attack by the Taliban to try and overrun the compound, they had been hit from every part of the camp, and had taken a direct hit by a mortar, the mortar had proved to be a deadly weapon and very effective.

This sent a massive blow to our platoon, no one knew who it was, but that didn't matter. We knew we had lost a fellow ranger, one of the 'Band of Brothers', it wasn't easy to swallow, but we still had a job to do, we were far from finished here.

Today was 2 September 2006, another day that would surely be filled with joy, at times I sat down and thought back to when we all complained to Spence that we had not been in a contact yet, and what he said to us, how stupid could we have been to think we wouldn't fire a single bullet.

With five Sangers and an ANP building to watch, we needed to spread the troops out equally to maximise the amount of rest time each man would get, it happened to work out quite well. We got Spence to give us guys from his platoon sergeants group, this would make it easier if we had Bolli and Al, it would mean every man got four hours off between sentry duty.

Most of the day was spent listening to British Forces Broadcasting Station, one of the radios that we had been tuning in, it's not turned up loud but we could hear the tune and that's good enough for me, especially after we had not heard music apart from call to prayer every night, and that's not exactly music.

The days passed yet again with another attack from the Taliban, this time mortar fire lands 200 metres out the back of the FOB, we heard the explosions followed by automatic fire, the front gate was now being attacked from RPGs, then from nowhere, all Sangers were engaged by the Taliban. Every man was told to get into cover, anyone who could, got to a Sanger and helped suppress the enemy positions. This attack only lasted forty minutes, that's long enough to get fast jets here. They arrived just in time, we were starting to run low on ammunition.

The building that sat 100 metres away from Sanger 4 got a J-DAM bomb landed on it, it was the loudest bomb I had ever heard. From the Sanger all I could see was a massive mushroom cloud, that's at least 100 metres in the air. This was followed only ten seconds later by the biggest explosion you could ever imagine to hear, then a wave of dust and debris came across the camp.

It had only been five minutes since the impact and already we were being attacked from the same position that the bomb had hit. This was now just plain crazy, we began to engage the position, but it's no use, the building was providing good cover for the enemy, we needed to get out there and fight the enemy.

The OC sent down yet more bad news to the troops. Spence had been left to give us bad news again. Musa Quala had been attacked again, this time the Taliban were even more determined to break the guys. They had more direct hits with mortars, resulting in numerous casualties, seven casualties this time. I felt like crying, I knew every one of the guys out there, and it must have been hell to see the amount of devastation caused by the ferocious attacks.

This was the bloodiest day my regiment had ever suffered, since its amalgamation back in 1992. They had never witnessed such courage and bravery by so few, and I'm sure it will never again have so many men that have a bond so strong that nothing will ever come between them.

I spent most of the night trying to keep the spirits of the guys up. Even though I looked okay, I was getting Spence to keep my morale up, he knew we were all at breaking point, but as a true professional, he kept on top of every one of us.

News back home was starting to look negative; the public were saying it's not our war and what were we doing there, for the first time the newspapers were very positive, especially the *Sun* newspaper, they were running stories every day about the battle for Helmand, it's keeping our morale very high, God knows we needed it.

I was starting to get bored with sausage and beans for breakfast. I thought I might try and wash the sausages and add another flavour, in fact I will cook the sausage separate to try and change the flavour, well, at least that's something to look forward to later on.

Today seemed to be a quiet day, for how long, I wondered. I was sure the Taliban only stopped to pray and eat, a bit like us really, at times I sat and wondered what the hell was this all about. I knew it's politics, but our mission was to enter Helmand and destroy the poppy fields, which was conjured up on a whim, you cannot destroy the only source of income that a country has to offer without replacing it with something that is just as easy to produce and expensive to buy.

What the hell were we thinking, it's never that simple to do anything. We had the best of the British army here and at times we were no match for the Taliban.

Whoooooosh . . . BOOM, BOOM . . . BOOM! *Rat tat tat tat tat*, I totally forgot that it was five o'clock, there was me sitting on a chair below the Sanger, I rushed up onto the roof to find three GPMGs all engaging positions at the same time, followed by the FSG tower engaging depth positions. This was all too much for the Taliban, our firepower was more superior.

The Taliban just seemed to go away after only thirty minutes. This was very unusual for the Taliban, they were a lot more tactical usually, well at least we would get a break tonight.

This gave Spence a bit of time to organise what he wanted to do. It also gave me a bit of time to sort out thing out with Sanger 1. It was starting to annoy me the way Luke was going on sentry, I caught him earlier walking to the Sanger wearing shorts, with his helmet strap hanging loosely and his body armour undone, and I had been waiting to get relieved so I could speak to him.

Dougal came on sentry, after a quick brief on what was going on within our arcs, I grabbed my rifle and made my way to see Luke. He was not surprised to see me, I gave him a bollocking from hell. 'Listen, you idiot, you're supposed to be the commander of this Sanger, so act like it, if the guys see you going on sentry not giving a shit, they will copy you, you're a complete dickhead, get a grip, before I get a grip of you.' He went red and started to act like a commander.

I didn't like doing that to Luke, but sometimes you have to set an example. I knew deep down that when it came to the crunch in battle, he was very reliable and always produced the goods, but I was not willing to let complacency settle into the section.

I noticed that Luke started to stay away from me; it didn't bother me as long as he was doing his job, we would get on fine. The platoon sergeant went away for another brief from the OC, he was gone sometime, more than usual this time, it must have been an hour before he summoned the commanders to the orchard. With a shake of the head, he began talking about the Americans, 'Listen, fellas, there has been a monumental fuck-up by the Yanks, the Canadians came under heavy enemy fire today way up north.'

So they asked for close air support and that's just what they got, something went wrong with the grid reference that was sent across the radio, it was meant to take out and kill the enemy that were in section plus strength, but the Yanks engaged the Canadians on the other side of the mountain killing one and wounding thirty-three. It's a massive operation to get them all extracted off of the mountain.

I hate to say it, but it's become normal on operations to hear this type of action carried out by friendly forces.

Then he ended his brief on a good note. 'And just in case I forget to mention, tomorrow we are going out on patrol, we leave here around ten o'clock and make our way up the pipe range, and fellas, this will be as hard or as easy as you make it.

'Speedy, your section are on point, you move up the road 50 metres then go firm. Davey, you are on the extreme left flank, give cover for Speedy to move into the area of building 4. Robbie, your section will move hopefully undetected on the rear right and provide flank protection, gents, we have unmanned aviation throughout the patrol, is there any questions? No, troops, be aware we have CVRT vehicles in the wadi just in case we get casualties, let's have a good patrol.'

The troops now were all in good spirits, especially now we had Desert Hawk 3 on station throughout the patrol. This would give the ops room live feed on the area that we were patrolling. It was great to know that other people were looking out for you. The patrol had made it out safely, we were all on edge, the Afghan National Police were at the end of the road. This should have made us feel at ease, but to be honest, none of us had faith, let alone trust in these so-called police officers.

The thought of working alongside a police force who were using drugs constantly put me and the rest of the platoon on edge. I spent the whole patrol scanning my arcs, all I managed to see was empty casings from previous attacks. The amount of devastation within the town was unspeakable, everywhere you looked was destroyed, we had dropped so many bombs, it had to be the case, every single bomb that was dropped in Sangin was in fact justified.

There was no other way to save the lives of British soldiers than to drop bombs on specific targets that had enemy forces in them.

We made it back up the pipe range in one piece, keeping one foot on the ground at all times. On return from patrol, we had to attend another briefing in the ops room, more rubbish news, there had been a mine strike in Kajaki, resulting in one soldier Killed in Action (KIA) and another soldier had been seriously wounded (WIA). It seemed that good news was never going to happen, it followed with the news that Musa Quala was yet again attacked by the Taliban.

The Royal Irish based in Musa Quala was being attacked on a daily basis, now that the Danish had left them on their own, they didn't seem to have much in support, the one thing they did have was mortars, and that was only because the Royal Irish had taken their own with them.

I was looking forward to the day coming to an end; I had lost count of the amount of times that OP MINIMISE had been called, it was the way we conducted business, it was hard that we couldn't call home just to say I'm all right, can't speak now take care, but some guys would always speak to the wrong person, so we just handed the satellite phones back into the ops room.

Well, at least I would have a break from everything tonight, the troops seemed in good spirits after the patrol, the only thing that was starting to get on our nerves was the lack of choice with food. I thought the best place to go would be my bunker, it was a great place to sit and reflect on things, especially as I had my complete mosquito net in there. I could relax and take off my helmet and body armour in complete safety, even if it was to take a direct hit by enemy mortar, I would be fine with the amount of overhead protection it had in place.

Once in the bunker, I could get a hot brew on the go and some food, no one would be able to see any light coming from it, and the sentry list that was up and running took into consideration where every man slept, so I could just fall asleep and when it was my turn in the Sanger someone would come and wake me.

When you are alone at night in a place like Sangin, you have a lot going through your mind. It plays games with your emotions, a weaker man would have fallen apart by now, there is a lot of self-induced stress placed onto you, there is an element of fear, but I seemed to love the fact that I was in this position. I felt at home in Sangin, after all I knew every street, where all choke points were at, where the vulnerable points were, and where we would be contacted from if we turned certain corners.

I fell asleep shortly after getting into my mosquito net. The roll mat I lay on felt a bit hard, but my body was used to the comfort of just a piece of sponge to lie on. I think everyone used their own webbing or chest rigs as pillows. It made it easier to sleep and was very quick to put on, it was as good as it got.

The next morning was 6 September 2006, a day of tranquillity, a day to sort out administration, and most of all, I had planned to go for a dip in the river. My boots needed a clean and I had planned to wash the T-shirts that I had in the top of my Bergan.

After breakfast in my bunker, I made my way to the surface and started to chat with the other guys, the craic was great, the guys were taking the piss out of each other, and this became the normal routine, in order to get you through the day.

Lunch seemed to pass with only a few engagements with the enemy, back at Bastion reports were coming in of other outposts being in contact with the enemy, but that was just second nature now, I'm sure every patrol base was either loving this experience or hating every minute of it. We just wanted it to end, enough was enough, been there, seen it, and got the T-shirt, so let's just go home.

I was sitting there beside the biggest tree in the orchard, when Spence looked across and said, 'Davey, get the commanders together for a brief.' Some of the rangers got up and moved to the different Sanger locations to let the commanders know of what Spence had said, it was now 1645 hours, I was already there, so just remained where I was.

Spence waited for a few minutes until all the guys had sat down in a line, the threat from attack was always there, after all it was Sangin, but from previous intelligence briefs and from experience of the time in Sangin, we had never been attacked at this time, it was always after the call of prayer, and on cue.

It wasn't long before the guys had all sat down. Luke came and sat down to my right. I looked at him and shook my head, he just smiled at me, he was eating a vegetarian meal. I said, 'Luke, all you do is just eat, you fat bastard.' He smiled and said, 'Yip', and continued to eat during the brief. On my left was Stella, he was just sitting there taking in everyone's conversation, he was a very intellectual person, he kept himself to himself.

The brief was about what Spence had been told by the CSM, Mick Bolton. There had been a lot of activity in and around the battle groups' locations, and it didn't look good reading, statistically we had killed hundreds of enemy forces, but it meant nothing, to be honest I personally did not feel that we had gained anything, especially when the majority of the time we couldn't find any bodies, just blood trails.

We had come to the end of the brief. Davey was finishing his service support, he wanted the weapons cleaned, and the orchard area looking respectable, there were too many clothes hanging up off everyone's mosquito net, basically he wanted us to smarten up a bit, and he had a point. With everything that goes on in a place like Sangin DC, you tend to let something slip, it takes a person like a platoon sergeant to keep a tight grip on things you think that do not matter.

Davey finished off his brief, then said something that will never leave me. I still to this day remember every single thing that took place that day. He said, 'Right, fellas, it's near time to get your helmet and body armour on, so get to it.' That was repeated by Spence, who added, 'STAND TO.'

We never got that far, just as I looked up, I could see Davey and Spence walking over to their kit, and then, Whooooooooooooosh . . . BOOM! It was followed by silence, or it felt like everything around me was quiet, the orchard was filled with dust, I saw what I can only describe as a white flash.

My ears felt like nothing was going in. I couldn't hear a thing, the explosion was the loudest thing that I had ever heard, it had been a Taliban mortar. They had been firing during the day, having had one land out the back of camp, they had been judging distance and worked out exactly what they needed to get it right in the middle of our camp.

It had landed right in the orchard, and only 20 metres from where every single commander was sitting, a direct hit, the red-hot burning metal had flown straight at every single one of us. The tree I had been sitting against had taken a lot of the metal that had been directed at me. It wasn't the end of the attack, it seemed to go on forever.

Once the dust had started to settle slightly, I was in fact in battle shock. I looked at my combats and I was covered in blood, my legs and arms were red. I was numb, I didn't know how I felt at that exact moment, my ears were not working properly. I didn't even know that Robbie was screaming for me to get into cover. I looked at the floor beside the tree. Luke was still there, he was lying on his side, his spoon was still in his mouth.

I looked at the other side of the tree and Stella was still sitting there. I was being screamed at from the other guys, I started to get a grip of myself and tried to help Stella, I could see that he had shrapnel in his back and stomach. It looked really bad, I helped him do up his body armour and then he limped into the trench. Robbie began shouting at Luke to get up, but he never responded.

Then I was grabbed by Robbie, he came running from cover and shouted to grab Luke's legs. I began to come around, while Robbie had his arms along with Craig, I cannot remember anyone else at this time, I was as soldiers call it 'in the zone'. We dragged Luke into what was a trench, but big enough for about a complete section to take cover in.

We were screaming for a medic, the enemy mortars were still landing in the DC, I could now hear slightly.

It sounded like we were being overrun by the Taliban, every single Sanger was engaging the enemy, and the amount of ammunition that was being fired was colossal. After what seemed like a lifetime, I saw a shadow appear from the dust, it was the company medic Billy Owen, he was a big guy, so to see him run through the orchard while bombs were still dropping around the DC was amazing and showed that he was a very brave and courageous paratrooper.

Just as Billy was about to enter the trench where we had moved Luke into, an explosion threw Billy straight into the trench and on top of Luke. He didn't even flinch, he began to carry out lifesaving drills, he even carried out a tracheostomy, he didn't even know that the explosion had blown his sight completely off his weapon, his combats were burnt a bit and there was a piece of burning metal on his daysack.

He worked on Luke for a few minutes and then told us to get him to the medical room. I cannot remember what I was thinking, I just knew Luke was in a terrible way, the attack was still in full motion, my ears were still not 100% but at least I was okay. I could hear Spence shouting for a head count. He wanted to know how many of the platoon had become casualties, but at this early stage and amongst the chaos, no one knew.

The only thing that was certain was that Luke had lost a lot of blood, my combats were covered in it. I remember the look on his face, his eyes were wide open and the dust had begun to settle on his pupils. The medic had to sweep the food from his mouth where he had been eating the vegetarian meal earlier during the brief, the look on everyone's face was that of worry and confusion.

It seemed very fast, but we quickly got him on a stretcher and began to run through the impact area and into the medical room. We were still under heavy fire from the Taliban, it wasn't until I had reached the medical room that the severity of the attack was noticed.

There had been four other soldiers injured during the attack. Stella had back and stomach wounds, his face was pure white, he looked in serious pain. Another young paratrooper who had only recently joined the company had a hole in his right hand, where the shrapnel had gone straight through, and to top it all off, Spence had been wounded, shrapnel had hit him in the legs, arms, and buttocks, he was bleeding badly.

The only drama now was that Spence was pissed off, his platoon had been hit and he wanted some payback. With all the confusion now in Sangin DC, he picked up an ILAW (anti-tank rocket) and ran back into the contact area, there he managed to fire it straight into the area of where the Taliban had been firing from. He arrived at the medical room, I thought he had come for some treatment, but Spence was not even thinking about himself. He wanted an update on Luke, he looked at me and I just shook my head. There was nothing we could do, his fate was with the medical teams and the surgeons at Bastion Hospital now.

The operations room had now informed JOC of what was happening at Sangin. They had already sent the immediate response team (IRT) to our location, a Chinook was in the air along with two Apache helicopters as support. I quickly realised that there was no way that we would be able to extract Luke across the small bridge without either being hit ourselves or dropping him into the Helmand river, so I decided to make a run for it. I ran out of the building and made my way as fast as I could across the open ground and to the Household Cavalry Regiment (HCR) soldiers.

They were in their vehicles, I explained that I needed them to bring their vehicles back to the building so we could put Luke into it. I wanted them to drive to the Helicopter Landing Site (HLS) as quick as they could so we could get him extracted ASAP.

I helped put the stretcher onto the back of the vehicle, I could see Spence now arguing with the CSM. He wanted Spence to make his way to the HLS so he could be evacuated to Bastion for medical treatment, but he was refusing to go, he did not want to leave his platoon behind, that was the way that Spence operated, he was a true soldier, nothing would hold him back, he had to be ordered onto the chopper by the OC and the CSM.

Once the stretcher was on, I ran across the bridge and waited for the vehicle to arrive. It only took about one minute to get there, the rest of the wounded soldiers had made their way there, and were now spaced out in case of another mortar would land on the HLS.

It was another couple of minutes before the Chinook could land, the HLS was taking a lot of enemy fire. I could see the Apache helicopters engaging with hellfire missiles and 30 mm chain guns, it was total chaos. I was still running on fumes, I was soaking with sweat and blood, my mouth was dry and I was still confused, the Chinook eventually landed, with the IRT security soldiers still sitting on their seats. We got Luke out the back of the vehicle and carried the stretcher onto the Chinook, I could see the look of pure panic on everyone's faces.

The nearest IRT soldier to me was just staring, his mouth was wide open and he looked scared. I handed him the oxygen bag and screamed at him to start to squeeze it. I shouted breathe for him, fucking squeeze the bag, at this stage a medic came running to me and took control of the breathing apparatus.

Just before the Chinook took off, Spence shouted out at me, 'Speedy, I will be back in a few days, tell Davey he is in charge, look after the troops, get amongst them.' I was still on a high, I just said yes, I will keep an eye on the troops.

The Chinook lifted off very rapidly, as the two Apaches still engaged positions, the fire support tower was still in a massive fire fight. It went on for what seemed like forever, I ran back to the ops room to tell them that Davey was now platoon commander, and that had come from Spence. The CSM was still pissed off, he had taken this badly, we were meant to be under his command. I think everyone was still in shock with the amount of damage the Taliban had inflicted on us in one strike.

I went from Sanger to Sanger to see how the guys were dealing with things. Davey and Robbie were already sorting out the troops, and morale had taken a massive blow, the three of us commanders left in the platoon spent that night walking from Sanger to Sanger talking to the troops. We wanted to make sure that everyone was okay, Robbie had a word in my ear, he told me to get my bloody combats off, I agreed. Davey wanted to know if I was okay, we looked after each other in the platoon.

This was the worst day that I had ever witnessed. The troops were mentally not in the right frame of mind. It took a few days to lift everyone just a slight bit, it was not great, our boss was in England on

R&R and was pissed off. He had not been there for us, he felt that he had let us down, but we all knew that he hadn't. Our platoon sergeant wasn't there and he too was pissed off that he had to go, and Stella was gone along with Luke. Morale couldn't get any worse.

We had to have a brief with what command element that we had left. We quickly changed the teams about so that we had at least an NCO in each location, so we could keep an eye on the troop's morale.

Once we had sorted ourselves out, I took myself away for a bit of peace and quiet. I needed to be alone to get my head together. I went to the area where I had been sitting and looked at the tree, exactly where my head had been. There was a large piece of shrapnel in the tree. I had been given another chance. I was so close to death, I got a lump in my throat, I could still see blood lying on the ground, so I got dirt and water and began to wash it all away. I didn't want the guys to have reminders of what had happened.

From this day forward, every member of the platoon became close. Every single time I think about the attack, I get it in 3D. It plays over and over in my head, it never goes away, it keeps happening every single day.

The next day went with not much interaction within the platoon. The guys were at an all-time low, we just wanted the tour to come to an end, either that or we wanted the opportunity for some payback. The morning passed with no patrols going into the town, we were all sorting ourselves out, the OC sent a runner for me. 'Speedy, the boss wants you in the ops room.' I immediately thought, what now, I am trying to keep some of these guys together. Dougal was taking it badly and Tam was just about holding himself together, their eyes were bloodshot, where they hadn't slept properly.

I walked into the corridor at the ops room, the OC approached me and put his hand out. He just smiled at me and said, 'I apologise on the timing of this, but I want to be the first to congratulate you, you have been awarded the Military Cross for your actions in Baghdad, so you are now officially Cpl Coult MC.' I just looked at him, and said, 'Are you being serious?' He said, 'Of course, go in the ops room and wait by the phone, the brigadier wants to speak to you.' I walked into the ops room and just stood there looking at the map on the wall.

The radio was going berserk, Nowzad was in a battle with the Taliban, they had been hit by three mortars and RPGs, they were taking in a lot of enemy fire. Musa Quala had taken 1 x T1 Casualty and had 1 x T2 Casualty. Kajaki have had 1 x killed in action, 4 x T1, 1x T2, and 1x T3. It's been a terrible day, then the phone rang and it's the brigade commander. He said, 'Congratulations, Cpl Coult, on your prestigious award, it's of that your regiment is famously known, enjoy the moment.' I said, 'Thanks, sir', and I put the phone down.

I walked out the ops room and I felt like crying. How the hell was I supposed to celebrate with what was going on in my platoon? I told Robbie and Dougal, but kept it from the rest of the guys, they didn't need to know, they needed time to sort their own heads out after such a furious couple of days.

An officer came across to us today. No one seemed to know where he has come from, or how he got here, but he wanted to speak to the command element of our platoon. We gathered the guys up and made our way to an area so he could talk to us. He looked very ragged, his hair was gingery and wavy, his beard was quite long. He explained that he was on special duties and wanted to take control of our platoon. He then said he was sorry about what had happened to our platoon.

He explained in great detail that he wanted us to run the platoon the way we have been, but he would be our top cover. If we needed anything, he would get it for us. It felt great to think that other units could understand the pain that we were going through, we were not alone.

He then looked at each of us and said, 'I'm sorry that it's me that has to break the news to you, but your colleague Luke died of his injuries before he even got to Bastion. If there is anything I can do, guys, please let me know.' I physically felt sick, it hit everyone hard, we all just walked off in different directions. I remember walking off on my own.

I needed some time to digest this whole situation. I headed to the river and sat down, I remember crying, it was the only time I have cried during the tour. I actually felt guilty, it was only a few days ago I was shouting at him, well, at least I stayed true to myself, I kept 100% professional.

That night was very difficult, I didn't sleep again. I spent the whole night going around the platoon making sure that all the guys were okay. Robbie and Davey did the same, it was a very testing time, a few of the guys broke down crying, it was hard, especially as every few hours we would be attacked.

My head was now messed up. I knew I had been awarded the Military Cross, but I didn't feel like celebrating, my platoon had taken a massive blow; it would be a while before we got over it.

The next day was spent with the guys moving everything they owned out of the orchard and into hard cover. There were a few outbuildings that we cleaned out, we then split the platoon into three equal bodies of men, this would make sure that we all had somewhere to go if we were attacked. It seemed to help bring the guys back together, it meant that we all had to talk, and it helped us to come to terms with Luke's death.

It wasn't long before the engineers began to dig in the orchard; they dug three massive trenches, which would afford the platoon more cover if attacked, it also made me and the guys feel more comfortable. It was what we needed at that time, these trenches would be where I would live during the remainder of this tour.

We were sent out on our first patrol by the OC, he needed to get us out of the rut that we were in fact in. It was now 9 September, the patrol was led by Davey, we had no key elements, but were thirsty for blood. We wanted a chance to kill Taliban fighters, but it never seemed to happen during that patrol. We got back in and had to supply two sections for QRF. The CSM was doing his best to keep us busy, and that was exactly what we needed.

Keeping the platoon busy was the best way to get everyone over what had happened, every so often I would hear one of the guys having a cry. I seemed to spend a lot of my time in Sanger 4, and for some reason it was always Dougal that was on sentry when I was on. We talked for hours, it was his coping mechanisms.

I looked forward to the nights on sentry, even though my eyes were stinging with the fact that I spent hours scanning the night-vision goggles. After a while I lost my night vision, we took it in turns to scan. It was worth the pain if it meant that everyone else had a quiet night's sleep.

The night seemed to pass without incident at the DC, however the battle group net was kept very busy, with dickers being killed throughout the AOR. Every outpost was being heavily dicked by the Taliban. It looked like they were yet again preparing for an attack, the feeling amongst the troops was, bring it on, we were all ready for whatever they could throw at us. We all just wished that our re-supply chain at Camp Bastion would be able to get more rations and ammunition to us.

I thought it was time to inform my family that were back in Northern Ireland about my award before the news back home broke the story. I went to the operations room and grabbed the satellite phone, I then made my way to the roof, wearing my helmet and body armour, after dialling the sixteen digits before the phone even rings. I just sat there looking out into the Sangin wadi, I didn't know what was going through my mind, I was just glad that operation minimise had been lifted, this also meant that his family had been informed of his death. I was numb inside, then my dad answered the phone, he said, 'Hello, who is this?' I said, 'It's me, Dad, Trevor.' 'What's up, son, is everything okay?' I said, 'Are you both sitting up in bed?' He said no. I then asked them both to sit up as I had good news.

My dad said, 'Okay, okay, we are both sitting up.' I really didn't know what to say at that moment. I had just lost a friend and great second in command NCO. I really felt like crying, but I kept it together, I said, 'The brigade commander spoke to me yesterday and congratulated me on being awarded the Military Cross, I've been awarded the MC, Dad.' He sounded completely shocked. He said, 'Stop pissing about', and handed the phone to my mother. He didn't believe me, and to be honest, why should he?

My mother was of the same mind. I told her that I was having a hard time in Sangin and that I had lost one of my section, and a few others had been injured. At that second if she could have reached out and hugged me, I think she would have. I told them to read the newspapers and they would see for themselves. I tried to have a conversation, but we started to take heavy fire again. I hung up and moved into cover, the fire fight lasted a few minutes. Once it was over, I could hear faint shouting coming from close by. I picked up the sat phone and my mother was still on it, she now was more worried than before. I ended the call by saying, 'I love you both and hopefully see you soon.'

I should never have said that. I was mixed up, I think everyone was in the same way, it could be anyone's turn to be killed in a place like that. If your number was up, then it was up.

Davey returned from an O Group. We had another task, it was to move out past the ANP building and clear buildings 74 and 75, conduct a quick battle damage assessment, and move back in through the pipe range, pretty simple task, but nothing was simple in Sangin. It was a nightmare to do anything, I remember reading up on Helmand and how the Russian-Afghan war had claimed thousands of lives, especially in Sangin where the Russian army had lost 100,000 men. Sangin was known as death valley, and now I knew why.

The patrol went without incident, it was the first time that we had nothing to report. Soldiers always go to the ops room on return from any patrol, it was unusual, the atmospherics were not good, there was no locals outside, the children that usually play outside were gone, there was definitely something going on, what I'm sure we would find out soon enough.

It's nearly a week since Luke was killed, the atmosphere within the platoon, you could cut with a knife. We need morale, even a letter from home would be nice at this time, but mail isn't even getting to us, it's only mission essential kit, like medical and rations, ammunition. If there is room on the choppers, then mail is last to go on, and that's how it should be, the guys understand.

The OC wants Ranger Platoon to patrol into the bazaar and show a presence, in the hope we can start to get amongst the locals and get some vital public relations carried out. This had me laughing inside, what the hell was he thinking, we had the town in rubble, it's completely destroyed, our fast jets, Apache gunships, A-10 bombers, and mortars had turned this mud town into the world's biggest rubble heap.

The patrol moved out and began to move cautiously up the pipe range and out into the bazaar, we started to leap-frog across the open ground. Locals who noticed us just turned and walked in a different direction, no one wanted to be seen talking to ISAF soldiers, they looked angry. It didn't help with the fact that we only spoke in broken Pashtu, we did try and communicate, but they didn't want to know.

We patrolled back into the DC and reported to the OC that the locals ignored us, he didn't seem surprised, but at least we were still trying to engage with the village.

Musa Quala have had more casualties, the HCR were out in their vehicles, when one was involved in a mine strike, this had resulted in 3 x WIA. It seemed like this was never ending, after a while it just became the normal routine. I've mentally prepared myself for the worst, it took some time, but I'm now in a dark place and at peace with myself, but let's just see what will happen, I'm with some of the army's best soldiers.

Ranger Platoon now had been given another task. We were to move south out of the DC and push approximately 300 metres south and hold it there. The ROE now gave us the power to kill anyone who is a fighting age male that poses a threat. This was a lot of power to hold, we now decide who lives or dies, as long as we can justify it in a court of law, and I'm sure we can justify every single bullet that has left our weapons.

The engineers were coming with us on the patrol, their mission was to move out with Ranger Platoon, then drop off the back, then they will place bar mines in the J-DAM building as it is now known, this is a big task, we have the HCR on the flanks, they were out the back of the DC and towards the mountain area. This will be early warning if the Taliban decide to attack, we also had one of the parachute platoons on the other flank, this was just the start, we also had two F-18 fast jets on station throughout the task, what more could you ask for?

We remained on task for little under an hour, the engineers had to place five bar mines into the compound. They found it hard to bury them and had to use their bayonets to dig away part of the wall. As soon as they were happy and that they had left no ground sign, they moved out back onto the track, this had been rehearsed back at the DC. No one was allowed to use their radio until we had got back in camp, due to the bar mines being set up with the use of electrical detonators, the use of radio could have set them off, risking the lives of the engineers, and no one wanted that.

The engineers looked like they had the weight of the world on their shoulders, they were soaked in sweat, it must have been nerve wrecking putting those mines in place, but someone had to do, it was a job I wouldn't have wanted to do. They might have had a lot of support, but they still had to crawl all the way out there and place them in position without the enemy knowing that they were there.

They had managed to do it, the electrical detonator cord had been run all the way back into the Sanger and was carefully put into a green box, with buttons and a computer, and it was now armed. After a quick brief, we were given strict instructions that it was not to be fired unless we could clearly identify Taliban moving into position in the J-DAM building.

Once back inside the DC, I took the time to phone home and see how my parents were coping with the news that I had broken to them in the early hours of the morning, they seemed ecstatic that I had been awarded the Military Cross.

My dad apologised for having doubted me, he was over the moon, my mother was crying, she didn't know what I had done. I never really tell them what I get up to, I just go home and eat their food and relax, it's what most soldiers do. If you told your parents that you got excited at the thought of killing enemy forces, they would think you had something wrong with you.

I knew I had something wrong with me. I was enjoying seeing dead Taliban, and it gave me a sense of satisfaction and for some weird reason it also gave me a sense of purpose.

I know it sounds wrong, but I actually felt great when there were blood trails and parts of them lying around. It also helped with the lifting of morale, it made my men feel like we were actually getting somewhere with all this nonsense.

Today we received great news from the O Group. It seemed the Taliban had decided to have a ceasefire in Musa Quala, this must be of great relief to the Royal Irish (easy company) that were based up there, they have had everything thrown at them, and to be still fighting just showed what type of men they were.

It didn't take long for the news of the ceasefire to spread amongst the platoon, it was great to know that the guys were at least safe for now; the question was how long it would last.

Another typical day in Sangin, started off with RPGs being fired at the front gate from across the wadi, this was short lived as a fast jet dropped a bomb on the launch site. It was probably overkill, but I'm sure the pilot had his reasons, reports from him stated that the Taliban had been extracting in strong numbers, so he took out all threats, just what we wanted to hear as well.

At the same time as we were getting attacked, they had attacked FOB Robinson, this meant that if they attacked more than one camp at the same time, we would find it hard to give top cover to different locations at the same time, the only way that we could achieve this was by prioritising who was more expendable. It seemed that they had taken three Taliban prisoners of war (POW), then out of nowhere an RPG hit the front gate again, it was now just becoming a pain in the ass.

The OC now wanted Ranger Platoon to take over all the Sangers in camp, he had tasked 8 Platoon to go out on patrol, they seemed ready for a good battle

Morale was beginning to lift slightly, just as we took over the Sangers, two F-18 jets flew over the district centre. They must be only 200 feet from the floor, my ears nearly burst with the noise, it was great to see the guys began running in diagonal lines to avoid being shot, then they got into cover.

It was another BDA patrol, I never really understood these patrols, as we had Desert Hawk 3, this could have flown over the area and taken pictures, thus not putting soldiers' lives in danger by going out, but at the end of the day, we do whatever we are ordered to do.

They didn't seem to hang about, that's how the Parachute Regiment operate, they don't waste time, out, task complete, and back, job done without any fuss. When they got back in, we didn't want them back in the Sangers yet, we wanted them to get themselves sorted out, with food and some personal admin time. After all we are all part of the same team, and I'm sure they would appreciate the time to sort out their kit.

The news coming from the operations room was that FOB Robinson now had six prisoners of war, they were being hit hard by the Taliban, and especially as intelligence was suggesting that they had just had a re-supply of mortars, this was not great news to hear. I personally now fear mortars; it's a very cruel and deadly weapon.

They were using the mortars to full effect, they had attacked Nowzad coalition bases along with Gereshk, resulting in two soldiers killed and another two soldiers seriously wounded. The numbers were seriously mounting up now, I never thought I would ever say this, but after a while it just goes over your head, it becomes expected.

It's not long before we hear the news that the Taliban in Sangin have had a re-supply of mortars and RPG, it was expected; now it was just a matter of time before we are attacked from every possible direction.

News that Nowzad and Kajaki had come under heavy attack from the Taliban has spread like wildfire across the battle group, this was amazing no matter how much you hate the Taliban, you have to admire their perseverance.

They are a disciplined and well-prepared fighting force, some of us have grown to respect their ballsy approach, but on the other hand, we despise them, we both have beliefs and ways of executing our orders. I suppose it is the first person with their sights on a target who will win.

Word from the top is that our commanding officer and RQMS had been trying to get to us, they had been stuck in Camp Bastion for a few days trying to get on a flight to Sangin, they were coming to have a chat with us and maybe try and lift the mood or the morale slightly.

It sent out a good vibe amongst the platoon, the fact that they had made the effort to visit us meant a great deal to all of us, especially as they were putting their own lives at risk to do it. I suppose it is one of the perks of leadership, getting to see your men and motivating them is the best way to lead, however listening to them is also a great way to relieve their burden from battle.

Morale had now lifted with the thought that the CO and RQMS were flying in, then the mood slightly changed too. I hoped they bring mail and goodies from home, I just laughed, it was good enough that they were coming without putting the added pressure on them.

Let's just hope that they could get here especially as the threat was constant that we could have a heli shot down at any given minute.

I'm sure that The RQMS will be able to lift our spirits; he was a well-respected soldier throughout the regiment.

A man who has completed nearly every course that the army can throw at him, a man who we all fear that any question he may ask us will be one that we do not know the answer to, he will ask me a question and I'm sure to go blank,.

I won't know the answer, I'm bound to freeze, but everyone is like that with him. He was the only person who continually hounded me with the principles of administration to such a degree that I will never forget them. I look back at my time working under him with some pride and respect, this as a soldier I would never tell someone as it would come across as a weakness and soldiers never admit to weakness, unless it is fear leaving the body.

Luke McCulloch extracting from a contact in Zumbelay

Ian Getty & Robbie Walker, across the river from the platoon house outside the ANP building, they were always prepared for a fight.

Stevie Weir on the left with Grant Brown, they
carried the big guns within the platoon.

Alan O, Driscol & Ian Getty, standing up in their accommodation.

IN MEMORY OF THOSE KILLED DURING OPERATIONS IN SANGIN, AFGHANISTAN.

CPL 'PETE' THORPE LEW.T.14 SIG REGT(EW) 01.07.06.   LCPL 'SEAN' TANSEY LG, D SQN, HCR 12.08.06.

LCPL HASH' HASHMI LEW.T.14 SIG REGT (EW) 01.07.06.   CPL 'BRI' BUDD A COY, 3 PARA 20.08.06.

PTE 'JACKO' JACKSON A COY, 3 PARA 04.07.06.   LCPL 'LUKE' M°CULLOCH D COY, 1 R IRISH 06.09.06

AIRBORNE

The wall of remembrance, Brian Budd would later receive the Victoria Cross;
this would be later painted over by the next unit due to their lack of respect.

A Chinook lands to re-supply the Company, as you
can see the Camp still has no exterior wall.

My platoon stacking up against the hesco wall, before a patrol.

Ranger platoon sergeant, Sgt Spence, "man of fire" he ruled the platoon with an iron fist, he would later be seen running towards the enemy with a 66mm rocket launcher, with shrapnel wounds

Ranger platoon gathered for a photograph, this is the tree were Luke was killed.

O,Driscol made this out of a piece of wood & a permanent pen, outstanding!!

Another J-DAM bomb dropped by our friends in the RAF.

A beautiful sight of yet another compound being destroyed by a J-DAM bomb.

Ian & Me taking time out to relax before another patrol into
Sangin, this is now an Operations room in Sangin D C

The crossing point on foot in Sangin D.C, all there is
between you & the Taliban is that brown sheet.

Calm before the storm, Rob, Sean, Me & Davy,
taken in the Oman on final preparation.

Sangin valley wadi, this is the centre point for all battles in Sangin.

This is my section standing beside where Luke was killed;
I am standing on the right next to the tree.

Ranger Platoon at the start of the tour in FOB Robinson,
this was taken in the American part of the camp.

The three amigos trying to smile to the camera, OD
is in the background sorting out his kit.

Another Chinook packed with soldiers, Davey is sitting centre
with the Boss on the far right in front of Dougal.

OD sorting out the section ammo

OD giving me an ammo state, he was always on top of our section admin, this was the last day for us in Sangin, we had just returned from a fire-fight.

The platoon house in Sangin D.C, this was taken
on the 12th May 2006, it looks peaceful.

I am back right, Luke is taking the photo.

Lt Kelly & Ranger Bacon carrying out first aid on
a local child, Sangin early May 2006

Davey Strain on the left along with Robin.

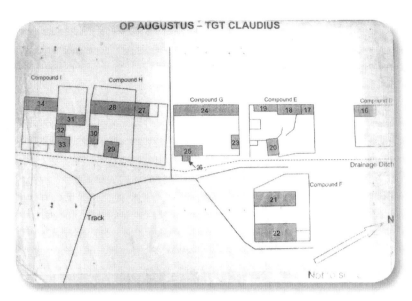

This is my target map for clearing these compounds.

One of two presentations that I received from the people of East Belfast,
John is talking on the microphone; he made & presented them to me

BUCKINGHAM PALACE

19th September, 2006

Dear Corporal Coult,

The Colonel-in-Chief has asked me to write and say how delighted he was to read, in the Armed Forces Operational Honours List, about the award of your Military Cross for services in Iraq.

His Royal Highness sends his warmest congratulations and best wishes to you for the future.

Yours sincerely,

Caroline Clark

Lieutenant Caroline Clark, Royal Navy
Equerry to The Duke of York

Corporal T R Coult, MC

Letter from Prince Andrew, Colonel-in Chief of the Royal Irish Regiment

Outside the back entrance to Buckingham Palace,
my mother & father are with me.

Being presented by the Military Cross by the Queen, Dec 2006

Ian Getty & Spence have a condor moment before Ian
gets told he is on Casevac duty at the D.C

The platoon Commander, Mr Kelly who hates having his picture taken

Davy Miller with the remains of a suicide bomber on HERRICK 8

7 platoons CMT, Caylie she looked after us all like and had some testing times

This was built up by 7 platoon who filled over 150 sandbags
in a 2 day period; it would be called PB PYLAE, named
after Justin cupples who died not too far from there

Members of C Company pay their respect to ranger Justin Cupples; we got them to fly into Bastion so see him on his last journey out of Afghanistan

It's not much but it is all we had at the time, a proper sign was made later

Myself sitting beside Dave Heyhoe author of *"it's all about TREO"*

This is Dave and Treo DM during a routine Patrol,
they were never apart and always alert

This sign was made by 2 Para, for our company
group, 2 Para did a lot of great stuff for us

This is what a rifle looks like after an explosion

My radio op Mac and Paddy Burry the Boss and author of *"callsign Hades"*

7 Platoon react to a Taliban strike from across the river

Another close call, I was sitting 1 metre away when this exploded
in the ground sending hot pieces of metal into my daysack.

Chapter 8

RANGERS VISIT

Today being 19 September, we were all waiting to see if the visit was going ahead. It's been a few days now, but I'm sure they will understand if they can't get here. It was very dangerous, I already knew that they tried to get to Musa Quala, and that was never going to happen, that place was a nightmare. Let's just hope it all went to plan, until they come we will just continue with routine.

I was going to just crack on with what I normally do, but I was kidding myself, for some reason I couldn't be doing with any sort of arguments that might come my way. I decided to have a shave, I knew water was scarce, but I was willing to use a bottle to shave, to save my commanding officer from giving us a stern talking-to.

News came from the ops room that our CO and RQMS were on the flight coming in from Bastion, it was due in thirty minutes, this gave us enough time to receive quick battle orders (QBOs), the OC wanted our platoon to push out through the helipad and into depth, this would help with troops out on the ground and give the Taliban a scare if they tried to attack the Chinook when it landed.

I quickly got the guys to tidy up. I knew this was a trivial thing to do, but I just couldn't be dealing with any hassle directed at me. We had been through a lot and I'm sure I would explode at the RQMS if he started trying to de-brief us on administration. I used to get it from him when I worked in the training wing, he would come in and say, the principles of administration were flexibility, foresight, simplicity, cooperation, and economy, it must have worked as I still knew them.

We got the platoon together and moved out into position, we had to push further than normal. The threat went up on helicopters, we knew from intelligence that the Taliban wanted to shoot one down, the pilots had been warned off not to land in the district centre, an alternative HLS had been marked on the map, it was right out the back of camp. The HCR were told to move their vehicles out onto the flanks, and provide fire support, into the area towards the mountain range and south of the DC.

We could see the Chinook flying low as it approached the HLS, just then I turned to O,Driscol and started to talk about how quiet it was, the Chinook started to turn when all of a sudden an RPG came flying from the tree line. Whooooosh . . . BOOM . . . BOOM! *Rat tat tat tat*, we started to get attacked, the door gunner was engaging targets just past us. I don't think he knew that we were hidden, this began to piss me off. We were being fired at by the Taliban from the front and being fired at by the troops getting off the Chinook, now the HCR were firing at us. I got up and began swearing at our own troops. I then fired a single shot at the HCR vehicle, I was completely snapping at everyone.

I looked across and could see the dismounted troops spread out across the ground. Some of the guys were trying to grab their bags and get across the ground, they were under fire and running as fast as they could, my section started to provide support for the troops and ushered them into safety, the Taliban had been waiting for the Chinook to land, the guests had a very warm welcoming.

My RQMS was actually in contact. I could see that he was firing back into the direction of the Taliban, I'm sure he wasn't expecting to be doing this after all those years, but good on him, now he was part of the platoon; this would take his mind off trivial stuff.

The contact lasted about forty minutes, it took forever to get the kit off the HLS, and by the time we had everyone back in camp safely, we were all exhausted and ready for some rest, we made our way back into the old district centre location. The OC and RQMS headed for the ops room as to show some sort of respect to our boss, once finished they came to our location, it was great to see new faces after all this time. I was chuffed that they had made it all the way out here, it had taken them four days to get here because of the air threat.

They had brought mail and goodies with them. Spence was with them along with Stella and two other Battle Casualty Replacements soldiers (BCR), it was a good feeling to know that Spence and Stella were okay. The morale lifted through the roof, the troops sifted through the mail and began to make food in the kitchen area. I walked out the back of the building and decided to make a hot brew, I wasn't really in the mood for socialising.

The RQMS came over to me and shook my hand, he congratulated me on my Military Cross, he told me that the whole battalion was proud of what we had achieved and now we had to stay focussed. He had a point, we didn't get to finish the conversation, the Taliban had better ideas, they attacked again. I grabbed my kit and ran to the roof, I was followed shortly by the RQMS, he stayed in cover, he was watching me bring direct fire onto the target area. He wanted to know what we were firing at, I explained that we were hitting the school and the pharmacy.

He looked shocked that we were engaging a school; I explained that the Taliban used it to attack us, so we had to hit it. He wasn't convinced, he then left the rooftop and made his way back down the stairs, the attack lasted about twenty minutes. Once over I made my way back down into the room, the CO wanted to chat to the platoon, he gave us a brief on what had happened in Musa Quala and the feeling back at the regiment, he then went on to praise our professionalism and courage, he congratulated me on being awarded the Military Cross, I just nodded.

The CO spent the next few days with the OC, he would see first-hand what we had to put up with, the attacks were relentless, the RQMS began to see how we coped on a day-to-day basis. It was hard work trying to stay alive, some days I just wanted to scream, but never did. I was a commander so, I had to set an example to the troops. It was good to chat to the RQMS, he explained that the RSM was too busy dealing with the families of the soldiers that had been killed in action, so he had sent the RQMS in his place. We totally understood, it wasn't going to be easy dealing with the chaos back at camp. I'm sure the guys would be practicing every day on how to conduct a funeral. This was not something I had wanted to go through, however I had prepared for it, my No2 uniform was hanging up in my room ready for such an occasion if it was to be called for.

I was now in touch with one of the officers back at camp, Jim Berry. He was trying everything possible to get out on this tour, and he knew this was going to be a tour of tours and he for sure did not want to miss out, after all he had just spent nearly a year at Sandhurst being told about leading men in battle was the biggest privilege of all. He wanted this bad, he had tried on several occasions, but it was not to be. I suppose it didn't help me telling him how much trigger time we were all having.

I'm sure deep down all the officers back at camp were jealous of our platoon commander. He was in fact the only officer in the history of the regiment to have led men in combat, he would forever now be part of the history, along with every soldier. Ranger Platoon was now steeped in history, we had in fact done what every other soldier had wanted to do, this was our time and the fate of it lay in the hands of the Taliban.

The Taliban seemed that they would never go away. Intelligence suggested that there were actually over 80,000, this was just crazy, we didn't even have an army that big anymore, most of us were just holding on for dear life in this Sangin outpost. After all we now felt like we had just been dumped here and forgotten about. I heard numerous conversations from the troops all stating that they felt like they had been dumped in this ferocious place, just waiting for death to creep up and grab them. Let's just hope we could hold on until the relief in place (RIP) gets here.

I was getting used to the CO and RQMS being around us. I know it was just for a few days, but it let them see what we had to put up with on a day-to-day basis, they were proud of what the Irish Ranger stood for, and the courage that we were showing in the face of the enemy.

The next few days consisted of being fired upon by the Taliban from every angle imaginable. They were relentless with their attacks. My RQMS was flabbergasted by the way his soldiers were taking to this with ease. It was now second nature to grab your personal protection equipment and get to a Sanger and engage, it actually felt great as a way to de-stress as well.

Today a lone man walked into the wadi and fired an RPG at the camp. As soon as he placed it onto his shoulder, we hit him with an 81 mm mortar, there was nothing left of him. I saw the whole thing from my Sanger position, it looked bloody amazing. I know I shouldn't laugh, but it really did feel good, on the other hand I find myself not caring about life now. To me life is precious, but if you decide that you want to try and kill me or my colleagues, then I will kill you.

We found ourselves today on guard in Sangin DC. It's 22 September and this tour did not seem to be ending. We now knew that Royal Marines were coming to Sangin. They would relieve us. I just hoped that they were ready for a hell of a battle, because the Taliban would take anyone on, this was their backyard and we were intruding.

It's not even lunch time yet and they were engaging the front gate with mortars. They were landing just short of camp, but we knew it's just a matter of time before they hit the camp. We were doing a line-of-sight appreciation, hopefully this would enable us to kill the mortar team. We had Apache gunships now firing into the area of the mortar team. That's the end of them, now we were being fired upon from wombat wood. We hit back with 81 mm mortar, the general purpose machine gun was now firing into the area of the pharmacy. Just as I started to scan with the range finder sight, a Javelin missile flew over the Sanger and into a target. **BOOM**! Devastation was everywhere in Sangin, this town would take years to recover.

I managed to get time to myself; I decided to make a call on the satellite phone to my brother. It took a while to get through, but it was worth it. He was excited to hear from me, he knew what I was going through. It was never off the television, every channel was talking about the war in Afghanistan, the newspapers were doing front-page articles on how many of us had been killed fighting. It was being compared to the Second World War by some papers and Korea by others, I told him that it was very hard work, the guys were exhausted from battle.

Just as we were fully engaged in conversation, I heard someone scream, **'STAND TO!'** I then heard automatic gun fire and explosions. I turned the phone off and got into cover, the fire fight lasted only a few minutes. We managed to get the upper hand on the Taliban, again I heard whispers, it was the phone, my brother was still on the other end, he heard the whole contact, I told him not to mention it to Mum, and he agreed.

The same day, NOWZAD was in a battle with the Taliban; we had killed two Taliban and wounded two others, not bad for a day's work. It was just a pity that it wasn't more. When there is an upside, there always has to be a downside. We had taken casualties as well, three more wounded in action, three more families given bad news. I just hoped it was not serious injuries.

I now can't even remember what it's like to just go on a normal patrol, this had turned every soldier into a combat strategist. We now do things without being prompted, we look for ground signs and top signs, we then check for potential threats before moving. We have changed as a platoon.

The OC and RQMS had now managed to get onto a Chinook, they had spent a few days with us, I'm sure they would report back to the battalion on how we were getting on. They had seen how we had matured as men. It was good to have them here and experience what we had been experiencing from a day-to-day basis. We also had shown that we were as good as they come, as far as commanders go.

It's time to start to sorting out my section, there were a million things that I needed to start to do, one being serial number checks. I knew that the Marines will be on final training, in fact they were already in Bastion sorting out their weapons and vehicles. We did not have much time left here in Sangin, one thing was true though, it will be a mother of a battles to get them here and get us out, a day the Taliban will relish, I'm sure.

Intelligence has indicated that Anti-Coalition Militia (ACM) had begun moving from Musa Quala, Nowzad, and Kajaki, towards Sangin, this may be due to the ceasefire in Musa Quala, or the fact that they knew that we were vulnerable. There was only a few days left now, so it might just be the last time they got to have a go at us, and to be honest we were looking forward to some payback.

News travelled very fast in Helmand, we knew that the Marines had now taken over command of Kajaki, and that it was a fight from the minute that the Chinook came into view. The Taliban hit them with a ferocious array of weaponry, I didn't think the Marines were expecting such a warm welcome, let's just hope they are ready for the battle they get when they arrive here in Sangin.

Again another night of sporadic fire from all angles hitting the district centre, we returned in kind, I started to think about shooting that speaker off the mosque, it was annoying. I thought if I shoot it off, will the Taliban know when to attack if they cannot hear the call to prayer? I'm sure some do-gooder would complain about it, I might as well just leave it hanging, as I'm sure someone else would do it for me.

It's now 29 September, and we had confirmation that the Royal Marines main body will be here tomorrow. Orders would be at 1530 hours, so all commanders to the operations room, or as it's such a big O Group, it would be done around the OC's bed space. It would take some time to orchestrate with all the attached personnel, we had to make sure we get the Marines in here in good order, and get them straight into position without any fuss.

The orders group lasted just over two hours; I could tell that everyone was threaders with this place, we knew it was going to be a day that would test us right up until the last man was on the Chinook safely. I just hoped we would be without any more casualties, it's in a place like Sangin that you start to question whether there is a God or not, because if there is, he isn't showing much compassion towards us.

It's now coming up to 1740 hours, and the arrival of the Marines' first packet of soldiers is imminent, so we started to move into the positions that had been allocated to us by the OC. I found myself with my section pushed out into the west and along the Helmand riverbank. We spaced out evenly and began to scan the tree line to our front, we knew from experience now that all targets were red, which means open season, and I'm making sure that my section gets home. We had come too far to be killed on the last few days, as the saying throughout the brigade goes, better to be tried by 10 than carried by 6. I for one would rather be in court than in a box, we had already lost one of our warriors, and we didn't intend to lose another.

The HLS was now secure, we were just waiting on the chopper to come into view. We knew it left Bastion and was on route to here. I bet the Marines in the back of it were shitting themselves, I knew I would be, especially having watched all this unfold on the television back home.

News came in that B-Company was in contact with the Taliban, they had two casualties, by an explosion. That's the only news that came across the battle group net. It made the mood amongst the troops lower, just as we thought, even now we were about to leave, the Taliban were still strong right to the last second, it gave you a reality check.

The Chinook started to come into view, it's hard to see because of the backdrop of the mountains, but the noise from the engines was heard across the valley. It's flying very low and was zigzagging to avoid direct fire from the Taliban. Above it to the left and right were two Apache gunship helicopters, they had begun to strike targets that were deep in the green zone, then the Chinook door gunner started to engage. It seemed like time had stood still, from peaceful silence to a battle within a micro second, my section was now engaging enemy forces trying to cross a bridge.

We hit them with 40 mm grenade rocket launcher, it looked spectacular as I got to see his legs explode into red mist, his so-called fellow Taliban fighters ran off and left him, he fell into the river and was taken by the strong current. I got a sense of achievement that day.

The Marines grabbed their Bergans and grip bags and started to unload the Chinook, all hands on deck. The Chinook wanted to get off the ground, there was screaming from every soldier and Marine, the HLS was taking incoming fire, it needed to go and go now. It eventually lifted off with the two Apaches firing 30 mm Canon into compounds. It's been a great day for the company, we had killed enemy fighters and not lost anyone so far, so good day at the office had by everyone.

The Marines were starting to slowly take over the operations room. It's just some of the command elements that had arrived, and the main body and the rest of the company would arrive tomorrow, it would be a great day when we lift off from here, but I would feel a lot better once we land in Bastion. I don't think anyone of us will be able to relax until we are sitting having a coffee, only then we can let our guard down.

That night I sat down with Dougal and started to talk about Luke. He too had a lot of unsaid things, so it's not just me who felt bad about shouting at him; it seemed we all had unsaid things we wish we could have told him. We sat there for about an hour cleaning our weapons and sorting out our webbing, we also decided to have an all-in-one meal. We threw what rations we had left into one big pot, remembering to keep at least twenty-four hours' emergency rations in our belt kit.

Throughout the night we continued to stag on the Sangers, it's not over until we all land in Bastion, and the Taliban brought us back down to reality with an onslaught of fire from the J-DAM building. It kept us on our toes and brought back the reality of war, it just took one of us to fall asleep on duty or start to waver from what the threat was and we would join Luke.

The next morning I was woken up by the .50 calibre, they were firing into wombat wood, the UAV had spotted men carrying a barrel and preparing to set up a mortar. The Fire Support Group took no chances when it came to putting our lives in danger. The 3 Para Mortar team had been outstanding during this tour, they had proved to everyone that they were the best in the brigade, they had deterred the Taliban from countless attacks onto the district centre and killed hundreds of enemy fighters, they all deserve a medal.

We were given a brief by Spence, he explained that we cannot get complacent, remember that this was as real as it gets. He was proud to have served with every one of us, and he was determined not to lose any more soldiers, keep on top of your game, stay together, and watch each other's back. We took his words on board. I didn't think anyone wanted to let him down, or ourselves.

We were told to prepare for a ferocious battle with the Taliban, they had been reinforcing Sangin with fighters from Musa Quala, Nowzad, and Kajaki, so as expected everyone was nervous. I used to think this would be weak of me to believe such a thing, but when your life is in someone else's hands, it makes me nervous, it makes us all nervous.

Just as the Marines were getting onto the Chinooks back in Bastion, they must be nervous about the prospect of coming here to Sangin. I would not want to be starting off a six-month tour in Sangin, it's hard to explain to someone what goes through your head when you know that you are about to fly into an area which is swarming with enemy that are trying to kill you.

At the same time as they are boarding the Chinooks, my platoon was moving out slowly into the west of Sangin district centre. We were scanning everything that moves, the branches that move with the wind quickly had weapons pointing at them, the guys in the platoon knew only too well how vitally important this last task was, our kit was all packed up and waiting for us to grab it, this could well be the last operation that we do here.

We moved out into a tree line as it gave us good cover, but more importantly it provided great arcs across the green zone, we settled into position, hoping that the Chinooks would land on the HLS or even behind us, but the first Chinook actually landed some distance in front of us, it was a very good deception plan. If it was the plan that they had been given, we heard them come under fire. It seemed like a battle for hell, we could hear screaming and shouting, then another Chinook landed to our rear, more troops ran off and headed towards the FOB.

We got orders to extract back into the FOB. We moved back inbounds towards the rear of the HLS, there was pre-fire going into different parts of Sangin. My ears were hurting, my shirt was soaking with sweat, and I was exhausted from not only lack of sleep but from lack of food. I think everyone was feeling the same at this point. We made our way back to the old ANP building, which was right next to the HLS. I could see the first wave of the Marines run off the ramp, the first Marine that ran off was carrying heavy kit, he ran so fast and jumped that he fell over and broke his ankle. He was quickly dragged back on, his tour of Sangin was short lived, well at least he wasn't shot.

The Marines sorted out their kit very quickly and we were told to get to the Sangers and conduct a RIP. It was shocking to see that they had only rifles and light support weapons; they had no GPMG or mortars, what the hell were they thinking, to think that their commanding officer and numerous other ranks had been here for a recce. They had taken nothing on board, now we had to leave our mortars and GPMG for them to use. If we didn't, then they would have been destroyed by the Taliban.

We could still hear the battle being had by B-Company. I was told that Jim Berry was with them, it didn't make any sense, why the hell was he with them, I'm sure he had done everything that he possibly could to get here, and if it meant going out on the ground for the final mission of the brigade, then that's what he had done. He was at the front leading, maybe that's a noble thing to do or just plain insane, only he could answer that question.

I made my way back to my section's sentry position. Some of the echelon troops within the FOB had been stagging on while we were out on patrol. I stayed there until we had been relieved by the Marines; we had handed over our Sanger position while in contact, it was the fastest ever relief in place I had ever done. I pointed out the arcs of fire, prominent points, places of interest, and the areas of possible threat. Once the Marine NCO was happy, I left him engaging enemy fighters, our job was done, we could all head across the rickety bridge and wait for our lift to come in.

Some of the guys had been told that B-Company had taken a casualty, it wasn't what we had wanted to hear. The media were standing amongst our platoon and were hungry for yet another story. I heard Robbie say that it was Jim Berry, one of the Royal Irish officers. I felt my heart sink into my chest, I was speechless, how could this be, what the hell had happened. The company was still clearing compounds, the explosions were now every few minutes, shortly followed by automatic fire. It was one hell of a battle, part of me wanted to go and help, but we would just be getting in the way, the paratroopers knew how to handle themselves, they were the best.

It wasn't long before we could hear a quad bike coming towards us from the canal path, it was being driven by John Hardy, who was the Regimental Sergeant Major (RSM) of 3 Para, and he was respected by all the troops. On the back of the quad he had Jim Berry on the trailer, he was being shouted at by some of the guys. They were telling him to slow down, he started to swear at them and picked up speed. He then hit a bump and Jim Berry's limp body was thrown from the quad and into a ditch, at that point I think he embarrassed himself.

The RSM reversed the quad back up the canal path and was greeted by numerous helpers who had lifted Jim back onto the quad; he then drove it slower towards the medical room.

They gave first aid at the scene and then helped to move him onto the HLS, where we waited for the IRT to come in. This was not accepted by the platoon, we had seen how one of our guys had been thrown off the quad and the fact that the RSM didn't seem to give a shit about what he had done, this may not go down well with others, but I had seen it with my own eyes.

I started to have a drink of water, when the media began to try and interview some of the soldiers, the party line was, 'How do you feel about leaving, and do you think that you have achieved anything here?' One of the guys in the platoon replied, 'I think you should ask Speedy.' He then approached me with the same question. I was exhausted, I didn't want to talk, I said, 'You should ask someone who is a lot higher in rank than me, but from my perspective, we haven't achieved anything here, we've just turned ammunition into empty casings.'

That was not just me that thought that. I've had it from every single soldier who I have asked who took part in the defence of Sangin district centre, thousands of rounds of ammunition expended, blood, sweat, and tears wasted, and numerous soldiers killed, not to mention some innocent civilians that may have been caught up in the conflict, along with hundreds of Taliban fighters, and it felt like for nothing.

The Chinook landed and we ran on for one last time. I placed my weapon facing downwards and strapped myself in; the Chinook was packed with the remaining soldiers from my platoon, the look of sheer relief etched across everyone's face said it all, some troops from 8 Platoon filled empty spaces on the chopper, the centre was packed with Bergans and other serialised kit, it lifted into the air and headed west towards Bastion. I felt like screaming at the top of my voice, thank God, and relax in the seat, it was the RAF's turn to look after us, let them take some responsibility for our safety at last. They took control and let us rest, we were given the five-minute warning that we were arriving at Bastion. I looked out of the window and was in shock, the camp was now massive, it had grown so much since we had last been here, then again troop numbers had doubled also.

We landed in Bastion and walked down the ramp, the look on our faces took a different story, a story of pain, heartache, worry, stress, relief, and most of all, loss, loss of a comrade in battle. I felt like crying, no one would ever understand what it is like to lose a member of your section, especially a 2 i/c. I'm sure one day time will heal.

Our accommodation was a tent, with the amount of troops now in Bastion, there was not enough space for us. I could see they had begun to build permanent air-conned blocks, and the NAAFI had moved from the tent to a proper building. I was looking forward to sitting there and just relaxing, people-watching was going to be my next task, and I was ready.

We made our way to the tented area, Spence had briefed us to do personal admin before we all bomb-busted to the NAAFI. We cleaned our weapons and sorted out our kit, the boss came down and told us we still had work to do, and we were going to FOB Price tomorrow in Gereshk, so enjoy the night and make sure we were ready to go at 0700 hours. This was another way of saying don't rest on your laurels, it's not over until the fat lady sings.

We put a stag list together and made sure that everyone got a chance to get to the NAAFI. It was one hour on and ten hours off. I waited for Robbie, Tam, and O,Driscol and then we walked over together, we grabbed a cold drink and other bits and pieces from the shop then sat outside just staring at everyone. We had long hair and beards now, well, I had stubble from when I shaved it off for the RQMS coming out on his visit, some of the girls that Luke had spoken to came across for a chat with us. They asked where he was, silence fell amongst the table, then Dougal said he was killed in Sangin, at that moment it hit everyone what had happened.

We never had the chance to grieve for Luke; it was work, work, work, now was not the time to show emotion. I would cry in my own time and by myself. I will never let my men see that I am weak, it would be justified if I did, but I was too strong a person to break down in public, especially as the tour was not over yet.

The next day the platoon all attended breakfast together, then made our way to the flight line. We got into two chalks and waited for the Chinook to land, Gereshk would be a place to get the platoon to talk again, we knew that some members were still finding it hard to come to terms with Luke's death. Robbie was bottling up a lot of stuff, his stutter had got a lot worse since that day, he nearly broke his back early on in the tour and had taken it badly. Time would tell how he would react.

The Chinook came into view, most of us made sure we had our goggles on, this would stop the dust and sand getting into our eyes. We had also learnt a lesson reference to our weapons, we had them all wrapped in black bin bags to prevent them from getting dirty, especially as we spent some time yesterday cleaning them, you learn very quickly that time is precious.

We ran onto the Chinook and strapped ourselves in. I couldn't find part of my seatbelt so I pretended to put it on. I actually just wrapped it around me, I was too embarrassed to ask for help from the other guys. I didn't really care about the seatbelt to be honest. We flew into Gereshk got off the Chinook and slowly walked to where we had slept nearly a lifetime ago, our tent was empty and the fridge that we had bought when we were there was still working, it felt great to be there. It wasn't long before I noticed the empty bed facing mine that belonged to Luke, everywhere I went there was a reminder of him, it was weird to be without him, but OD was doing a great job. I would never compare them to each other again, they were both great at their job.

It wasn't long before we found ourselves on guard in Gereshk, we still knew that we were not free from danger, there always is a threat from attack, or maybe a suicide bomber coming in the shape of a vehicle at the front gate. We had to still be fully aware of our surroundings, the thing that was not going to happen to us was we would not be sent into the green zone and have to use close air support to get us out of trouble, so that was a bonus.

We spent the next few days just stagging on the Sangers in FOB Price. I used this time to walk around camp, and I walked towards the operations room which was beside where the other government agencies worked from.

I stood there just looking at a memorial monument, it had the names of special forces from America who had been killed in the Gereshk area since 2001. There was not many on the wall, maybe ten soldiers had died there, it had been built near the sniper tower. It was a place in camp that you could guarantee some peace to look at it.

I think every member of the platoon had been there to have some peace and quiet, some of the troops took this time to call home and advise their families that they were all right, others decided to go and hit the gym.

Davey and Robbie were there as per usual any time they had free would be spent lifting weights and beefing up. It was their way of dealing with stress and traumatic days at the office, it seemed to work as well, because every time they came back from the gym, they were in good spirits and refreshed.

It's now 5 October and it was starting to feel like this will never end, we were out on a vehicle patrol with the Marines, the patrol moved across open ground just outside Gereshk and we were welcomed by automatic fire. This time it was not aimed at us, it's actually the Afghan army who were engaging the Afghan National Police, how the hell would we ever get this place sorted when they can't even identify each other, never mind the bloody Taliban, it said it all.

We finished the patrol and made our way back to FOB Price. I didn't even have to fire my weapon, and it was still clean. On return from patrol we were starting to now get the feeling that we were on the home straight at last. I headed to the shower and decided to just lie on my cot bed. I thought I would write down some notes in my diary, I had a lot to write, there had been a lot that happened.

That night I couldn't sleep. I hadn't told anyone in my platoon but I was constantly living through that fateful day on 6 September over and over again in my head, why was I slow to react, my ears had been deafened by the blast and I was in battle shock for a few minutes, it was actually Robbie who got a grip of me that day, he had made it into the bunker and was screaming for me to get in it, but I didn't even know he had been screaming at me, how the hell was I supposed to get over this.

I knew it would haunt me for the rest of my life. I spent the day sorting out my webbing and Bergan, our grip bags were in Bastion in an ISO, we had to leave them there with clean clothes and spare kit, due to us moving around so much there would be no chance that we would be able to carry it around with us especially at the speed we had been moving around the battlefield.

There had been significant changes in the FOB, one being a NAAFI complex, workers from an American firm had brought in a flat pack building and assembled it in just a few days. It was a breath of fresh air and a great place to watch sports and relax, Afghanistan was changing for troops and it was for the better, no wonder it was costing the taxpayer so much money back in the UK, but when you're faced with death every time you go to work, you need somewhere to forget about it, so it was money well spent.

We began to carry out serial number checks and pack away sights that we didn't use. My section was in good order, as for the other two, some sights had been damaged, but were repairable, my wrist Garmin global positioning satellite (GPS) was broken, so I got that exchanged with the CQMS. He had a spare stockpile for such an occasion, the check took me little under an hour to complete then I let the guys thin out until after dinner. It was after all our time to sunbathe and relax, so I let them do just that.

After Spence had briefed us on our flight times from Gereshk to Bastion, we all packed away the last bits and pieces, only leaving out washing and shaving kit, spare socks, and clean combats for the travel back to Bastion, this was definitely the last time we would do anything remotely dangerous and thank God was on all our lips.

We enjoyed our last night in Gereshk with the night off, the Royal Marines had now fully taken over the camp and it was now their tour. Herrick 5 had officially begun, we could see some of the Marines had never been on operations and they were the ones that looked fresh-faced straight from training, then there were others that looked war-hardened already and raring to just get on with the job.

The next day we all assembled at the HLS waiting for our flight to whisk us off, every few minutes the boss and Spence would make sure that we had carried out 100% serial number check.

The last thing we needed was to look like a bunch of idiots on the last day, we had achieved so much and brought the name of the Royal Irish to the surface, every unit in the army now knew how good we were as soldiers, we had held our own against the elite Parachute Regiment, we were not better than them, but we sure showed them that we were as good as them.

What we had achieved would live on for the foreseeable future, as famous generals have all said in the past, 'You will only be remembered for the last thing that you achieved, people tend to forget about the dozen or so other things that you have carried out.'

During our stopover in Bastion, we had to wait for a few days for our flight to Cyprus, this would be where we carried out decompression, and a place to seek professional counselling if needed. The problem was I don't think anyone wanted to be seen as a weak person by coming forward.

We had all been through a lot and some of the guys were suffering from stress. We would need this time to get out frustration that had built up during the tour. Alcohol was probably not the answer at this time, but it would be gratefully received by nearly 150 paratroopers with a Royal Irish platoon, I feared the worst but was willing to stand up for my platoon. This might be as big a test as fighting the Taliban.

The day of the flight was now here, we all made our way to the movements control checkpoint (MCCP) to hand in our grip bags and Bergans. We still had about eight hours before the flight, so as we had nothing to do but think and ponder on the past, we all headed to the NAAFI.

So the NAAFI became the focal point for everyone, as there was nothing else to do in Bastion, we must have drank over a dozen cans of Mountain Dew and Coca-Cola while clock-watching, we spoke about things that had happened over the tour and Luke was the topic most of the time.

I think that no one wanted to talk about Luke, it was still a tender topic and fresh in our minds. We needed to come to terms with it first, it was very frustrating to listen to people going on and on about how Luke died, when to be honest I had been sitting beside him, the image of both soldiers being hit by shrapnel would play over and over again in my mind for the rest of my life.

Just then the female nurses and female soldiers started to arrive at the NAAFI, we were told that we had to report back at the MCCP area. On arrival at the MCCP we heard our names being called out by the movement's corporal, who then ushered us into another part of the tent again we stood around with no direction from anyone until the tent unzipped and we were pointed towards coaches as a nice lady clicked away on her counter to ensure she had the correct amount of personnel on each coach.

Chapter 9

DECOMPRESSION

Before we were all ushered onto a coach, I sat beside OD. We were talking gibberish, we were very excited to be going home, we must have thousands in the bank by now, and if anyone had earned their money, it was us, every single penny was fought for. God help anyone who said it hadn't been.

We sat on the coach for about ten minutes before the engines started up, with a massive cheer from everyone we began to move around the dusty roads of Bastion and towards the runway. I could see that there was a lot of construction under way and they were actually extending the runway, this operation would take some time to achieve.

We boarded the C-130 and began the flight out of Bastion and towards Kabul. This was where we would get the flight out of Afghanistan, it would be a Tri-Star, the crew would be RAF and the food would be a change from rations. The flight took just over two hours, we landed on a very well-lit runway surrounded by US Marines, this was like a place that hadn't seen war. I don't even think they had to use weapons here, it was a culture shock, there was an ice rink, coffee shops, clothes shops, it looked like a proper town. I could see they had KFC and Pizza Hut, this was not a tour, they hadn't earned their Herrick medal, at least we could hold our head high.

We spent that night in a tented hangar, before being called again outside where we had more coaches waiting to take us on the final leg in Afghanistan; we boarded the coaches and began to drive towards the plane.

The coaches began to park up in a diagonal line just short of the steps to the aircraft; we sat there for a few minutes before being given the thumbs-up from the RAF ground staff, then it looked like everyone was trying to get up the steps first, most of the soldiers on my coach waited until the other two coaches had emptied. We then walked up the steps and were ushered to the back of the plane, it looked packed already, the difference between civilian planes and military is that you don't see soldiers in beds with drips and nurses, that's what greeted me at the top of the steps, I could see how everyone had had the smile wiped from their faces just before we sat down.

I slowly weaved in and out of people before finding seats right at the back of the plane, we packed away some of our kit, but were quickly reminded that we had to keep our body armour and helmet on until after take-off. Just as you are trying to forget about this place, reality hits you time and time again, we sat there in our seats with smiles etched across our faces. The pilot then announced that he was honoured to be flying us all home, he told us that he would be joining us in Cyprus then flying the last leg home, sit back and relax, we would be stopping off in Akrotiri.

I tried to sleep most of the way there, I wanted the flight to seem very quick, I was only woken up for a meal, and that was not even worth it. I didn't care though, as I knew that I was going to get a pizza and a beer in fact lots of beer, this is where we would be able to toast farewell to Luke, and the other fallen soldiers from easy company. I knew them all, I was concerned about the state some of them were in, my good pal Dee had been injured and none of us knew how they were getting on. This would be a good opportunity to make a few calls and find out, let's hope it's great news, Jesus, we could all do with some.

The plane took some time to taxi to the runway before coming to a stop; it was a good 200 metres from the terminal, but by the look of all those coaches, I don't think we are walking anywhere, the pilot gave us a warm welcome to RAF Akrotiri and told us to enjoy our time here. We all cheered and waited to be called off the plane, lots of the guys began to stand up and get their helmets and body armour from the overhead lockers, this would be the last time that I grabbed mine. I was going to pack it away in my Bergan first chance that I got.

The coaches began to fill up rather quickly. I think we all just wanted to get off and have beer and just relax, we began to head away from the terminal, when a voice came across the speaker on the coach, he told us that we would be stopping off at a hanger, here we would get undressed and put on shorts and T-shirts, our uniforms would go into a laundry bag along with socks and underwear, it would be taken away and washed and dried, we would get it back tomorrow night so we could travel home in clean uniform. They had thought of everything, we could just relax.

I moved across to where there were a series of bunk beds placed out, it didn't make any sense considering that it was a flying visit. We were moving straight out to bloodhound camp, it was a small camp around from Episkopi garrison, I remember being based there when I finished training in Strensal back in 1994. It was my first posting, I had not been to Bloodhound camp before, but I remember the television programme *Soldier Soldier* being filmed there.

The drive from Akrotiri took another thirty minutes. We drove past Cyprus's one and only KEO beer distillery, and then past my old barracks. It had been upgraded since I was last there, it brought back some memories and helped take my mind of a hellish tour. I looked out the window and could see a football match under way down the cliff side in happy valley, the waves were smashing the beach up and the day looked to be good. We drove up the other side of the hill and down a straight for another 2 miles. I looked out and could see a small camp with a 7 foot fence around it, we were there.

The coach turned left and made its way towards the camp gates, it began to slow down and then the coach stopped, I grabbed my back pack with my iPod and wallet then began to get off the coach. We were greeted by staff that were part of the decompression team. They all wore T-shirts like Butlins yellow coats, it looked like a good setup. We had a brief about what was on offer then got taken to our room, this was where we would spend the next thirty-six hours, it was full on. We got ushered into the building and received information about stress management, then if we needed it, there was a padre on offer for all of us to have a chat with, numerous counsellors were there along with psychiatrists, and by God, some of us needed to get a lot off our chests.

Then there was the coming home brief and how it would be extremely hard to settle back into home life having been through what we had. It was then when we realised how we might struggle to keep what some of us had seen locked away in our heads, let's hope I wouldn't do something stupid, to be honest I had hoped that this decompression would just help me to forget some of the atrocities that I had seen, and this decompression team wanted us to talk about it. I know that's their job, but I didn't really want to bring it to the front of my mind again.

I went for a walk around the camp and discovered an articulated lorry that had been transformed into a cinema. It was amazing, it was showing the latest films that had been released, I had a look inside, but I wasn't used to sitting down for two hours watching a film. I needed to be keeping myself busy, but that didn't involve sitting still. I went to the decompression office and asked for a phone card. They were handing them out like confetti, I grabbed two cards and made a call to my parents' house.

It was the most annoying thing to call home. I was grateful for the free minutes, but it took forever to get through. I had to dial twenty-seven digits and wait for someone to pick up, I just hoped there was someone at the end of the phone, it didn't help the fact that I now had serious issues with rage, the smallest thing would set me off, I would need time to get this under control, and would need my family to help me.

My mother answered the phone, there was a slight time delay but it was good to hear her. She was very excited about what had been happening back in Belfast. She had been interviewed by the local news station Ulster Television, and a famous news reader from Belfast called Paul Clark had been to our house to interview them. They were well-known now, for being my parents, and so they should be, they also knew that they were going to Buckingham Palace to see the Queen give me the Military Cross, it would be a great day for the Coult family.

My dad came on the phone and told me that he had kept scrapbooks of everything that had happened in Afghanistan. He had six of them and one of them was full of newspaper cuttings about me winning the Military Cross, how the hero had done this and how the hero had done that. I wasn't a hero, I had done what other guys had done, it was just the lucky guy that had been written up.

My dad told me of how people in the shops were talking about me, and the fact that I had been to two war zones back to back. They may have felt that I was strong, but inside my head was a very mixed-up person. I just needed time to put everything into perspective and it wouldn't be easy, but having been through what I had over the last twelve months, I'm sure I would cope.

I spoke with my mother who was still overwhelmed at my award, I knew from this day forward I would either be respected or hated by some of my fellow soldiers back in battalion, only time would tell. I felt excited at the prospect of meeting the Queen and receiving my medal, it would be a day I would cherish forever.

I hung up the phone after telling my parents that I had a few things to do before I actually flew home. I did let them know what date it might be, just in case they were out when I arrived at the door. I spent the remainder of the day just relaxing and having time to reflect on a ferocious tour, the next morning we all attended breakfast and boarded the coach for the beach, the drive took about twenty minutes as it weaved its way around the dangerous Cyprus roads.

We then had to drive through a manmade tunnel and onto the beach, as the coach pulled up we were greeted by numerous staff who were all lifeguards. They would come in handy due to the large amount of troops descending onto the beach, they gathered us all onto the beach and gave us safety brief on the dos and don'ts. We then grabbed a reclining chair to put our towels and kit on and proceeded to the beach were a man stood with an air horn waiting for us all to line up.

I made my way to the middle of the group where I stood beside Davey, he was the fittest guy in the platoon, so it was a bad choice to stand beside him, he would show me up, as soon as the horn sounded everyone ran towards the sea, we had to swim out 50 metres around a buoy and back in. This would decide who could go on the jet skis and canoes and other inflatables, it was for safety reasons that they did this and rightly so.

I started off quite well, but it had been a while since I had done fitness and I was beginning to struggle. I made it all the way out and half way back before I began to doubt myself, I may have had battle fitness, but this was different. I started to swallow lots of seawater and began to have thoughts of drowning, I then panicked and nearly went under. I looked at the shore and had about 10 metres to swim, so I tried to put my feet down but it was still too deep. I struggled for the next few metres and managed to make it in, I was relieved that it was the only test we had to do.

I made my way into the shore walking the last few metres; I was red in the face from sheer panic that had set in just a moment ago, this would make me a laughing stock amongst the guys, having survived a tour like Herrick 4, only to drown on a military swimming test in Cyprus, thank God, I made it in. I headed towards the sun lounger and caught my breath, Robbie kept insisting that I go out for a swim, but I just wanted to mong it.

We spent the whole day on banana inflatables and other equipment that they had put on for us. I signed out the mobile phone again and made a few calls, one to my brother and another to my sister, they kept telling me how proud they were of what I had achieved, it was nice to hear, but I just wanted to listen to a friendly voice. It was good to hear what they were getting up to back at home, it also took my mind off some terrible thoughts that were going around in my head. I knew they would never go away, I just needed time to process them away from the front of my thoughts. I walked in to a lounge area and was able to go onto the internet. This did me no good whatsoever as I spent 20 minutes deleting junk mail. I had 768 unread messages, there was no way I would read all of them. I deleted all but 5, then replied to them. This would start to get my life back on track, after all it had been on pause for nearly a year now. I would miss working with such a high-calibre professional platoon, but we all would move on to bigger and better things.

I was enjoying the sun beating down on my white body, when some of the guys were shouting for me to play volleyball. To be honest I just wanted to be left alone, this was my time to reflect on what my next step would be as far as soldiering was concerned, the rest of the platoon at this stage were playing volleyball, canoeing, and trying to wind-surf, myself and a few others along with the boss Sean, Spence, and Alan Baxter were enjoying listening to music on the sun loungers.

We spent the next few hours just relaxing in the sun, before the coaches returned to collect us. On the way back up towards Camp Bloodhound, the jokes were now in full swing, everyone seemed in a good mood, the morale had lifted considerably. We had laundry bags to collect and the tailors had turned up to measure us for suits, who the hell would want a suit made on decompression. People were cashing because we were loaded from a long tour, we each had a minimum of about £4-5,000 in our accounts, with a hefty leave in front of us, I was sure that this would be blown on cars and top of the range clothes.

I sifted through the mountain of laundry bags until I found mine. I then went to a room that had six ironing boards set up and a few irons. I then began to press my uniform, it smelt fresh for the first time in God knows how many months. I have obsessive cleaning disorder (OCD), so I wouldn't be able to relax until I have everything ready for the flight back to the UK. I finished ironing and carried my uniform to the twenty-man room that I was sharing with a mixture of Royal Irish and Paratroopers. I neatly placed it on the top bunk which I was using as my admin bed, my boots I had washed and were now sitting out in the sun drying. I felt great, everything was looking okay for tomorrow.

One of the guys returned from the shower looking relaxed, he said that the showers were roasting, so I took his lead and went for a shower. He was right, I didn't want to get out, but I knew we were still on timings, so I headed back to the room and put on a Ranger Platoon T-shirt that we all had made, it had the badge of the Parachute Regiment, but the writing of Ranger Platoon etched across it, it looked good and I was proud to wear it.

We all headed down towards the tented area and waited for the barbeque to commence. It was another twenty minutes, so we just mingled with the troops and started to spin stories about the tour. Some of the guys had done some really funny things, Spence kept telling me that I had called in fast air to drop a bomb on him, and he was right to a certain extent, I had been given the grid reference by a lance corporal in 8 Platoon. I had asked him if he was sure and I got back, 'It's right, mate, just send it', so I sent the grid reference to the pilots. Spence came on the net and asked us to confirm that grid and quick, at the last minute I had said, 'CANCEL, CANCEL!' The pilots had flown straight by over Sangin, it had been a close call, and I think that Spence will never let me forget it. If it was me, I would be the same, at least it had a happy ending, well not for me as this would be used in the Sergeants Mess for years to come.

The barbeque started to commence and we were all starving by this stage, the food looked and smelt great. I filled my plate with as much as I could possibly lift before the paper plate collapsed onto the floor. I then made my way across to the tables that had been laid by the decompression crew and began to tuck into the feast. Before the night started into a drinking fest, we had a moment's silence for Luke, then we had a toast for him before we continued to drown our sorrows.

Davey was already there with Tam and Stella, they were drinking some of the many cans of beer that had been piled up on the table. Al Baxter was taking the mickey out of Dougal and Girvan, the craic was fantastic. Big Mo Morrison was starting to take the mickey out of McBride about something he had done back at the kitchen in the DC. It was the start of a great night.

The boss brought over a crate of beer and we all began to drink heavily, the stories all came flooding out about what we had done in Helmand, and then there was the exercise in Oman and the nights out in Colchester. Robbie started winding Dougal up because he was always doing funny things, then there was the time that the OC sent out our platoon to spring an ambush that caused some trust issues between us and the OC, who the hell would send out a platoon to spring an ambush, especially as we had UAV and mortars to confirm it.

The stories continued to flow all night. We had Denni from the paratroopers joining in, he was a strong soldier, no one really crossed him as he could handle himself rather well. There was a paratrooper called Mike who had transferred into 3 Para, who was the only one that was calling us all hats. It had gotten to the stage where some in the platoon were going to knock him out during the night, but some of the paratroopers had heard about the situation, they were not happy especially as we had grown to be great friends. It was the paratroopers who took it amongst themselves to knock him out in our honour, it was well appreciated.

As the night progressed, there seemed to be a lot of scuffles, some of the guys had issues dealing with what they had been through over the last six months, and the best way to deal with it was to fight everyone that walked past. I decided to yet again use the phone, it took up another twenty minutes or so. Once I had come off the phone, I started to cry for some unknown reason, this was not normal, I never used to cry while on beer. I knew I needed help, I had a lot of issues that needed addressing and quick.

The night passed away with thousands of cans of beer being drunk. The place looked like a rubbish tip and a lot of the guys didn't even make it from their seats, let alone back to their beds, the next morning was spent with groups of us being sent all over camp to clean up the rubbish. I noticed that a few guys were sporting black eyes and bruises across their faces, these had been building up for some weeks on others' minds. A lot of the guys used the alcohol as an excuse to fight with people that they didn't like, it was a bit out of order, but after what the guys had been through in combat, it was justified and well received by everyone. Today was a new day and what had happened yesterday was now forgotten.

We handed over the accommodation and made our way to the coaches where the CSM took the nominal roll, he had to account that he had everyone before we could continue our journey to the airport and get on the final leg to England. After about five more minutes, the coaches began their engines and we drove out of Bloodhound camp and onto RAF Akrotiri. It would be only a few more hours before we landed on British soil, we couldn't wait.

The drive to the airport took a little over twenty minutes before we turned into the RAF camp, the coaches were directed straight onto the runway where we waited to be called forward to the foot of the steps. We then had one of the ground crew call us off the coaches. I made my way towards the steps and walked along side OD, Dougal, and McBride was walking with Davey in front of me, with Spence and Al Baxter walking behind me. The conversation was starting to build on what was going to be a holiday to New York. Spence was planning to go there with Robbie, Ian, and Stella, it was early days but it was now the new topic of conversation.

I thought about going with them, but I had plans already in place that would take up most of my leave. The regimental colonel wanted me to meet him in Ballymena for lunch, then there was Councillor Jim Rogers OBE, who wanted to arrange for me to be received in the city hall, then there was Alderman Michael Copeland MLA, who wanted me to join them in their members room at Parliament buildings for lunch in Stormont buildings. All this was because I had been awarded the Military Cross (MC), so how was I supposed to go anywhere, I was in demand, on top of that the people of East Belfast wanted to host me in the Welders Club, that I was looking forward to, a few drinks with family and friends.

I got a seat on the plane with a spare one beside me, this was fantastic as I could sprawl out for the first time and actually not get pins and needles for the third time in a row. It felt great, I knew as soon as I got home my life would never be the same. I was now expected to be of a certain type of soldier, I needed to live up to the reputation that comes with such a prestigious award.

Then the flight landed at RAF Brize Norton and we were greeted by numerous members of the brigade. There was a pipe band and news reporters everywhere, the amount of flash photography was overwhelming, television crews were everywhere I looked, we walked quickly towards the terminal and waited for our bags to be unloaded by the ground crew. It took another thirty minutes before we could pass through the terminal and straight onto the awaiting coaches, where we sat chatting until the other coaches had filled up, only then we would move as a packet towards Colchester.

As soon as the coaches moved off, I tried to listen to the radio, but excitement of being home was keeping everyone on edge. The conversation revolved around going out on a pub crawl, the guys wanted to get wrecked, however the boss and Spence had other ideas, they insisted that we carry out a 100% serial check and hand in our Para helmets, we had loaned them from C-Company 3 Para, so it was time to say goodbye to the light ally-looking helmet and get used to the heavy hat one again.

The coaches drove slowly through Colchester, the public were clapping their hands as the coaches drove past, it brought a lump to my throat, the paratroopers were a well-respected fighting force as everyone knew it, as we approached the gates of Hyderabad barracks.

There were banners and flags hung up everywhere, families and members of the public had come to see the troops arrive back safely. There were injured paratroopers with missing limbs in wheelchairs clapping the guys back, it was a very emotional moment to be part of.

The coaches pulled up onto the parade ground and again we were greeted by over a hundred reporters and television crews, the flashes from the cameras were almost too much to bear. I was trying very hard to hold myself together, we had no one to directly meet us off the coaches, it was a little bit disappointing to say the least.

We grabbed our kit and headed to our accommodation, I was asked to go and speak with a reporter. I would become very friendly with this journalist over the next six or seven years. His name was Robert Kelloway, and he was asking me all kinds of questions, which I kindly answered to the best of my knowledge.

He reminded me of things I had said to the press, Baghdad was a walk in the park compared to Sangin, this place is like the Alamo, we have to fight to get out of camp, we have to fight to get into camp, all these things I had said were now being repeated back to me, it was surreal.

He then wanted to know what I had planned for the future and to be honest at that stage I didn't even know what was planned for the night ahead, let alone the future. I was just glad that I made it here in one piece. After my interview I headed to the block with the others and grabbed a tin of beer.

While we waited on the baggage truck to arrive, it took less than an hour, so we assembled the platoon together while the boss and Spence gave us a pep talk about not letting ourselves down at this last hurdle, he didn't want anyone to mess up before we travelled up the road back to camp.

We all wanted to go out and get totally wasted with alcohol, it was a way of letting off steam and toasting Luke, and in a way, it would help put some bad images to the back of my mind, and well I hoped it would anyway.

I sorted out my kit, then checked up on the rest of the platoon. I went into the room where Luke had been living, his box was there still packed. I waited for Spence and the boss to give direction on what was to happen with it, I knew he still had things belonging to 3 Para in it, but I wasn't happy to go into it without permission.

I made sure that the rest of the guys were sorting out their kit, some of them had already begun drinking. I wasn't worried, after all they had earned it, I quickly reminded them that they were not to get into fights or mess up downtown, at this late stage, it would be a disaster if we were to let ourselves down.

We had agreed to meet downtown in a pub called Weatherspoons; it was the focal point for many a nice girl, the doormen were decent blokes and the staff were very pleasant towards soldiers. This is where I tried to race Luke on a pint of beer called a 'HULK', it was a pint of Carlsberg with a bottle of WKD poured into it, it turned green and was like drinking instant vodka. After three of those pints no matter how big you were, you ended up on your hands and knees.

Myself, Robbie, and Luke had been on our knees six months ago in here, it would bring back happy and sad memories again, just then reality seemed to hit everyone at once, with a bunch of grown men just staring at each other, it was a rather emotional moment.

As soon as we all got a grip of ourselves having just burst through the doors, Dougal ordered three HULK drinks. He turned and said, 'TO LUKE.' We had no choice but to drink them, this was going to be an early night, we continued to have a laugh in there and knock back a lot of alcohol until a good friend of mine entered the bar, it was Grant Mundy.

He had been one of the RMP who had spent a lot of his time taking statements from me or one of the guys for having killed someone, and we had killed a few people by mistake, but it had been justified at the time.

He bought me and a few others a beer, and joined us for the remainder of the night, we continued to go from pub to pub until reaching a nightclub called the Hippodrome. This was a place that I enjoyed to hang out, it was always packed with good-looking women, it had great dance floor and atmosphere, it was now only about 11:30 p.m. when Grant wanted to go to another club, so I decided that I would join him. We went outside to be greeted by an RMP van, he quickly pointed out that the RMP corporal on duty was a guy he didn't really like, Grant and the RMP did not like each other, this was not great news.

I was standing beside Grant laughing my head off at his not-so-funny jokes. I think it was the alcohol making me do it, when the RMP came across and told me to quieten down a bit, I was confused by his lack of manners at this stage.

Grant began to tell him that we were not doing anything wrong, this then was starting to turn into an argument. I explained that I was just laughing, whereupon he told me to be quiet. He then said, 'Shut up, you are drunk.' This then made me laugh and get angry as I explained, 'Of course I'm drunk, it's nearly midnight and I'm outside a nightclub.' As I continued to laugh, he got upset and arrested me for breach of the peace.

No wonder the RMP is hated by every soldier in the army, if this is what they are like. Grant kept telling him that he was making a big mistake arresting me, but he was just glad that he had made an arrest, well done him.

When we reached the police station, he asked for my name., I then told him CPL Trevor R. Coult MC, he then asked me to repeat it, so I again said CPL Trevor R. Coult MC. He looked confused and said, 'I will ask you one last time before I charge you for wasting police time.' I again stressed I was in fact CPL Trevor R. Coult MC (Military Cross). He shook his head and threw me into a cell, he didn't even believe me, even when I had handed him my identity card, he still refused to believe me.

I spent that night lying on a wooden bed. It was a terrible night, I just lay there half-drunk thinking of how I would get my revenge on him. I would seek revenge through the RMP lads that I knew, there was no way I was letting this go, and all because he didn't like Grant, what an idiot.

The next day I had to tell Spence what had happened. He didn't seem too pleased but there was nothing that I could do about it, I had to explain why I was arrested, I don't think he actually believed me, it was just a typical excuse that we used on most days so it didn't stand out amongst the rest of the platoons' excuses.

We continued to hand in the rest of the kit and equipment that we had signed off from C-Company 3 Para, the OC and CSM had a presentation that they had given the platoon, it was a fantastic picture frame and it was a great reminder of the tour, that would be the first and last time that any of us would see it. I think it went to the boss, we all thought it should have gone in the corridor in C-Company outside C-Company office, but it disappeared like the whiskey that the commanding officer had given the platoon. Looking at what the boss had achieved, he deserved them both.

We spent the next few hours sorting out kit and then got onto a coach that was waiting on the parade square. We had said our goodbyes to the paratroopers and were now making our way back towards the top of Scotland. It would be another twelve hours before we reached Inverness, the coldest part of Britain. It was an old Fort which looked out towards the sea, now owned by Historic Scotland but leased out the British Army, this also helped for the fort's upkeep and it was a tourist attraction.

We had been there for some time now. I liked the nightlife, the only thing that put the troops off was the distance from camp to town, it cost us anything between £12 and £17 depending how drunk we were and how greedy the taxi drivers were, the only good thing about the place was that the airport was only 2 miles from camp and you could fly directly from Inverness to Belfast, very handy for visiting family and enjoying your social life back home.

The journey back up towards Scotland began to show when the guys started to pull out their warm kit. I think I ended up having to put my softie jacket on, the coach driver was driving the coach with no heating on it, it was bloody freezing, what kind of idiot does these type of things, it was making it hard to fall asleep. We got the driver to pull over and we went into the services to get coffee and hot food, this would at least help with keeping our bodies a little warm, it would be another four hours before we reached camp.

I managed to drift off asleep listening to the latest hits, the Kings of Leon had just released another hit, so I fell asleep listening to it, and Porky was telling the guys that he was going out to jonny foxes as soon as he had sorted out his room.

I heard them all say that the coach driver was stopping in the tiny village before we got to camp so the guys could buy a stockpile of beer; it wasn't long before we were coming down the home straight past the training wing, and we were finally there.

I bought a few beers myself, I just copied everyone else I suppose. I didn't really have anything else apart from sit and ponder of what could have been and why we have carried out the things that we had done my head was full of emotions and I just wanted to drink myself into a drunken mess as the saying goes, a problem shared is a problem halved.

Some of the guys were already on their phones trying to organise girls that they knew to meet up with them for a few drinks. It wasn't a good idea especially as the guys had a lot of baggage and emotion to deal with. The best thing for everyone was to leave us all locked up in a room that had been filled with alcohol and let us deal with things our own way.

I could feel the start of my OCD beginning to kick into effect, with the build-up of tasks mounting like a shopping list. Bergan emptied out in the corridor, followed by grip bag and webbing, everything needed to be scrubbed and re-packed for whatever would be coming next.

Chapter 10

FORT GEORGE

The coach drove over the old concrete bridge and came to a stop just outside the fort, the entrance to Fort George was not wide enough to enable the coach to drive in. We stopped at the side of the roundabout and began to get up from the seats, then Spence had a word. He said, 'Right, fellas, just in case some of you lunatics try and do a bunk downtown, you are all gated tonight, so once you have unpacked and sorted out your rooms, by all means have a beer in the NAAFI.' It wasn't what we had wanted to hear but it made sense.

This was so we could be monitored and see how we would react on alcohol back home, so we had a few beers in Cyprus, but that was to get out a lot of frustration before we actually got home, now was going to be the biggest test of all. I headed to my room with my Bergan, the corridor was empty, it felt strange. When I walked in, my room was bare, I had packed everything into boxes, over a year ago, it was time to unpack and this would take some time.

I started with unpacking my grip bag, my washing and shaving kit and essentials first followed by underwear and socks. I gave the room a clean and sorted out my bed, I then began to hover the floor, and my OCD was now in full affect. I had to keep busy, I began to put up pictures on the wall, I then sat there wondering where everyone was. I wasn't aware that most of them were out downtown, on leave, or on course, it just felt weird. I'm sure the others guys were going through the same thoughts as me.

I spent a further two hours in my room, sorting out my kit. Once I had done the main bulk of stuff, I decided to re-pack my webbing. I have no idea why I did that, I just thought that I would need it again, and it was good to be on top of your admin, I then made sure I had enough rations in my webbing for the event of emergency. By the time I was finished with it, I was ready to re-deploy with it, I could now relax slightly knowing it was sitting below my sink ready to go, I then washed my body armour cover and helmet cover in case I needed them.

I still wanted all my kit to be ready, for some reason I needed to be kept busy, this was weird, for nearly a complete year I have been alert ready for anything and now I found myself being left alone to just reflect on what had been the toughest operational tour that the army had been involved in since the Falklands tour, and in some cases since Korea, what the hell was I supposed to do now.

I stopped what I was doing and went to see Davy and Robbie, they were going through the same thing. Robbie was just staring at his Bergan, his grip bag was emptied on the floor and he was wondering where to start. Davy was just making a fitness drink and had decided to go to the gym on camp. None of us knew what to do apart from get drunk, there was nothing to do at Fort George.

We decided to go to the NAAFI, in there I found Tam, Dougal, Stella, and Al Baxter. Ralf was sorting out his kit, I don't think he actually had come to terms with what he had achieved back in Sangin. If it hadn't of been for him running out that day and taking incoming fire, we might have been hit. I'm 100% sure that one of my section could have become a casualty, his courage and sheer bravery had saved us on that occasion, then there was Tam, who had shot the dicker on the motorbike just seconds earlier. O,Driscol having done brave actions at least twice a day, how the hell would this ever leave my head.

Just as I had decided to put a pound in the internet machine, big Mo Morris walked in, he was laughing at the fact that he was going mad with boredom. He bought a pint of beer and sat down using his phone to text a friend back in N. Ireland. We had a few of the guys that were on camp say hello to us, but I think that a lot of the guys in camp didn't know what way to engage us in conversation, how the hell could they after the bond that the platoon now had. Everyone would find it hard to break down the barriers that we had now naturally built up.

That night I found myself getting extremely drunk and crying in my room, the alcohol had started to kick in and I had no control over my emotions. I even found myself making a board for my wall, it was approximately 3 feet wide by 4 feet in length. I began to rule lines on it and started to check through my notes, on this board I had every member of the battalion who had been injured or killed on Herrick.

I then put them in order of date injured. I had their Zap Numbers beside the date and how serious their wounds had been, whether they were a T1, T2, T3, or T4 (dead), below the board I had my webbing and helmet, it was a stupid idea but it made me come to terms with what had happened. It took a while, but every time I looked at it, it reminded me of reality.

My room became a place where I was left alone, no one would come near me for some time. I think the rest of my platoon were weary of me in case I snapped, my platoon sergeant was a tough guy called Strawman, he would quickly get a grip of me, but even he gave me time to sort myself out, it was appreciated at the time.

The next day we were told that we were to parade upstairs in the NAAFI. This would be our first brief on stress management within the battalion. I'm sure it would be someone that we could all relate to, or I hoped I could, we all entered the room and took a seat. A guy stood there in a suit, this was his first mistake and he looked too official, we would not interact with him, he then began to speak and it went in his favour as he was from Belfast so he had a friendly voice.

He then started by trying to put sense to what we had all been through, he began quoting what the news channels and papers had said every day back home. 'You are all wondering why I'm here to speak to you, well I'm here to try and make you understand that what you are all going through is completely normal, what you feeling is a natural process, some of you are angry, distraught, and even guilty for what you have done.'

I was guilty for shouting at Luke only hours before he died, so he had that right at least, he then said that he understood us, in fact he explained that while he was in the Ulster Defence Regiment (UDR) that a member of the IRA put a gun to his head so he knew what we were going through. I had to hold myself back from running up to the front of the room and physically strangle him, how the hell did that put him on power with what we were going through, typical idiot. From that statement that he made, he had already lost the respect of our platoon.

I'm not saying that members of the UDR didn't go through hell back in Belfast because a lot of my friends had been there and back, but don't send someone who had a gun to their head and compare it with fighting every day in a war zone, with proper enemy who attacked you with every weapon under the sun. There was no comparison, if anything he had made himself look stupid.

He continued with his presentation for another ten minutes or so, before he stood at the door and shook everybody's hand, he even handed out leaflets on how to cope with stress. I was happy that he had made his way all the way here for the brief, we needed it, but just think before you speak, it may save you embarrassment next time.

After the brief I made my way back to my room, where I continued to drink a few cans of beer. I went on the internet and read stories about myself about how I had been awarded the Military Cross, and how brave I had been, it made me feel like shit. My whole platoon in Afghanistan had done things worthy of an award, Tam and Stevie Weir had been on the patrol with me in Baghdad, they knew I hadn't done anything that brave. I had just fired my rifle from the top of a snatch, with my OC writing me up to be a hero, as Sir Winston Churchill once said, 'Only those who wear the medal know of its true value', that was true.

What he also said was 'those with the shiniest medals cast the darkest shadows', that was also true. I started to notice that an individual from my battalion would have jealousy etched across his face, he had fired more rounds than anyone else during that patrol and members of the unit believed that he should have been given the medal. It was the talk of the battalion for a long time, he wasn't the greatest of shots and his rounds had not been accurate on that vital day in Baghdad.

When it came to commanders, he was in fact a good guy, we had been friends in the past, but during these testing times, we began to drift apart, mostly due to others putting ideas in his head.

If it not have been for a good friend of mine called Dee, I would have probably strangled him to death. No one ever asked him how many rounds he had fired apart from the day where he had to explain why he had fired so many, he would have trouble explaining and justifying it in a court of law, he had just been a bit boisterous on the day.

I was still waiting to find out how the guys were. I bumped into one of the young soldiers who had been sent back from Afghanistan as a casualty, he was still a bit shaken up, he would take some time to heal. Sometimes the deepest wounds are those that are on the inside.

I continued to look at things on the internet and see the scope of what we had achieved as a platoon, it was still the top news story in Belfast. It was saying that Belfast soldier returns to collect medal, the Hero was home, it was overwhelming, my platoon deserved a lot of the glory. I was ashamed that what Ralf had done would go unrewarded, in fact not a single soldier from the Royal Irish Regiment would receive a single award, not even a mention in dispatches (MID), it would become apparent that Luke would receive a posthumous MID for his outstanding bravery in Zumbelay.

Every award would go to the Third Battalion the Parachute Regiment, our OC would receive the DSO and his unit would take all the glory. I believe they deserved every award that they had received, but Spence, Mr Kelly, Nafrue, and Ralf should have received an award also, this would not go quietly back at Regimental Headquarters, they were as disgusted as the platoon.

There would always be the next Herrick when we went as a battalion. We would not be brushed aside the next time, I was trying to find out how Dee was, he had been seriously injured in Musa Quala and I was worried to know that he would be okay. It took a few days but I finally found out that he was home on sick leave, that was music to my ears, on the other hand the battalion had been going through a lot of changes. The guys had been conducting funerals and bearer parties, the families officer Brian Johnston had been the busiest families officer that the regiment had ever had, he had done a fantastic job getting in contact with the injured and killed soldiers families.

He had approached me and asked me if I wanted to meet Luke's mother and brother on Remembrance Day. I was reluctant, I didn't want to ever meet her. I just wanted to stay at home, I didn't want to go to the parade, he insisted that I go to it, it was a battalion scale x parade, no one was exempt. I didn't take this news well, I just wanted to forget about everything that had happened, I believe that everyone has their own way of dealing with death, my way was to block it out with alcohol, not a very good way to be honest, but I didn't care at the time.

After talking to Robbie and Dougal, I agreed to meet with her. The families officer was pleased that I had come around to his understanding, he was under a lot of pressure from his superiors to get the parents from the injured soldiers properly looked after.

I was given my flight details by the duty clerk in BHQ and would now be able to go home at last, I didn't tell my parents when I was flying in. I always liked to surprise them, it kept them on their toes. I waited for the rest of the guys to get their flight details and other travel arrangements. Spence, Ian, and Robbie were off to New York, with a few others from the platoon, so everyone had a place to go to. I ordered a taxi from the guardroom and waited about twenty minutes for it to arrive, it then took me to Inverness airport where I had a flight straight into Belfast City.

The flight was only an hour so it didn't serve food; in fact it was a cheap airline so it just had wings and a seat, that's all you can expect from cheap airlines. I began to read the in-flight magazine, but it was ripped and had food stains on it, the air hostess looked like she had been dragged through a hedge backwards. It wasn't a great flight.

We began to descend into Belfast, I looked out of the window and instantly felt great. It was always great to be back in Belfast, it's hard to explain what feelings you get come over you when you fly into N. Ireland, but anyone who has been away for some time will understand that it's great to go back for a visit.

We landed and began to taxi yet another runway, would I ever get home, we pulled up into the flight bay and waited there for only a few minutes. Everyone started to stand up and get their bags from the overhead lockers, I waited for people to barge past like it was about to explode if they didn't get off first, then with more room to manoeuvre, I got my bags and made my way off the aircraft and into the many winding corridors before coming to the bags carousel.

I stood there staring at everyone, wondering who was who, what country they were all from, and just thinking about the biggest rubbish that sprung to mind, then I started to wonder what it would be like when I got home, what would the bar be like when I went in for a pint, how my friends would view me now that I had a Military Cross. Life was about to change forever.

I grabbed my bags and made my way out of the airport and to a taxi rank. I knew my parents were expecting me, my father had asked to collect me but I didn't want to put him out. I got into a taxi and he drove me all the way to station road, he was asking me about the demonstrations in Belfast that had been taking place, to be honest I didn't give a toss about who walked down whose road or what religion somebody was, it was way down my scale of pathetic things to think about, I just wanted to get out of his taxi and go home.

We pulled up in front of my house. I paid him £7 to drive only 2 miles, the world is becoming a rip-off. I noticed that my parents had banners up on the front of the house saying welcome home, there were balloons up as well, it looked great. I grabbed my bags and walked up the driveway, my mother came out crying, she hugged me as my dad waited his turn, they were pleased to have me home. It was now a reality, they had letters from Members of Parliament congratulating me on my award, Paul Clark from UTV had sent a DVD on the interview that they had made at the house, and a neighbour called John had invited me to the Welders Club to celebrate my award. It was overwhelming to say the least.

I walked into the house and tried to settle down, I was still on edge slightly. My dad began to show me the many hours of footage that he had recorded, it was great that he was interested in the war in Afghanistan, but I was home now, I watched the footage for a short while then became a little frustrated with it. He then showed me the many scrapbooks he had made, they were fantastic. I would keep these to show my son, in the future, my dad and mum kept telling me how proud they were and that they couldn't believe that I had been awarded the Military Cross. It was very surreal.

I stayed in for a while and then asked my dad to drive me to see my sister and her family. He agreed and drove me there. I told him I would give him a ring when I was finished. I didn't call him, my nieces were happy to see me, they gave me a big hug and my sister started to cry a bit. It was very emotional. Craig, my brother-in-law, insisted that my sister let him go to the pub for a drink, she happily agreed and briefed him not to be late and to be sober.

We walked to the pub in Dundonald village, it was just over a mile and it gave us a chance to talk. He wanted to know what it was like, I explained that it was the best and worse tour that I had ever done, best for getting to soldier and worse for friends being injured or killed. He couldn't understand why anyone would enjoy that type of work. I agreed with him, I knew I was not right in the head, why did I enjoy it, to be honest I was finding it hard to settle back into civilian way of living, I found it easier being in Afghanistan, at least I knew who my enemies where.

When we arrived at the pub, Craig shouted, 'I'm with the Hero, here, Ralf, get him what he wants.' Ralf was the father of a soldier that I used to work with called Orsy, he was a very robust soldier who left the army only a few years earlier. Then Cavey came across and shook my hand along with other people that I didn't even know, I found myself being bought drinks by people who knew who I was from the television, it was a weird feeling, I felt great actually.

I went outside the back of the pub to have a cigarette and was greeted by Mickey. He was one of Craig's friends, usually he was a decent bloke, but not this time he was saying smart comments directed at me.

I took it for long enough, then eventually snapped, 'Right, Mickey, let's go outside.' He wanted to know why, I told him I would rip his head off, he was a waste of space. Craig and Cavey stepped in. Cavey knew he was winding me up and told him to go home, that was a warm welcome I thought. Craig then told me that he was jealous of what I had done. I understood to a degree, but there was no need for his behaviour, maybe this was the start of things to come.

I decided to get a taxi back to my parents' house. When I got home I explained what had happened to my dad, then his male ego got upset slightly. He wanted to go back to the pub and rip Mickey's head off. My mother had to bring him back down to earth, we sat there the remainder of the night just talking, they wanted to know everything that I had done. I would tell them in time, there was far too much to talk about. I started to show them photographs and trying to get my head around the forthcoming events.

I told my mother that I had to return to camp for Remembrance Day and that Brian Johnson wanted me to meet Luke's mother and brother. I don't think she wanted me to, she explained it would be a hard day and if I thought was ready. I knew I wasn't ready, but I was being pressured into it, I had no choice, I would be made to do it.

I asked my mother to get in touch with Jim Rogers OBE and organise that meeting in the city hall and Parliament buildings. She asked if I was sure, I just wanted to get all these functions out of the way and start to sort myself out. I then arranged for a meeting with the regimental colonel in Ballymena and a meeting in the city hall in Belfast. It was great to be in demand, all functions went really well, the only one that still annoys me is the meeting in Belfast City Hall, this is where the Lord Mayor refused to host me. It was strange, all the MLA members were making excuses on behalf of the Mayor, but the damage had already been done.

My parents had the letter that they had sent out, but the Lord Mayor of Belfast now did not want to be seen hosting a British soldier, especially one from the Royal Irish Regiment, and the fact that he was Nationalist did not make it any easier. He asked the High Sheriff if he would do it on his behalf, it just went to show that the Members of Parliament in Belfast were still living in the past.

I have since meet many members of parliament from N. Ireland and this view is not held by all of them, especially the Members of Parliament that I spent time with in Washington DC, where we all went to the White House and spoke with the President, but that's a different story.

The night that will stand out forever was the night that I was hosted in the Harland and Wolf Welders Club in Dee Street. One of our neighbours John and his wife Mandy had been keeping an eye on the news about Afghanistan, he had gone out of his way to work on a project for some time, and he was going to present it to me on the night. I had arranged to go there with my parents and my aunt and uncle along with my cousin Harry and his wife. The night was great, I was introduced to old war veterans, they were all wearing their medals, they looked great.

I was sitting amongst some of the veterans listening to their stories of how they had fought many years ago. It was humbling to hear them say that they were proud of me, just as I was about to go to the bar. John came across on the microphone and introduced himself. He then began his speech by telling everyone why they had gathered there, and he announced me as the local War Hero.

I felt embarrassed. I walked up to the front where he then presented me with a massive mirror, it was a picture of me charging forward and a miniature Military Cross on it, with an inscription saying 'Duty demanding Courage outstanding', it was a fantastic gift.

Just as I was about to say thank you, he then pulled a cloth off yet another one. This time it was a mirror with the three soldiers that we had lost in Helmand. It took my breath away and I had an instant lump in my throat. It was fantastic. It had the Royal Irish Regiment's cap badge in the centre of it, with a poem below their photographs. He asked me to make sure it was placed in the Corporals Mess back at camp, I promised it would be, and today it sits pride of place there behind the bar.

That night I had to give a speech, I didn't have anything prepared, so I did what I am best at and I cuffed it. I thanked everyone for attending that night and thanked John and his wife for making the gifts, but it wouldn't have been fair if I didn't mention the sacrifice of every soldier who had gone before me. I thanked the soldiers of the Home Service battalions who faced threats and bombings every day. I might have been brave on one day, but every day in Belfast as a soldier you have to be brave to wake up and just get on with it, with the constant threat of being killed just going to the shops.

That night I spoke with a former 7 Royal Irish colleague at the bar called Robbo. He shook my hand and said that what I had said about the UDR was touching. I had meant every word of it, there were some great soldiers that I had worked with back at Malone road. I had only worked there for a year, then had to be moved back to the First Battalion due to an idiot that I let move into my home who had got himself involved in terrorist activities, it turned out to be the best move I had ever made.

That night as I was leaving with my parents, we decided to put the mirrors in my dad's car and walk back home due to the amount of alcohol that we had drank it would be a lot safer. As we walked back up the Newtownards road, my dad had his arm around me on one side and my mother on the other side. I don't think they could ever be as proud of me as they were that night, it was great to see them both having fun, I even think my mother had a little drink that night and that's a rare sight.

The next morning my mother made us a cup of coffee after which I walked with my dad to collect the car. When we arrived home, we unloaded the car and brought the mirrors inside, they were a lot heavier than I had thought and very big, we just sat there for a while staring at them. They were fantastic. My parents decided that it must return with me to camp, but I wanted them to have it, so it was mounted on the living room wall for everyone that visited to see, it was also a talking point for guests.

For the next few days, I stayed at home helping with the washing up and going shopping with my parents, when out shopping they would bump into someone who knew them and I would be introduced as a Military Cross winner. They were very proud of the fact that I would be getting one from the Queen, it was great to see them so happy.

I would pop up to my sister's house for a chat and end up in the bar having a pint, on the outside I looked burnt from the sun and very gaunt from lack of nourishment, however I was a lot worse, because on the inside, I was messed up inside my head.

I would get down behind cars when I heard an exhaust from a car back fire and fireworks made me nervous to the extent that I was willing to kill the person that set them off. I was trying my best to keep all this hidden from my family, I think I was doing a great job until they started to notice that I was a different person from the one who left home to go to Iraq.

After having so much to cope with and dealing with it very easily, I now found myself surrounded by a lot of friends and family who just wanted to help me; this was starting to freak me out almost to the extent of just screaming, 'Would everyone just leave me alone!'

I needed time to come to terms with the death of Luke, and the list of endless things that had happened to me on operations. I do not think to this day anyone in the history of the Royal Irish Regiment has ever done two tours with such intensity back to back. This would go down in the regiment's history as to what an Irish Ranger can do when he puts his mind to it.

The proud history of the Irish Ranger dating way back through history, when Sergeant Labalaba, a Fijian soldier who served with the Special Air Service and had fought at the battle of Mirabat in the Oman against hundreds of rebel fighters, was with a small number of SAS soldiers and was one of the remaining men left who was firing the 105 mm cannon when he was fatally wounded.

I was proud of what we had achieved as a body of men, my platoon commander had done what no other officer had managed to do and that was lead a platoon of men to war and back with having killed enemy forces, this was something that many officers could do but had never had the privilege to carry out.

My platoon sergeant was now renowned as the only person who had experienced the full spectrum of battle and had himself become a casualty and had proven that when it came to the crunch he did not waver in any way shape of form, in fact he was a tough as they came, a man that could be relied upon in the heaviest of enemy fire he would come through for his men.

I for one would always look up to such a strong charismatic person; I had achieved nearly everything there was as far as soldiering had to offer, yet I still wanted more. I wanted to do the complete soldiering experience, I wanted to have the all-round package, platoon sergeant in battle. Once I had that under my belt, then I could sit back and relax, that was me saying my body and head had done enough, no one could ever say that I hadn't done my bit, I would hold my head up high and show off my medals.

Chapter 11

A LIVING HELL

I spent some time at home talking with my parents and trying to make sense of all the nonsense that was going around in my head. They were doing their best not to snap at me, they told me that I may need to seek professional help, but I didn't believe that I needed any help as long as everyone left me alone I would be fine.

My parents were getting cards off people that wanted to say well done for being awarded the MC, it was great for a while, but I was having to pay for suits to attend functions and galas. They didn't say what was expected of you when you won such a prestigious award, you're supposed to know how to react straight away.

I was starting to receive mail from war veterans, these guys had fought in World War 2 and had received the Military Cross for defending positions against the German Army. These letters I would keep forever, and they were proper heroes with proper stories, I was just a guy who did top cover in a snatch land rover.

My leave was nearly up and I had to fly back to Inverness and get ready for the Remembrance Day parade. I was not looking forward to it. Back in camp I would begin to see who were my true friends and who were the jealous ones that I worked with, they seemed to crawl out the woodwork like worms, and for some reason stories began to circulate, it bothered me to a degree. But the true friends that I had were C-Company, as a whole they stood by me, along with Pablo and

Dee. There was a degree of loyalty from some of the other companies I had worked with many of them in the past.

Remembrance Day was fast approaching and I was beginning to get a little nervous, I became a recluse and started to stay in my room I felt comfortable just being by myself. I started to enjoy my own company far too much. I would sit there and drink cans of beer and play on the games console, it's where I felt I was not being watched, the drama I had now was that my CSM and my OC were starting to notice this also.

Remembrance Day was tomorrow, I had been spoken to by the families officer. I now had Luke's mother's number, I knew she had been asking difficult questions to everyone that had even crossed paths with her son. So this would not be easy, I had to man up and just go, so I rang her and explained who I was, she knew of me already. So we arranged to meet in Wetherspoons for some food, it was early on 10 November 2006. I travelled there with Dee, he went on for a drink with Pablo, while I waited for Luke's mother to enter the establishment.

It was a further fifteen minutes before she arrived. She was happy to see me, we sat at a table and chatted for a while, everything she asked me I answered honestly, there were a few things that I held back with. But that was to keep his dignity intact, we ordered some food and chatted some more, his brother was a very smart young man, I could see the pain he still had over the death of his brother. I felt awkward now, but carried on smiling, she said that she wanted to go to the nightclubs that he went to. I agreed that I would go to them. At this stage my head was a little messed up, I offered to pay for the food, but she insisted that she would pay. I said thanks, a short time later we said goodbye and I walked away relieved that it had passed without incident.

That night I was in a nightclub called G's, it was one of the only decent places to go at night in Inverness. I was with Dee and Pablo, we were having a few beers when we noticed Luke's mother was dancing on the dance floor. I was up there along with some friends, I pointed out who she was and some of my mates thought it would be nice to introduce themselves to her, they wanted to let her know that they too missed Luke, it was a good night.

The next morning we were all on parade in our No2 uniform, we had an inspection that was carried out by the platoon sergeants and it seemed to go well, we then went back to our rooms and relaxed until called onto parade. We then were ushered down to the church which was behind the Warrant Officers and Sergeants Mess, it was very small, but big enough for what we needed it for. At this stage the fort was beginning to fill up with tourists also, I wished for the day to be over as quickly as possible, but we still had the annual get-together in the NAAFI to go yet.

In the NAAFI I got to meet Paul Muirhead's mother Violet and stepdad, they put me at ease as they were great people to be around, they were still hurting with the loss of their son. I decided to make my way back to C-Company block, I had a few beers on my own, now I could relax at last.

Luke's mother was grieving badly at the loss of her son, it seemed no one wanted to upset her, her son had been killed in combat and that's how it should remain, that's all she should be told. We wanted to keep his memory intact, he was an Irish Ranger through and through.

The weeks dragged by, I was nowhere near forward from when I had returned from Afghanistan, well, I had nearly done two tours back to back in different theatres. It was to be expected, the platoon was starting to drift apart. Spence was now promoted to Colour/Sgt, Alan was now on Section Commanders Battle Course, Davy was about to leave the army, Grant had left the army along with Shankill, a lot of the guys had serious issues dealing with what they had been through.

I would be sent for by the CSM on more than one occasion and he would ask me to seek help through the medical chain. I reluctantly agreed to see a doctor who sat there telling me what I already knew, I was finding it hard to cope.

The days seemed to fly by and it was now 5 December, and I was travelling to London to meet the Queen, my unit had booked a flight from Inverness to Gatwick. The whole trip was paid for by the Military/Government, they would foot the bill on my behalf, I just had to keep receipts.

I landed at about 3 p.m. and decided to grab a taxi to the Union Jack Hotel, I didn't realise how far it was from the airport. But I didn't care, I was not footing the bill, the taxi took about thirty minutes to get to the hotel. When it arrived there my dad was there to meet me, he was smiling and chuffed, he would cherish this day forever. My mother was inside the hotel waiting for me, we hugged and I went to book in, and grabbed my key and dropped my stuff off in the room. I got my No1 uniform from the suit bag and hung it up, making sure that it sat perfect, I then brushed my Caubeen down and dressed my Hackle, it had to look perfect for the big day.

My shoes were already painted leather, they just need a wipe down. Once I was finished, we all went out to dinner. I took them to a great restaurant and insisted that the meal was on me. I later told them that it was actually on the taxpayer, we all laughed and enjoyed the expensive wine that we drank to wash down the fabulous meal.

That night I met up with another soldier who had been awarded the Military Cross for his actions in Iraq, he was a member of the Second Battalion the Parachute Regiment and he was with his wife. We went out for a few beers then returned to the hotel for a good sleep before the big day, the next morning we all attended breakfast and began to clock watch.

It was now only one hour before we were in front of the Queen, we started to get ready and tensions started to rise between my parents, I was now fully dressed and nervous, I was wondering what they were upset about. We headed out into the hotel foyer and waited for a taxi to the Palace, my mother was cursing my dad, he had forgotten to take his invitation with him, it was still in Belfast, and my mother thought everything would be ruined on her great day.

We got out of the taxi and made our way through the tourist crowd that had gathered outside the Palace only to be greeted by a police officer at the Palace gates. I explained what had happened with my father's invitation and he then asked me if he was my father. With a slight laugh, I said, 'Do you think I brought fake parents?' He laughed and let us into the Palace grounds, we walked right through the centre of the grounds and into the rear entrance.

From here my parents were ushered away from me and into a seating area where the Queen would come out. I was taken to a room where all the recipients would be gathered. It was weird, I was chatting to Charles Worthington, the famous hairdresser, he was being honoured for his work, it was weird. We were all given soft drinks and briefed on etiquette within the Palace, we were then shown a small video of what the procedures were when we got called forward.

I would be one of the last people to go through that day. I waited for what seemed like forever, then the last ten people were called, we all lined up and were walked through numerous corridors towards the hall where the Queen was waiting. I felt nervous. I had to walk straight out in front of the selected audience, then stop. I would then walk a further 20 metres then stop, turn left, move forward, and bow towards the Queen, and she would acknowledge me and take the Military Cross off a cushion and place it onto my chest. She then grabbed my hand and shook it, telling me that I must be very proud, and that it was a tradition of the Irish Regiments to show such bravery.

I didn't know what to say, I was overwhelmed by her, she looked fantastic, it was a surreal moment. As she took her hand away, it was my cue to step back and bow again, I then walked off and stood by the exit as the national anthem sounded, everyone stood up and the Queen left the room. I walked out and was met by my parents. They were very excited and could not believe what had just happened to their son, it was a time that will live on in my head forever.

I was walking towards my parents in one of the grand corridors within the Palace, when a gentleman approached me. He had a table beside him with boxes on it. He gave me the box for my Military Cross and shook my hand saying, 'Congratulations, sir.' I said thank you very much and with that he pointed me the direction of the exit.

I walked with my parents towards the staircase when another gentleman said, 'Mr Coult, I presume.' I said, 'Yes, it is.' He then pointed towards the wall and asked me to follow him, he then pushed the wall and it opened into a door, which led into a room, the paintings were massive, they filled the wall and looked fantastic. We then approached a lift and we all got inside, he began to tell us that this was Prince Andrew's private quarters, the golf clubs in the lift belong to him, I was amazed.

As we approached the top of the lift, he began to apologise on Prince Andrew's absence, he said he was sorry that he could not be here, but wanted me to know that he sent his best wishes and had champagne on ice in his private office for me and my parents to enjoy. His staff were fantastic, it made the day even more special.

We continued to drink the bottle until it was empty, after all its not every day that this happens. Once finished we made our way back down in the lift and outside for some photographs to be taken. The day was outstanding for all three of us, we then left the Palace amongst the crowds of people and into a passing taxi. The day of excitement was over to the relief of my mother who cursed my father for leaving his invitation for the most important day he would ever have, at least it would make a great story.

I spent that night enjoying the moment, before I had to say goodbye to my parents and make my way back to camp. I couldn't stop smiling at such a prestigious award, I knew everyone back at camp would want to see it. I was the first person in the regiment to be awarded such an award, it would be the envy of most soldiers. I was just very lucky indeed to have it, I knew it was for the whole patrol that day in Baghdad. I was just the one wearing it.

I was sent for by my OC, he had asked me to his office which was in the company block. I made my way down the stairs and knocked on his door, he told me to grab a seat and relax, 'You're not in trouble, Speedy.' He knew me from when I was a young lad growing up on the Ballybeen estate, we used to do martial arts together, we were unstoppable back then.

I remember we were the N. Ireland Judo champions and we travelled to the South of Ireland and took on the Irish Judo Champions and we had won. We were now the ALL-Ireland Judo Champions and it had felt great, but that was then and this was now.

He had been given permission by the commanding officer to speak to me reference this topic, he had told the CO that he knew me well and he would like to break the news to me. As he went on I noticed that the CSM Alan Somerville was still standing beside me. I knew something was up. He then said that he had spoken with the commanding officer and they all agreed that I needed a career break, this was unheard of within my unit. I knew this existed but no one had ever been offered it before, so why now.

He then went on to explain that allegations had been made against me that I was a terrible commander and individuals wanted to know why I hadn't enforced him to wear his helmet and body armour. I was in shock with this news, I didn't know what to say or do, he said,

'You don't have to say anything, we both understand, go speak to the clerk and book a flight back home and come back when you are ready, and, Speedy, stay away from the papers as there might be something in there that will upset you.'

I said, 'Thanks, sir', and walked out the office and straight outside the block. I just stood there staring into the camp, and I went back upstairs to my room and began to pack my bags. Some of the guys were wondering what I was packing for, I only told Dee and Pablo what was really going on. They were as surprised as me, I continued to pack the rest of my kit and decided to go and speak to the families officer. I explained what was going on, he didn't look surprised, I think he had been going through hell himself. I could see he was as much pissed off as me.

My company clerk had booked me a flight and I was making my way to the airport, my parents knew that something was up but were still in the dark. I kept it from them, they just knew I was home for a career break which my commanding officer had given me, as a well done for completing two tours back to back and being awarded the Military Cross.

I took this time to sort my head out, or at least try and put things into perspective a little. I had arranged with my new girlfriend to go on a holiday, we had decided to travel to Tunisia. I hadn't been there before and neither had she. Due to her working for an airline, there wasn't many places she hadn't travelled to, so I was looking forward to it, it may just be what I needed to clear my head also.

My parents were keen to meet Luba, but it was early days in the relationship. She knew that I was a soldier, and ignoring everything that her family and friends were saying about typical squaddies, she still wanted to go out with me. It was great, she looked beautiful, we had meet now several times for drinks and meals, we looked like an odd couple as she had to stop wearing high heels as it made her look at least 1 foot taller than me, it also made me look like an idiot to a certain degree.

The holiday was fantastic, we had booked it to Les Oranges resort and it was full board. We spent every day going on long walks and enjoying what Tunisia had to offer, we even went on a Safari trip. Which resulted in Luba constantly telling that she had a coat made out of that animal and a handbag made out of this animal, it was very funny indeed, and this was followed by a tribal dance and great food.

The days seemed to be just perfect, we would have breakfast then go for a stroll along the beach followed by a swim in the hotel pool. It was great to be free from all the stress back home and in camp, the nights were just as good. We would have a magic show followed by drinks beside the pool. What came at the end of the night started to become a regular occurrence, I would get drunk and go to bed, only to wake up talking complete rubbish. I ran out of the room in front of Luba, whilst naked. I then got onto my knees and began to say I need to save them, help me, these were some of the weird things that began to go around in my head.

The holiday was fantastic, but now Luba knew that this relationship wouldn't be as easy as she once thought. I still have a lot of issues that needed sorting out. But this was not the place to sort them, I felt embarrassed about what I had done, but there was nothing I could do about it what was done was done.

The holiday was coming to an end, we had only booked it for a week, we wish it had of been two weeks as it was fantastic. We had bought lots of presents for family and friends, this was not a great way to end the holiday. But I managed to leave everything that we had bought in our trolley at Gatwick airport, this was not to the amusement of her mother and sister. Even though they were telling me it didn't matter, I still felt like an idiot inside.

I stayed at Luba's mother's house for a few days before we both flew back to N. Ireland and visited my parents. They were glad to see me again and more importantly wanted to meet Luba. My dad had already commented on the photograph that I had of her, he kept saying I was a lucky guy and that she was stunning. She was also the first girlfriend that my parents had ever met. Due to me living in England for over twelve years and only coming home on leave, they would fuss over her like one of their own. It was great to be back.

We had a great welcome awaiting us, we had only just walked through the door when my mother wanted to make a drink and food, and it was fantastic of her. But that's what she was like every time me or my brother went home. We arranged to go out for a meal to the Park Avenue Hotel, it had just been redeveloped and it looked great from the outside. From the inside it looked even better, the night passed without incident, when I say incident, it's because me and my father can get drawn into an argument over shopping queues at Tesco and people on the dole. The last time we argued it was about something that was on the news.

He was explaining to me what he had seen in a news footage and I had said that it was just for the press. He told me that something had happened in Afghanistan and that Prince William probably lived in some great accommodation. He had a point but there are no great rooms in Bastion apart from the two-man air-conditioned rooms, which none of the front line soldiers get to enjoy. They are for all the rear echelon personnel who run the camp and carry out medical operations, I believe that other personnel who come in from the ground injured should be given those while going through their healing process.

We had drank a lot of wine and talked about Luba's job in the airline industry. She was a No1, which meant she controlled the rest of the cabin crew and checked safety while flying. My parents were amazed that she could speak fluent English and Russian along with Latvian, what the hell was she doing with me, my dad said and he had a point.

We finished eating our meals and continued to chat about anything and everything, until we started to feel a little tired, so my dad paid the bill (he insisted) and we left the hotel. It was a good night so we decided to walk the short distance to our house. It was great to spend quality time at home and in good company, on arriving home the first thing my mother said was, 'I will put the kettle on while you all sort yourselves out.' It made me chuckle, that's what mums do.

Luba went up the stairs to our room while I went into the kitchen to help out. I had had a few beers now, so it was just on the edge of coming out, I couldn't watch television without crying at a sad story. My emotions were mixed up, I knew something was up with me, but I wouldn't admit that I needed help. I also knew that if I wanted to stay in a relationship that I would have to take ownership of my actions, I just didn't know how to.

We spent the next few days driving around N. Ireland and visiting the Giants Causeway and other areas of interest. Bangor's new Marina looked fantastic and the shopping centre was okay, I guess. But it brought back memories when my mother's sister had walked past with her daughter, we ignored each other, due to what had taken place when my uncle had passed away. It was still very painful and raw subject to bring up, so we all avoided it for her sake.

The following few days were fast and furious, we had to visit my sister and her family up in Ballybeen estate, the place that I had grown up, they were really pleasant to us, we enjoyed a chat and a drink. They hadn't meet Luba before and now they were really pleased that I was starting to settle down at last. They thought I would never settle down due to me loving tours and fighting so much, but everyone of us has to settle down at some stage.

The holiday was coming to an end, I gave Luba a kiss and we drove her to the airport, where she had to catch a flight back to Gatwick airport, she had work to do. I left her there and returned with my parents to their home, I would sit there and stare into the wilderness for a while. She would ask me what I was thinking about, I would try and laugh my way out of it by saying something silly. The truth is I was struggling to come to terms with the death of Luke.

I did learn to deal with it through blocking it behind other memories; I would try and put happy thoughts into my mind about my MC and the Queen. The reason that Luba had to fly back on her own was due to the fact that I had received a phone call from my unit and was informed that more allegations had been made towards me. It was not good, I did talk things over with certain military personnel about getting a solicitor to stop these false allegations.

A lot of things go through your head about such serious incriminations, but I stopped myself from doing this. I let the situation just develop almost to the point of no return, I was a strong individual.

I had spent some time at home now, I had been to Tunisia and visited everyone that actually mattered to me, and now I was ready to go back to battalion. I picked up the phone and phoned my company commander directly, Jamie Humphrey. He was pleased to hear from me, he asked if I was all right and I was, I told him that I was ready to return, he explained that this topic hadn't come to an end yet and was I sure that I wanted to come back now.

I gave him my word that I was ready, he then threw a curved ball right at me: Do you think you're ready to do Pre-Course Senior Brecon? I paused for a moment and gathered my thoughts. I could hear him laugh. 'It's okay, Speedy.' I then replied with, 'Yes, sir, I'm not 100% fit, but I will become Senior Brecon.' He said, 'Great, I will put your name down for it, and by the way it starts Monday.' There was no way I would be ready, but I would die trying.

I came off the phone and told my parents the news. My dad just shook his head, if you think you can do it, then go for it. My mum was pleased that I was beginning to grip life again. I started to try and do something that I think most soldiers do and that is make crib cards to prompt me and help me grasp platoon sergeants' considerations.

I knew what was expected from me, but how could they break me now. After all the shit I had been through, there was nothing that would ever break me now, in fact the only thing that could break me was me.

My target was to lead a platoon back out into enemy territory. I wanted to go back to Sangin, this way I could lay to rest all those demons that were still running around in my head, it would also give me a chance to visit where we had lost Luke. I was hoping this would be the start of a new chapter in my life, I was relishing the challenge that was to come.

I started to sort my stuff out and prepared myself mentally for what was to come. I got a phone call from my best friend Dee, who informed me that he was helping run the Pre-Course for Senior. He told me straight that there was not to be any favours for friends, I totally understood that, and it was that kind of honesty that had made our friendship. He then explained that Neil Horner and a few others were on the course also, we were all fighting for only two places, I would do my best.

The following day, I said goodbye to my parents and caught a flight back to Inverness. I then got a taxi back to camp, it felt weird to be there. I would bump into a guy whose father used to be the RSM, he too had gone through the ranks and was my platoon sergeant when I was on my Junior NCO Cadre. He hadn't spoken to me in over a year, he would normally ignore and walk past me, but now he was going out of his way to make conversation with me, it was all too much to take in.

It was great that everyone appreciated what an outstanding award I had been written up for, but it felt very strange to be the centre of attention. Normally I would love to have everyone laughing at my jokes or something that I had done for a laugh, but a lot had happened over the past year and my head was now full of traumatic experiences and tactical nonsense.

I had in fact taken on a lot of ideas and fresh learning points, I knew that in future on patrol in high-risk areas I would want a CMT-1 with the platoon sergeant at the back of the patrol and a CMT-3 with the boss at the front of the patrol, this would enable the platoon to react to any type of incident ASAP, hopefully giving me more time with a casualty.

These were the type of things I continued to work on, I would want at least a minimum of fifteen team medics within my platoon and a further two to three trained signallers, this with experienced soldiers throughout the platoon.

I spent a lot of my time now drawing up plans of what I would need to get me through another tour like the one that I had just had. I kept referring back to three strong section commanders and a good boss and last but not least someone who could speak the local language.

Chapter 12

SENIOR BRECON

Now I was getting soldiers that never really knew me saying, 'All right, mate.' The Military Cross was turning some people into friends, I was not gullible. I knew some only wanted to be friends because of what I had achieved. I said hello and walked into the block, up the stairs I bumped into Dee, he told me what the dress was for the following morning. It was fitness all the way, I just hoped that I wouldn't let myself down.

I spent the rest of the night sorting out my webbing and packing my Bergan. Dee kept calling in from time to time seeing if I was okay, or if I needed anything, he knew what I was going through and how certain individuals within the battalion had been treating me. He was as upset as me, I would now have to learn to block everyone else out of my head. I would spend time going on the phone or talking to Luba on the internet. She kept my mind off Afghanistan.

The next day was enjoyable, the lessons were very easy, but I was still lacking physical stamina and endurance along with some knowledge. I was going to have to learn and revise quickly, I knew my OC had high expectations of me. Along with other members of my unit, the young soldiers in my company had seen me on the television talking about being involved in combat missions, some of the young guys looked up to me, I had a little bit of pressure on me.

I had to prove to myself that I deserved to be a platoon sergeant. A lot of the senior NCOs within the battalion had bags of experience from Bosnia, Iraq, and N. Ireland, as well as Kosovo and Africa, they all knew I had it within me to do well. But there were also the bunch who knew I would break or cream in, I had to prove that I was the real deal, I knew the orders process, and I just needed to remind myself of them.

The fitness came as a shock, Dee was fit as hell and leading from the front as usual, Neil was running with him. It was obvious that he had trained for the pre-course. I tried my best but could not match the speed or pace of every single person on the course. I was making myself look stupid, on the Infantry Combat Fitness Test I found myself running just in front of the jack wagon. Dee was shouting at me to get into it as I was weak. I couldn't do it, I was known as Speedy and was one of the fittest soldiers in the battalion and to be told to get into a jack wagon was soul destroying.

I lasted the whole pre-course, every day being mocked by Dee; I knew it was going to be an uphill struggle to even get selected from the battalion, let alone pass Brecon. I continued to come last on the 4 miler and then come last on the Brecon 2 miler. I was not what they had expected, I then went on to give a set of orders. But this time my OC and CSM, along with the RSM had come to listen to me. I struggled through them, leaving out key things that made my orders sound like that expected from a lieutenant corporal, not what's expected from a platoon sergeant. I knew I was dammed unless I could come through with something and quick.

Dee knew I could cut the mustard, it was just a matter of time, I went in front of my OC and convinced Dee that I would be ready for Senior Brecon. I just needed a little more time to sort out my fitness and read up on tactics. It would take me a few weeks to be back on top of my fitness, everyone in my battalion knew I was fit, the fact that I classed myself as unfit was weird. Considering I was still able to run 9 minutes 20 seconds, this was by far in Speedy Coult terms unacceptable for an infantry soldier. How can you lead from the front if you are a fat soldier?

Dee knew what I was like with my fitness, I believed that you should be an all-round good example to your rangers, it just took me too many years to work that out. Having wasted so many drinking with the boys and partying just as hard, I was trying to mature, and there's nothing like a gallantry medal to speed up that process.

I had only four weeks to sort myself out, I would seek permission from the CSM to start training, and I would go for runs with Dee and practice my navigation at a park in Inverness. I would go on weight runs carrying 35 lbs and no more, I believed that it would injure you rather than build you up, I started to develop my tactical mind again. Dee had already completed Senior Brecon so he was up to speed in everything that I needed to know, I would depend on him a lot over the next couple of weeks.

My body was starting to feel better the next morning after gruelling sessions, this meant that my recovery time was dropping dramatically. I could train more, I was even looking forward to hard runs and gym workouts. I was proving not only to myself, but to those people that doubted me, it was a rare sight within the battalion that I got beaten in runs. For over ten years I had led the battalion in basic fitness tests. This was to the dislike of an old running enemy John, he could only beat me once in a blue moon, I was so fit at one stage that I would turn up to races completely drunk and still beat everyone, and it was the talk of the battalion.

I wish I was still young but those days are sadly over, I still compete for everything that life throws my way, including Senior Brecon. I tested myself on a basic fitness test before I travelled to Wales, I was sort of happy, I had ran it ¾ speed, and finished it in 8 minutes 25 seconds, that was me getting back to my best. I knew I would come in the top 10 on Senior regarding fitness. I just need to lift my knowledge.

I collected my hire car from the MT Platoon and parked it outside my accommodation in order to pack it with my kit, it took me about an hour to sort it the way I wanted it. My Bergan and grip bag, followed by my quilt and spare pillows, then my laptop and printer with laminator for Live Fire Tactical Training (LFTT), finally my belt kit with civilian clothing. I packed so much combats that it looked like I was moving into Dering Lines. I was finally ready, and it was only ten o'clock in the morning. But we had to be booked in by 1500 hours, it didn't make sense, but that's how they did things there. I booked in and was told where my room would be, it was top floor in the Sergeants Mess. I was sharing with Robbo from 3 Para mortars and Neil from the Special Forces Support Group (SFSG), they were good guys and I learnt a lot from them, Neil was sharing his room with the Ghurkhas.

Senior Brecon would be the last course as an infantryman that you would put your body through such demanding terrain and physical pain, it was right up there with Special Air Service selection.

Well, not as hard as that, but on power with the amount of self-determination to achieve a pass, it was regarded as the pinnacle of an infantry soldier's career, without it you would not promote past the Sergeants Mess. If you failed it, you were regarded as a mong in the infantry, in fact in my book you would be better off leaving the army if you failed.

I had a lot of things still to achieve and I was more determined to pass this as anyone, how was I going to have my own platoon in combat without it, I would become known as a Brecon orphan over the next few months. As I stayed there over the weekends, this time was spent carrying out administration and preparing for the following week, it also gave me a chance to relax and recuperate, most of the military surplus stores made a fortune from soldiers buying pointless crap. I think I must have given them money for sake of spending it.

The course was very daunting from the start, but like all courses in the army, you always weigh up your competition on the first day, even knowing what a robust course Platoon Sergeants Battle Course (PSBC) is. Some units sent some utter idiots, every section had a complete mong, my section had at least two, so it took the pressure off straight away knowing that they would get picked on and not I was a massive relief.

We were assembled numerous times and seated in the Falklands hall theatre; this was where I spent many hours staring at my eyelids, a lot of the lessons were about defence policy and history of previous battles. We analysed many wars and came to conclusions on why many wars were started, they all resulted in the same way, greed, dictatorship, and money.

After opening addresses by the OC, RSM, and the directing staff, we were placed into sections for Live Firing Tactical Training (LFTT), this was where I got to know the rest of the guys. We were taught everything from how to conduct range safety, to running the different types of ranges as a Range Conducting Officer (RCO). This was interesting to know how all the working parts came together, but rather boring as well.

The biggest pain in the backside came when we had to make our range templates; these were just small pieces of clear plastic, which encompassed a firing line and danger zone 'known as Full Energy or Reduced Energy' (FE and FER). A full energy range is where the bullet can keep going, for example, this would be in the desert or out to sea, a reduced energy would be at a range where there is a catcher to catch the bullet. These templates had to be exactly perfect, once completed we could then plan ranges from the map page that was produced.

Numerous written tests about ranges and maximum weapon ranges along with the famous Pam 21 open book test. Even with an open book test, it is still a pain to find anything first time, then again with twenty-four people in a class helping each other, it was rather simple.

I was looking forward to getting this phase over with and beginning tactics, having completed a Battle Lesson (BL) and a Battle Exercise (BE), all I had to do now was make sure that my planned live section attack went without a hitch. With all the guys on the range planning the game, it seemed to run rather well, even my SF gun was outstanding. I passed with flying colours, in fact everyone passed this phase, so we had the weekend to prepare for Monday. First thing was an Infantry Combat Fitness Test (ICFT), anyone who failed would be kicked off the course straight away.

The next morning we had to parade at the gym and complete a fitness test. I was shaking my arms and legs off. I noticed some of the guys were wearing proper racing shoes. This was making me uneasy as I thought they would destroy me on the run, we conducted sit-ups and press-ups in the gym, this resulting in me doing well. I managed to complete 70 sit-ups and 80 press-ups, there were a few that beat me, but I was really chuffed.

The QMSI then told us to go outside, he explained the run and took all of us for a lap warm-up, once finished he explained that we needed to complete two laps. He then said, 'Okay, on the line', then he blew a whistle and everyone raced off. I stayed within the group for about 800 metres, I saw a gap and went for it, I was now within the first group of runners, I was feeling great, I could see Neil behind me in the second group. I shook my arms off and picked the pace up, I was now in a group of only six runners, and I tucked myself behind another runner while we were running towards the wind.

Then just as we were about to run past the laundry facility, I moved out and passed another two runners, I was now in third place and running downhill, I felt great, I used the bends to pick up speed and continued to press hard. On the last few hundred meters, I passed another runner, this only left one to beat, I gave everything I could. I looked up and saw Spence staring at me, he shouted, 'You better not embarrass me, Coult', and smiled. I didn't let him down, I came second with a time worthy of the fittest soldiers in my unit. I ran 8 minutes 17 seconds, it wasn't my fastest time ever, but I was extremely happy.

All I had to do no was prove to everyone that I was a good soldier. I wanted to do well on Senior, there was no turning back, it wasn't the hardest course in the world to complete.

It was the most demanding course next to Special Forces selection, with sleep deprivation and CASEVAC being thrown at you every day and every minute, it was draining to get through the day. If you had a great section, then it was easy to get things done. I had a great section, and everybody pulled their own weight.

I started off the course on the right foot, I had to just keep my head down now and do what they wanted me to do. I had proven to everyone back at camp, just because someone hasn't done something in a while, you should never write anyone off, especially Speedy Coult MC.

My instructor was C/Sgt Spalding, a member of the Royal Regiment of Scotland, a very capable individual. He had no experience of Afghanistan but plenty of Northern Ireland and Iraq; he made no bones about what his expectations were and what he wanted us to achieve, it was great to know that we had a good instructor.

We all had to introduce ourselves to the rest of the section, this was rather funny. Farmer got up and explained that he was a member of Special Forces Support Group (SFSG) and that he had served so many years. Then Robbo explained that he was with 3 Para and had been shot by the Taliban in Sangin valley. Then I mentioned that I had worked in Baghdad and knew Farmer from there, and that I had worked with 3 Para and knew Robbo, pointing out that I had the Military Cross. Our instructor thought, 'GREAT, I am going to have fun with you lot.'

I look back at tactics with a lot of pride and self-dignity. I did not let myself down, there were times that I thought, 'Sod this, I am off', but it's will power that keeps you from walking off the course. Some of the instructors at Brecon are under the impression that they are gods, and the truth is they are far from it. In fact a lot of the corporals on the course had more experience than them.

The drama you have is everyone you talk to about this will agree, unless they have been an instructor there, which says a lot for them. I needed to do well, so I toed the line to a certain extent. When I looked at certain individuals that had passed Senior, I thought, 'My god, it must be a piss take', but I take my hat off to them, after all they did pass.

My section got straight into the basics, with individual manoeuvre, followed by pairs and fire teams; this lasted only a few days, we all knew the basics of section attacks, it was part of the course précis. So we just got on with it, it wasn't long before we all had appointments given to us and we had to work for each other. I found being in appointment came with a lot of baggage, especially the kit and equipment that they MAKE you carry, binoculars around your neck, now come on, what the hell is that all about!

The section attack week went rather fast, it sorted out who was a hard and aggressive worker while in the field and who the lazy members of the section were, cliques and bonds amongst the men began to happen. This I had always expected would happen, I just worked hard for everyone that was in appointment that way I thought they would work hard for me. Davy Walker from the Scots Guards worked hard, he was a breath of fresh air when it came to common sense approaches to simple solutions, he did not suffer fools gladly.

The platoon that I was in was a very professional bunch of guys; I got to know some soldiers that would remain friends for the remainder of my soldiering days, these would stay behind with me and have a few beers and share some of their own experiences.

Every Monday morning it was the same old sketch, on the square in a hollow square for kit inspections by whoever was the platoon sergeant, then appointment changes if needed followed by weapons from the armoury and rations dished out to the section 2i/c's, always an emotional time before we got onto the vehicles. This was my time for a snooze as the training area was a good forty minutes' drive away.

The only drama with sleeping on the transport was when you stopped and disembarked from the vehicle, you would be expected to know exactly where you where, the distance to the next RV, and give a complete brief to the directing staff within only two or three minutes of getting your kit together, this was why some of the guys choose to stay awake. Others would go across to the staff as only to stand out from the rest of us, these were also known as the DS watchers, they were soon noticed by the staff and told to clear off.

It didn't take long to find our bearings and move into the chosen wood for the exercise, these were known as Harbours, a place to carry out administration and plan missions from. Every man had a task, some of us began to work on a track plan, while others worked on defences and the stag positions, these needed to be built up from the elements yet defendable from an aggressor force.

I along with six others found an area just right for a model pit, we collected logs the exact size then began to de-turf. We needed a model in general and a model in detail, a north pointer and coloured powder paints, and some ribbons and moss, it looked good enough to use for a scaled-down area.

Once we had completed this, I moved back to my shell scrape which I was sharing with Farmer, he had been working harder than me, he had dug down considerably and looked very dejected with the whole idea. I just laughed and we took turns to dig while the other watched, it was painstakingly slow, we could not see the logic behind it but it is what we had been told to do.

We went through the night digging this bottomless pit, we were told to not have any light on, so we had now begun to dig in the pitch black. Every hour or so the directing staff would come across and shine his head torch into our shell scrape and tell us that it was not deep enough, we gave up in the end and just pretended to dig when the DS came over.

I let Farmer sleep for forty minutes and then he did the same for me, I knew it was wrong but no one was getting hurt and it helped us to get through the night. In the morning after we had stood to, I walked around the track plan to see the layout of the platoon's defensive position, it began to piss me off seeing that a lot of the guys had not even dug down a quarter the depth that we had, from there on I knew who the workers were in the platoon, me and Farmer just continued to do everything 100%, that way we would have no comebacks from the instructors.

That whole week seemed to go rather quickly, when you are constantly making models and preparing orders for platoon and section strength missions. It keeps you very busy, everyone receives the orders and writes them down, only two of us would actually give them, that would be the platoon commander and platoon sergeant, he would give the service support paragraph. That was the main meat of the course, so it would be very in depth, we would have to hit every heading that came under it. The casualty extraction plan would have to be plausible, after all we would be trying to sell this to a platoon of men on operations.

If we did not think the whole process through and could not guarantee the safe extraction of our own soldiers from the battlefield, then they would not trust or support you when you most needed them. Once you have proven to your men that you will do anything and everything that it takes to get them back in one piece, then these men would walk over broken glass for you.

After spending most of the week living in a harbour and below a poncho, we had been tested to the maximum as far as sleep deprivation goes anyway. With the recce patrols going out and fighting patrols going out, there was never enough guys left in the harbour for a decent rest, we did not get too many hours in our sleeping bags. The staff were relentless in their approach to making sure we had been doing something other than sleeping, the harbour and track plan were collapsed and we all began to tab back to a rendezvous to meet the transport back to camp.

I took full advantage of this drive back to camp by sleeping again, as soon as we got in the gates of Dering Lines, we all woke up, the vehicles all packed on the square as we unloaded our kit.

Next it was each platoon into a hollow square and a serial number check of the equipment and then handed in, this followed weapon cleaning. We spent at least an hour sorting out the platoon equipment and then handed our rifles into the armoury.

Now the weekend had begun, but like every weekend we spent it cleaning our kit for the following Monday morning, then we would deploy again into the field. This would become groundhog day many times, most of the guys had been on operations numerous times and this was second nature to the infantry, so it ran smoothly.

The following week would be the defensive phase, this was going to be a pain in the backside. The only good thing that came from it was that the trench system was already dug for us, and we just had to occupy the trenches. I was the platoon runner, and Davy Walker was platoon commander. It was getting rather dark and the DS had gone back into camp to do administration, this gave us time to sort our personal kit out. Davey asked me to walk around the positions to inform all commanders that he would be giving confirmatory orders at 2,000 hours. It was very dark, so I took my belt kit and helmet off and proceeded to walk around the positions, when I noticed two figures silhouetted in the distance, I quickly ran back to my trench telling Davey that the DS were coming.

I put my belt kit back on along with my helmet and sat there with my rifle on my lap, the two DS came straight to my trench wanting to know who I was. I explained that I was Sergeant Coult. They then said that they had seen me walking about with no helmet or rifle, I insisted that it wasn't me as I had not left my position, they then laughed at me and said, 'Listen here, Sergeant Coult MC, I bloody watched you getting in here.' Again I insisted that it had not been me, they both laughed louder. 'Sergeant Coult, I see everything so don't lie.' Using the darkness to best effect, I did the fingers at them both and said, 'Did you see that, Colour?' He screamed at me to get out the trench, he said, 'YES, I DID SEE THAT, I HAVE NIGHT-VISION GOGGLES ON.'

Well, holy crap, I wasn't expecting him to be wearing them, so I spent the next hour crawling up and down the position saying my DS watches everything to the amusement of the platoon, and when it came to the positions being attacked, I found myself carrying everyone on stretchers to the HLS for extraction, it was a long five days in the field. The C/Sgt from 3 Para who I had done the fingers to didn't seem to leave me alone from that moment onwards.

The exercise finished on Friday morning with a casualty extraction and tab, they kept saying as the platoon were carrying injured soldiers and all the extra kit the HLS had moved to a different grid, this was normally 1 or 2 kilometres away. Once the DS could see that everyone was working extremely hard, they called a stop to it, a quick debrief about how the phase went and then we had the vehicles come to us and conducted yet again a 100% serial number check before climbing onto the vehicles.

Time for a short snooze before we got back into camp, this time everyone was sleeping, I could hear some guys snoring on the back of the vehicle, everyone was wrecked it had been a hard week. We got back into camp and started to carry out all our administration tasks, by now we all had areas that we covered that made the tasks a lot quicker, it only took the platoon forty minutes to hand in all serial number items and clean our weapons.

As soon as I had put my weapon into the armoury and collected my weapon card from the armourer, I couldn't wait to get to my room and get on with some cleaning. I took all my clothes off and emptied my Bergan onto the floor, I collected up all my washing and began to stick that into the washing bag, I then handed it in to be cleaned. Once back in the Sergeants Mess, I headed straight for the shower and spent over twenty minutes trying to get the dirt out of my skin, eventually I gave up and just got dried. My room needed tidying up so I spent a short while doing that before deciding to just lie on my bed and relax. The sound of quiet was fantastic, I think most of the guys had gone back to their homes or they were down the town shopping, I was just happy with time to reflect, it also gave me time to gather my thoughts about the up and coming week.

I went over to the mess to watch the television and see what was happening in Afghanistan, it didn't take long to get that back in my thoughts, especially as my platoon had just deployed on HERRICK 8, and as soon as I had passed this course, I was taking over as the new platoon sergeant as he was being posted to Brecon as an instructor, so I had a little self-induced pressure to deal with. PJ was a good soldier, so I had big shoes to fill, I am sure he will help me out though.

I decided to head back to my room in the Sergeants Mess, it was great to have no one else there, I just lay on my bed and put a film on my laptop, something with motivation would be a good start, but after watching numerous films and sorting out my kit for Monday, the weekend was over.

Again a very rushed start to the week, everyone running to various destinations across camp, orders being screamed out at every possible opportunity, I was runner again and this meant that I was going to get a command appointment while out on the ground. We got all our kit and equipment and boarded the transport, this time we knew our destination was Fighting in Built-up Areas (FIBUA) village, here we would attack it and then defend it, the first few days were spent building it up and learning how to defend a village from an enemy force.

I must have placed out over 30 x 6 foot pickets and hundreds of metres of barbed wire, along with the whole company, the place was looking like a scene from a World War 2 movie. After nearly twenty-four hours building it up, we began to be given tasks. My section was given a house to defend, and then I lost half of them to a patrol tasking, then appointments changed and I was the platoon sergeant, so I quickly walked around the position to see if there were gaps that needed filling. I wanted a sketch of our defences and communications established with the other platoons and to the officer commanding.

Just as I was trying to find extra manpower, the patrol got into a contact and had taken a casualty, I was listening into the radio and identifying were they were so I could get my medic to them, then the OC came across the radio, he wanted a situation report (Sit-rep) on what was happening. I told him to wait out while I got the information. On top of all this, the DS was standing looking down at me saying, 'What you gonna do now, Coult, eh. . . . What you gonna do?' I was kneeling down and taking notes, I just looked at him and said, 'Not a lot with you rabbiting in my ear.' The rest of the guys just looked at him to see his reaction. I think I stunned him, as he just walked off.

Soldiers who are on a course and in command appointment do take things seriously, but there comes a point when nothing can be achieved through someone shouting in your ear, just back the hell off and let me get on with it, I am very capable with dealing with what's unfolding. It didn't take long for word to spread I shouted at the DS, other guys were smiling at me and saying I had a set of balls, which I was pleased to hear that they appreciated my sense of humour.

The FIBUA seemed to go on forever, we were attacked by Platoon Commanders Battle Course (PCBC), we then attacked them. By the time the battle was over, the village was in a right mess, we had been pretty good at placing out the defences, but from an attacking point of view, the village is designed that it could be hit from any side, it's only there for training value.

After every main exercise, there is always the cleaning phase, we all spent hours clearing the village from debris. Then we had to pick up all the expended ammunition, thousands of rounds had been fired and over forty smoke grenades, this all had to be accounted for, well, the rule of thumb is 10%. But we tried to pick up everything, just as I was starting to think this is just pathetic, I noticed that in one of the sheds there was a burger van, well, I quickly spread the word about, and soon we had a queue waiting for burgers.

I managed to scrape the money together for one and shared it with some of the guys. After eating rations for a few days, this burger tasted like luxury, it could have been the worst burger on the planet but there and then it was the best burger ever.

Just as we finished cleaning and the place was back to the way that we found it, a collective brief by the CSM, 'Right, troops, it's 2 p.m. now! At 3 p.m. everyone in three ranks ready to go for the ICFT, anyone wanting to go sick or who are lazy, the medic will see you now.'

I knew it was going too well; it is part of this course that gets you into a false sense of security then BAM! It hits you with one last thing; this was designed to test your strength and will power, who had some more left in the tank and who would fold under pressure, at the end of the tab would be fresh juice and the vehicles to take us back to camp.

The tab seemed to go well for me, my shoulders were in pain the whole 8 miles that we walked, but at least I finished it. My feet were fine, I sucked on some boiled sweets throughout the march. I could see a few of the guys put onto the safety vehicle, this just went to prove that many did not have battle fitness. It was a disgrace that these were supposed to be the best corporals that their units had sent to Brecon, well, in my eyes they were not natural leaders, and you cannot lead from the rear, only dictate.

When I get my platoon, I will have already proven to the corporals and the rangers that I am the fittest in the platoon, and that I will command respect straight away. Thus having already earned it from the men on previous tours of combat in two different theatres, the only person that could let me down now was me, and I was never going to let that happen.

On return to camp, I could see the ambulance parked outside the medical centre with all the injured guys hopping around like they had been shot in battle. Some were genuine and many were just plain malingerers looking for an excuse why they didn't finish the ICFT.

The weekend was again spent like the previous one, preparing for the coming week, and letting the body recover from what was a hard week, my legs were very sore and I had sores on my shoulders and back from carrying 80 lb of weight every day across the Beacons. I was looking forward to Monday morning, the challenge this week was to do the fan dance, and this is by far the hardest test that the British Army has to offer. In fact it is so hard they have put it down as a test for United Kingdom Special Forces (UKSF) where they have four hours to complete it. When the weather changes up in the mountains, it could destroy the strongest of will powers, many great soldiers have crumbled at the foot of Penny-Fan.

This would be a weekend where I would lie in a bath and rest, get some bath salts and crystals, and just enjoy the pure relaxation of it all before the storm of Monday would be amongst us. I decided to buy some energy bars and liquid food, this I would carry in my combat jacket pocket. I made sure my boots had fresh wax applied to them, as footwear is vitally important to get right in testing times. Without it being applied properly, it would be the failing of me.

I re-packed my Bergan and got rid of anything that would not be used, I only carried mission essential kit, and everything else I took out and kept in my room. I checked my A4 nirex to make sure I was up to date and had the full service support paragraph in there. This I was going to need in case I got the platoon sergeants' appointment for the excursion across the Beacons.

The weekend was again over too quickly, I bumped into one of the guys from my unit, and he had been on the pre-course with me and was on the same course as me, he was in a different platoon. At the weekends he would travel back to see his wife, he had prepared himself very well for the tab, with energy drinks and bars, his boots were brand new, so I hoped they wouldn't let him down.

The transport would drop us off in platoons, we would set off at intervals to enable that the whole course was not up there at the same time. This would be a little dangerous if too many were on it at the same time, the pace was just a tad too quick. I knew it wouldn't last, most people show off at the start then cream in coming to the end, so I just enjoyed the brisk pace that some lunatic had set at the start, it lasted only ten minutes before he was at the back.

The terrain was not good to us, the grass was very wet and the going was not good. The only good thing about the whole thing was that the air was damp, which helped to keep me hydrated and moving fast.

After a painstaking 4 hours 12 minutes, we had finished, well, the first group had anyway, a lot of the guys were still 30 minutes out. We waited at the finish with our lunch boxes that had been given to us. I ate everything that was on offer while I waited for the rest to come in. As soon as they had all finished, the OC gave one of his inspirational speeches on how motivated soldiers always do better that non-motivated ones, that was stating the obvious.

On the way back to camp, I sat there just thinking that, all there was left on Senior Brecon to complete was the final exercise, this was nine days long. It would encompass everything that we had done up until now, it would be gruelling and we would get hardly any sleep, but I was more than ready for it. The question was, would my bloody ankle play up!

That weekend the majority of the course stayed behind to prepare themselves for the final exercise. Some of the guys had begun to pack up as if the course was already over, well, I couldn't pack up even if I wanted to. My hire car for the end of the course would not be available until 1200 hours on the last day of the course. So I went and bought noodles and tuna for the final exercise, I packed as much food as my body could possibly carry, even then I still got more into the top zip of my Bergan.

I sorted out my belt kit and cleaned around my helmet rim, I rang Luba and had a chat about what our next step would be. She was happy that I had nearly finished the course, I hadn't been in contact much due to being out all week in the field with no phone, she totally understood what my job entailed, which helped me to just think about the course.

By the time I finished my phone call and returned to my room, I noticed that there was a metal shovel on my bed, apparently the platoon sergeant had distributed out the stores, I understood, but why didn't he do it when I was packing my Bergan, the bloody fool.

By now my whole room had their Bergans and kit sorted, so that evening, we all just lay about watching films on our computers and eating junk food, it was actually quite relaxing. I was falling asleep so I decided to have a wash and get into bed, this way I would have maximum rest, I knew I may not have any the following morning. So I set my alarm clock for 0630 hours, that way it would give me time to get up, sort myself out, and have breakfast, the guys all agreed. So we each set an alarm five minutes after each other, I don't know why we did that, it just meant that we could have a five-minute rest before the next five-minute rest before we had to get up.

I slowly drifted off to sleep, every so often I would wake to hear drunken guys coming in who were talking far too loud, with the warmth of my bed I was not getting up to tell them to be quiet, I just put earplugs in to reduce the noise slightly. I could see that Robbo and Farmer were soon behind me, I think we all just wanted this course over so we could relax for a bit. It seemed that I had only been asleep for an hour or so when I heard guys in the showers and talking, I looked at my watch and it was 0545 hours, Jesus Christ, where the hell did the night go!

I lay there for a further five to ten minutes and decided to get up, it was a weird atmosphere in the room which filtered out into the mess, and no one was really talking. I guess nerves had settled into most of us, we just wanted the exercise to be over. I quickly finished off breakfast and began to take my kit across to the already lines of troops in hollow squares. The troops knew who was in command appointment and the equipment was being dished out to the relevant key players in the first scenarios, I watched as everyone was passing out orders to one another.

Then I got handed the dreaded 94 mm rocket launcher to carry, it was an inert weapon system which had been fired many years ago, but for exercise play, it had concrete inside it to represent the weight of a live one, no one ever wanted to carry this. I strapped it under the flap of my Bergan and then began to bomb up my ammunition that had been passed across to me, now the kit seemed to just keep coming, where the hell was I supposed to put it all, I'm sure I will squeeze it in somewhere.

The DS had now begun to mingle with the rest of us, every few minutes screaming at the top of their voice, 'PLATOON SERGEANTS ON ME', it was a pain in the backside. 'Right, you have five minutes to give me a 100% accurate ammunition state.' As if the guys didn't have enough on their plates already, this always seemed to annoy me, especially as they should know what they just given out. I once tried to use that in my appointment, to the distaste of my C/ Sgt, when asked what ammunition I had. I replied using the Brecon point, 'Well, Colour, how much did you give me, well, take away 10% and divide the rest by 8.' I thought he was going to rip my head off.

After a further twenty minutes running around like headless chickens, we were told to get on the transport. I waited to be told by my section commander which vehicle he wanted us to get onto, as per usual it was the last one that arrived on the square.

We got aboard and instantly cigarettes were lit and flasks of coffee got passed around, our section was in good spirits, the thought of the next time that we came in would be our last was just fantastic. We all chatted about having an end-of-course piss-up, along with what we all wanted to do after this course. I was a little quiet for the first time ever, I knew I would return to Tern Hill camp and wait for a flight.

Then fly out to Helmand and replace PJ as the new platoon sergeant of 7 Platoon C-Company, a role that some great sergeants had passed through in the past.

The drive only took thirty minutes before the vehicle came to a halt. We slowly climbed off and moved to the side of the road and got straight into herringbone formation. With every man facing alternative directions and now applying camouflage cream to break up the outline and take away the natural oils from the face hands and neck, we were ready for the enemy. The section commander got us all to make our weapons ready and prepare to move off in half attack, after a quick map and compass check, he pointed up the steepest hill in the valley. Then across my personal role radio, I heard it, 'Right, listen in, our section is rear left of the platoon, it's one section up and two back, as soon as we are all over this hill, shake out and prepare for a contact. The ground is very open with a wood block 250-300 metres in the distance, that's where we might get hit from, are there any questions! No, right, let's move.'

We all got up one at a time and began to move up the hill, the ground wasn't too bad and my boots were gripping quite well, which surprised me. After nearly fifteen minutes climbing up this gradient, we reached the top, the other section had moved forward approximately 30 metres which allowed for us to get into good cover, the ground was exactly what we had been told, it looked obvious that we would be contacted from that wood block in the distance.

Once the last section had gotten up and into position, the platoon commander gave us two minutes to grab a drink before we all moved off in formation. We had been patrolling for about ten minutes now, and I could see everyone scanning their arcs of fire anticipating the enemy to engage us. When we heard automatic fire coming from the wood, the point section had returned fire and was indeed sending a contact report across the radio. The rear sections had gone firm, and my section commander had moved up to the platoon sergeant for tasking, the section 2i/c had taken over.

By now the fire fight had gone on for a few minutes, the other section had been tasked with going on a right flank and assaulting the position, we were now the reserve section. We got a few guys together and began to distribute spare ammunition and bombed up magazines to the section who had nearly expended all their ammo. The platoon sergeant then moved us around the proven safe route and held us in reserve, then the rate of fire lifted, smoke bellowed across the front of the wood followed by an explosion and automatic fire. 'POSITION CLEAR!' . . . 'REORG!'

We had killed the enemy and taken control of the situation, it seemed to run smoothly from my perspective, the DS called us all in and told us to remove helmets. We had a drink and then we discussed what had happened and why we had taken the action that we took, it was all good positive feedback and lessons learnt from the first attack, it put us all on a high and ready for the next one, command appointments changes and we were ready to move off.

Well, that was short and sweet a command appointment that lasted only fifty minutes including a debrief, and he got a highly competent (HC) for not much work done. This was one of the things that I hated about Brecon, it was all too staged. I am sure that an appointment that lasted nearly twenty-four hours with numerous events would be more of a suitable challenge. That wouldn't even test a young ranger back in battalion, but if that was what they wanted, then let them have it.

We shook ourselves out and began to patrol towards a pre-designated harbour, we stopped short and carried out a snap ambush in case we had been followed by enemy forces. The recce party was assembled and moved off to the location and established communication with zero. The guides then returned to collect the rest of the platoon, and we moved off to our new home for the next twenty-four to forty-eight hours. On arrival I could see at least the ground was dry, this was a bonus, I thought things are looking up.

We were told to drop our Bergans and face out in the direction we had been travelling. This again was to make sure we had not been followed. After lying facing out for twenty minutes, we got the word to stand down.

The 2i/c was preparing a stag list and we all were given thirty minutes on it, this enabled the rest of the guys to begin the work phase, we had now occupied a harbour and the track plan and shell scrapes needed to begin. Each section was tasked with work, we completed the sentry position and fall-back position for night-time routine. After two hours of work, we could now relax for a bit, myself and Farmer got a hot drink on and had a meal, we sorted out our feet and wiped down our weapon systems.

At this stage the platoon commander was writing his orders down, and preparing to deliver what the next phase would be. For the next few hours it rained and it looked as if it would rain forever, we quickly got our ponchos up and relaxed below them relatively dry. The DS walking around telling us to be getting on with something constructive just for the sake of talking to us, this was the way Brecon was, pointless criticism most of the time, with the odd word of advice the key phase being 'IF I WAS YOU' that night dragged in.

The next few days were packed with command appointment changes and sleep deprivation. I was exhausted from lack of sleep and tabbing. My Tactical Aide Memoire (TAMS) were now in my Bergan, I had done my command appointment and passed, others had failed and I knew they would be tested again. I was safe now, then I noticed that a lot of the guys were going back into camp to see the medic about trivial injuries, this time was used to grab food for the remainder of the section.

I thought it was a great idea, now what happened next was not me pretending, but it was looked at as if I had faked it. On the next patrol I was walking on an incline and slipped over, with the weight on my back and with an already weak ankle I creamed in, I was in so much pain, I tried to stand up and couldn't. Some of the guys came across to help me up, but as soon as I put weight on my foot, I screamed out in pain. The DS got me with the help of two others guys onto the road, where he left me for the transport. My section continued the patrol without me.

This is probably one of the most embarrassing times I can remember, the vehicle collected me and took me into Dering Lines medical centre. After a quick assessment was made, I was then driven to Abergavenny hospital where I was x-rayed. I had torn ligaments and muscle in my lower leg and ankle, the DS explained to me that if I didn't finish the exercise I would fail the course. This was not great news. I had to pass it, he said, 'Right, Sergeant Coult, I will drop you off at the medical centre, there is a bed there with a medic on call, you have twenty-four hours to sort yourself out and get pain relief,

on my return tomorrow you need to come back with me and finish.'
I used this time to get washed and cleaned up, I got a plastic cast for
my ankle and over thirty painkillers, I also did not want to go back
empty-handed, so I bought lots of goodies for my section to have.

The following day I waited for the transport to collect me and
drive me back out to the rest of the platoon, the harbour had moved
and we were now preparing for the final company attack to end the
exercise. The end was so near, I hobbled into the harbour and met
my section, they were pleased to have me back amongst the troops,
and I dished out the goodies and filtered back into where I was in the
section.

Morale was a little low due to four guys getting injured and thus
not going to finish the exercise, this would result in them having to
come back on the next course, it had dampened the mood slightly
but I was able to lift it with Mars bars and fresh bread that I had
purchased from the shop in camp.

The final battle had been set, the forming-up point (FUP) had
been marked the model was finished and the platoon commander had
finished writing orders, we were now into enforced rest. This would
enable us to deliver a good final attack, I used this time to sort out my
ankle, I heavily strapped it up and took a few pain killers. Farmer and
I decided to make a massive meal which had meatballs and noodles
along with curry powder all over it, it was laced with biscuit browning
and was very heavy on the stomach. It set us both up for a good sleep,
only being woken up for sentry.

Farmer lay there telling me stories about working with the Special
Forces and how they got the best of kit just thrown at them, this is
what you would expect to happen anyway. He spoke about their first
ever operation and explained that it was Operation Barras in Sierra
Leone. I laughed at him and explained that it was half of my platoon
that had been captured by the west side boys. It's a small world, he
replied.

The hours seemed to fly by then the sentry walked around and
explained that it was reveille, we all had to start packing our kit away
and getting ready for orders. We spent the next thirty minutes sorting
our kit out and then made our way to the model pit. It was a good
model in general and a better model in detail, which had our specific

targets placed out, we sat down in section lines facing the way we would be approaching the positions.

The platoon commander then waited for the DS to appear so he could critique his orders, once that was in place the platoon sergeant stood up and described the model and what everything represented on the model. 'Any questions, NO, well, I have some for you, what did I say the black line represented?' pointing at me, I answered him with METAL ROAD, he said good and sat back down.

The boss started making sure we were all correctly seated and then moved on with the prelims, and explained the weather and moon state for the next twenty-four hours. Before carrying on with situation enemy forces, he gave a very good comprehensive set, explaining everything from strength, equipment, morale, and future intensions. Before explaining what we had as assets and strengths, I took a few notes along with everybody else.

I was only interested in passwords and phase lines and report lines, we listened for the next hour or so on what the plan was and what our part was, the company mission was straightforward. But even that was broken down into section missions, we needed to complete our own individual missions to enable the overall mission to succeed.

After the orders were given we had to sit through the service support paragraph, this too lasted over an hour, as it covered everything from dress, carriage of equipment to prisoner of war and casualty extraction plans. It was in some depth, then as he finished off with asking questions to confirm we had listened, the boss came back on to give counter-surveillance control measures (CSCM) and then synchronise watches.

Finally with the orders out the way we could conduct a rehearsal before moving into the pre-marked FUP, we spent thirty minutes practicing getting into position and hand signals. Before setting off on the 3 kilometres hike into the FUP, the patrol was littered with RV points, this was used to rest the troops and carry out map checks. We then reached an area which would become the Bergan Cache, it was a wood next to a small track, that was the best news I had heard it meant that we could be a lot more mobile going into the attack.

I had taken my Bergan off my back in micro seconds and then made my way best speed back to the rest of my section. We walked

another 400 metres and moved into the FUP, it was marked by
other troops. As soon as we had got into position the troops who
had marked the FUP then disappeared, we sat there now checking
weapons and making sure pouches were closed before the pre-fire
began to go into enemy depth positions. It was now H minus 5 and
the mortars where firing at H minus 4, the snipers opened up on
targets, then at H minus 3, the javelins engaged command vehicles.

It all sounded rather exciting except all this was being notional
pre-fire, in reality the enemy would be trying to extract as fast as they
possibly could.

At H minus 2 the other platoons had begun to engage enemy that
were on the flanks, then on H minus 1. the air assets came online
to hit bunker positions. Then it was H-Hour and we began to push
forward onto the enemy positions, we were met with heavy fire from
numerous points. We quickly began to suppress these and called in
fire onto those positions. We soon gained a foothold and pressed
forward always knowing where the link man was and what the bigger
picture was.

We had taken a casualty in the assaulting section and moved a
case vac team forward to extract him backwards, using smoke to cover
our approach. The DS were smiling as they could see that we had this
well-oiled machine running smoothly, once they could see we knew
how to deliver a battle, they left us alone.

The battle was not going well from the other platoon's perspective,
we were doing rather well, the boss then decided to send a fire team to
help the others achieve their objective. We had now reached our line of
exploitation (LOE) and our battle was over, it had taken us 1 hour and
40 minutes. While the other platoon were still trying to get a foothold,
with the extra fire team we had sent, they had more options now, and
pushed a point of fire out, they suppressed the position as three others
rushed it, it looked like a scene from *Saving Private Ryan*.

Eventually they took the position and started to change the
outcome of the battle, the sniper that was keeping them pinned
down was taken out by a javelin missile, maybe a little excessive, but
it did the job. After a further two hours and nearly all ammunition
expended, the OC came across the radio called ENDEX. Finally
Brecon was over, the clean-up phase kicked into full swing and

everyone was exhausted, the look of pure relief was etched across many a face, I for one couldn't wait to get the hell out of there and back to my unit.

Now back in Dering Lines, we continued to clean and wash everything, the stores were handed back in and the weapons scrubbed and given in, our rooms had to be cleaned and inspected by the DS. Once the block was handed back over and our kit placed into our hire cars, we had to go for a brief by the OC and the DSM, from there and after a 'Well done, you are now all qualified platoon sergeants', we went and got our certificates from our own section DS.

After a 'Well done, Sergeant Coult' and a course report on how I had done, I said cheers for that and left to drive back to Tern Hill. It was great to get out of that camp at last, I would never have to go back there again.

The drive back to camp was a quiet one; I kept the radio off as I gathered my thoughts about the tour back out to Sangin. I was looking forward to getting my teeth into it, but on the other hand I knew I was going to be tested fully on what type of platoon sergeant I would be. This tour would either make me known as a great platoon sergeant, or it would destroy me as a soldier. The army can be cruel, but if you are a weak person under pressure then the troops below you lose respect very easily and this can never be regained, I for one would never let that happen.

On return to camp I found myself quickly on guard commander, even knowing I was about to deploy as a platoon sergeant, the rear party CSM was not one for slacking. He made sure everyone pulled their weight, I spent just under a week on rear party before news of my flight came in, then I had to unpack my Bergan and repack it in a short space of time, I was now ready!

Chapter 13

BACK TO HELMAND

It was 18 April and the coach had been booked to drive us to RAF Brize Norton, for the first time in a long time I could actually pick a seat as it only had a few of us going. I sat near the front of the coach and began to listen to music that my girlfriend had downloaded for me, our plan was while I was working in Afghanistan she would work in Dublin. This way it would keep us both occupied and busy, I soon drifted off asleep listening to the sounds of Pink.

After a few hours we approached Oxford, this was our key to wake everyone up, so as we drove into Brize Norton, we would all be correctly dressed with our Courbeens on our heads. News from only a few days ago was starting to play in my head. Major Shirley who was the OC of A-Company had been injured in Helmand, and it just goes to show that no one is exempt when it comes to combat.

The coach dropped us all off at a hangar and disappeared back up the road, we now just waited for the plane to give us the nod. Lunches were handed out and phone cards, the remainder of us just lay about festering. I phoned my girlfriend and we spoke about trivial stuff, it was just good to hear a friendly voice at last. I then phoned my parents who again thought what the hell will he get up to this time, I just enjoyed the sheer excitement of combat, and I suppose I was not completely sane.

The RAF MCCP personnel called us all over and began to give their brief about carrying dangerous cargo and what to expect on the flight. Shortly after this we collected our belongings and made our way onto yet another coach, this time it drove us to the plane. It was an old DC-10, it was well looked after, this would take us all the way to our next stop which was in fact Cyprus, I knew it well enough to be able to sketch it.

We landed and spent a further fifteen minutes taxiing around the peri track before coming to a stop, the announcement came across the speaker that we would be here for two hours as the plane refuelled for the last leg into Afghanistan. We quickly made our way off the plane and across the runway to the terminal. Once inside I knew the format, so I went and signed for a mobile phone and phoned Luba and my parents. I must have spent an hour on the phone just talking rubbish, I was always guaranteed an update on the situation in Helmand when I spoke with my dad, and I think he was glued to the television for six months.

The two hours was almost up, so we were assembled and ushered back towards the plane for that final leg. I grabbed the same seat that I had been sitting in and put my earphones on, only to be woke up once and that was for a bite to eat. I quickly devoured it and fell back asleep.

'This is your captain speaking; we will shortly be flying over Helmand and making our descent into Bastion, can I ask you all now to place on your body armour and helmet as a safety precaution, thank you.' Reality begins to kick you up the backside in times like this, it was another reminder that you were in Afghanistan. With all the lights now turned off inside the plane and the window blinds all down, the only light was from the emergency lighting leading to the exits, no one spoke a word all of us waiting for our next instruction.

I felt like jumping up and going, 'Everyone wise up, if we got hit from this height, the f——king helmet and body armour won't help.' People just needed to feel important and add more shit to what you were about to face outside the aircraft, this was the RAF's way of saying we have a seriously dangerous job flying all of you in and out. Well, maybe you do, but so does the guy who works in Bastion 1 Pizza Hut as he deals with hot ovens every day.

The aircraft landed on the ever-increasing runway in Bastion and started to taxi towards the terminal, this was only tents with blast walls surrounding it. We came to a stop and were told to remain seated, and this just seemed to fall on deaf ears as everyone began to get their own bags from the overhead lockers.

Well, if you cannot beat them, join them. I grabbed my daysack and stood up, we then got told to disembark the aircraft and get onto the bus provided. Once aboard, the vehicle moved away to a waiting area, we lined up and got checked into theatre, numerous safety briefs on the likely event of attack and actions on followed by arrival procedures.

I collected my bags and was taken to the transit accommodation, here I stayed until I had completed the in-theatre training package, and this consisted of Rules of Engagements (ROE) zeroing my weapon system, local culture lessons, patrolling lane followed by a countermeasures lesson, and the dreaded roll over vehicle lesson. How to use certain pieces of equipment, this was spread over three days and you had to attend them all. Your name was called out each time and ticked off a nominal roll.

Once completed, I was dropped off at the 2 Para rear echelon accommodation, I went and found out when the next flight was into Sangin. I had to wait two days, I managed to get a message to Sangin via the ops room telling them I was in theatre and waiting for my flight, I got a welcome and, 'Will see you in a few days.'

I went to the tent and unpacked my sleeping bag and tried to make myself comfortable for the short period I would be there. I decided to cash a check for $50 and buy some goodies for when I was in Sangin, the place had changed a bit. I noticed that the hospital was now a concrete building and state of the art. I used this time to tweak my belt kit and prepare for a long haul. I signed for ammunition and morphine along with 2 x tourniquets and plates for my body armour.

Now the tour had begun to happen, it's only when they give you that kit that you know you are going to somewhere dangerous. I used what time I had left to get on the internet and check my emails. I sent Luba a message and made a few calls home, as long as I checked in with a select few, they would be put at ease, especially parents.

I then made myself known to Nigel who was the CQMS, he explained that getting mail to Sangin was hard as the priority was for medical equipment first. Then ammunition and rations, mail was a nicety and not a necessity, which to be fair was exactly right. I told him that I would take mail with me. There were a few guys on my heli all going to Sangin so I got each of them to carry a bag, if we had of gone empty-handed, it would not have been good for morale, plus as the new platoon sergeant, it would set me up quite well.

Brymer was working with Nigel in the CQ stores, which helped me out a lot, we got on very well, and if there was something that I had needed, he would bend over backwards to get it. However being new guys at Bastion meant we had to stay in the arrivals accommodation until we had fully completed our induction training before we could legally go on the ground. This meant that I would be used to my full potential by helping out on the range. I spent an extra few hours there going over 9 mm drills with the attached arms.

OP Barmer was high up on the list of things that I needed to know, it would set me in good stead for when I arrived in Sangin. I was very nervous about the whole thing, and it had so many memories and not all of them good.

The intelligence coming out of the ops room was not great, south of Fob Robinson there had been a mine strike, 1x KIA, and 2x suicide bombers had tried to kill the guys in Sangin, thankfully unsuccessful.

The Taliban had grown a big set of balls, they took on a convoy and attacked it even knowing there was an Apache flying over it, it seemed they had nothing to lose anymore, this meant it would be an even bigger challenge to keep one step in front of your enemy.

I would spend the next few days sorting out my personal admin, buying luxury items from the NAAFI, and a few Velcro badges as keepsakes, trying not to think about the past. Yet I never could stop comparing how different things where now, it was a complete joke now, I sat there outside the Pizza Hut just watching all these idiots wearing leg holsters and expensive shades, long sideburns and hair that had not been cut for months. All these guys trying to be someone else, most were working in Bastion and did not know one end of a rifle from the next.

It was now Friday, 25 April, and my flight into Sangin was in two hours. I went through my kit one last time to make sure I had everything that I would need, not just for work, but for comfort too. Any idiot could struggle for a few months, as soon as the Chinook had landed, I noticed that it was very relaxed, not many soldiers carrying weapons. This was not what I had expected, the ramp dropped and I ran off grabbing my Bergan and grip bag. I ran off the helipad across to the ISO containers, I was met by Joey, and he pointed over to my new bed space for the next few months.

The guys all met me and shook my hand, I placed my kit into a hesco square-shaped hut and made my way to the ops room to meet the CSM. Frankie was the guy that would help me get through the next few months. When I got there, I bumped into PJ, he was a great platoon sergeant and I would have big shoes to fill, after all I had flown into Sangin to replace him.

All I had to do now was shadow PJ for a few days and see how he ran the platoon then implement that, and when I had settled into my new job, I could start to change things that suited either me or the boss. One thing I promised myself that I would do and that was always discuss everything with the section commanders, after all they are the forefront of everything that takes place in Afghanistan and I personally believe they do not get enough credit for what they go through, it is always someone else that reaps the glory.

I had only been back in Sangin a short while before reality quickly hit home. PJ came and gave me a heads-up on how things had been amongst the platoon, a suicide bomber exploded too soon and his body parts were scattered across the field, leaving Davy with a grin as he explained to me that he found a leg, well, as long as everyone was okay, that was all that matters.

The brief was mainly about my role as platoon sergeant, the CSM needed a start state every week, an ammo state needed to be updated every time we expended ammunition towards the enemy. This would become a balls-ache if we engaged every day, but needed to be kept on track.

Maps need to be kept clean and not marked up, just in case they fall into the wrong hands, this would sure cause a complete battle group stand still. I make sure we are all singing off the same hymn sheet with this.

29 April and PJ and I were now sharing duties, this would give everyone more downtime and free up others for an extra few hours each day. Watchkeeper is where I monitor the company radio, as well as the JCHAT, this is an up-to-date data log that lets us know

who is on patrol and every single incident that takes place within the battle group. It also is a time where I get to know who the FAC and FOO are, getting some valuable face time with the guys that will be dropping bombs into areas that I have requested is vital.

This gave me a chance to attend the O Gp, at least I would be able to give the troops a full brief of what was expected from them, meal timings headed the list, the troops must be aware that meals were flexible and would work around patrols. The CSM and OC had decided to put on a fourth meal at night due to the guys losing too much weight. The heat was already too much for the guys, especially with the amount of weight that the troops had to carry, it's a great decision from the boss. I nearly fell off my seat when the OC mentioned that PJ had to wait due to his flight being delayed, this was a slight setback for him, however I was secretly chuffed as it meant I could learn a few more things from him. After all he was a very well-experienced sergeant who had been through a lot on HERRICK 4, he was bombarded by enemy fire for weeks and months on end in the infamous Musa Quala.

The briefs used to go on for up to two hours a night, there was always a lot of intelligence coming in from different assets that we had out on the ground. Enemy forces were now using compounds close to the base to launch their IDF attacks onto the DC, over the next twenty-four hours we had no patrols going out into Sangin. This all tied in with PB Tangiers doing a clearance patrol and the fact that Task Force (TF) 42 conducting a mission into Sangin. This was a code word for the Special Forces and would mean we had a no-go policy into the area they were working in.

The brief went on to mention that the engineers had conducted tests on the river that ran through camp and it contained salmonella and other diseases due to an area further upstream that was used by the Taliban as an execution area. This would mean that from here on in we would need a river supervisor (just another bright idea from the boss!).

The Afghan Army were now complaining that we did not show them respect, this made me laugh, as it seemed that every few weeks they got bored and shot some of us soldiers. I have no respect for them personally, I do have respect for my superiors but then again they don't shoot at me!

The brief finished off like every brief, it finished on a high by letting us all know how well the troops have been conducting their duties and that the brigade commander was coming here to visit us.

Just before we all depart to brief our respective groupings, the interpreter teaches us a new phrase in Pashtu, today it is Bolathe: which means, You can go.

I arrived back from the brief with PJ, the guys were all waiting with notebooks open, the brief was started by the Boss Paddy Bury (CALLSIGN HADES), he had a very broad Irish accent and had a way with words. He was a very talented commander, I saw how well he and PJ had bonded and just hoped I could bond this good with the boss. I started to pick up pointers that PJ used and locked them away for when I took over and began to brief the guys.

The boss took thirty minutes to give his brief and then handed over to PJ, he started by giving orders to the corporals, and then specific tasks to members of the platoon. He got a list from each section commander of kit and equipment that was needed or broken, then told them how he had loved being the platoon sergeant and then told them to work hard for me, before handing the platoon across to me.

I thanked PJ for his hard work with the platoon, then explained that I knew I had big boots to fill and I would do my best by each and every member. I also realised that the platoon was yet to be tested in combat and that would come naturally over the coming days, the one thing that I could guarantee was that my casualty extraction plan for the platoon would be watertight. I was willing to take a bullet for every single one of them, I would fulfil my role as platoon sergeant to the letter.

All I asked for in return was that they watched each other's backs and gave 100% in or out of contact and I would make sure that they all returned home no matter what it took.

I needed the whole platoon to trust me; once you have the trust of your men, they will do anything for you, and are then a platoon of soldiers who are professionals and produce quality even when they are resting, they talk about routes taken and possible vulnerable areas!

After what seemed like an hour of me and the boss talking, I finish off with questions to the guys, then this is where I met the famous TREO and his handler Dave Heyhoe. This would be the start of something special, his dog would go on to save countless lives from not only my platoon, but the whole company group. The dog was the best asset that we had, we had to look after each other. If it was too hot during the day, I would rather delay the patrol a few hours in order to take Treo and Dave out with us.

As my platoon was currently on guard in the DC, it gave me time to sit and discuss training with Matt, Ronnie, and H. We decided that each of them would conduct training with the guys. I wanted Cupples and Mac to continue to carry out signals training, Mac was my backup radio operator and a very good soldier. He would always be someone I could count on. Whereas Cupples was an ex-American sailor that constantly made me smile with his wit and sense of humour, very dry yet honest in his approach and outlook on life.

When I was settled into my new bed space and unpacked my kit and equipment, I had something that I needed to do, so I made my way across the man-made bridge and into the Orchard area. This is where I needed to see for myself what was left of the place that caused me so many nightmares in the past. It was where I had been sitting listening to Spence just before the mortar landed killing Luke, I sat there for a while enjoying the peace and quiet. Then Robbie came over with some of the remaining guys from HERRICK 4 and requested a photograph of us all. I said yes, and we all posed for a warry picture, once taken I walked back over towards the ops room for a brew.

PJ had now left on the Chinook and was back in Bastion waiting for his flight to the UK, his next post was going to be an instructor in Brecon, he would help to shape the next generation of section commanders and platoon sergeants, and I am sure with all his experience they would be an asset to their units.

The troops were now fully ready for the Taliban, the training did not stop for a second, and the section commanders kept every member of their section up to speed with weapons training and signals training. Not to mention the LASM and the 66 mm anti-tank weapon that seemed to change every two months due to shortages of it. I kept Joe on his toes with the 60 mm mortar that had two base plates; it was my preferred weapon due to the accuracy of killing area, I was not a great shot with it. However if I put the bomb to airburst, then I was guaranteed an even spread of 100 metres above the enemy threat and would surely get them and it gave me and Joe a warm and fuzzy feeling.

I would report to the boss every day in Sangin, we worked off each other and it was great that not only was he listening to me, but also teaching me at the same time. Now that PJ had left, he took it upon himself to teach me how he had been taught by PJ, this is what is known as mentoring, and I was very keen and willing to accept as much knowledge as I could get my hands on.

2 May and the news of casualties and troops killed in combat just kept growing. It seemed that five Scots had hit an IED up at NOWZAD while conducting a vehicle patrol. Resulting in 1 x KIA and another seriously fighting for his life, it seemed that the lucky one had a cracked pelvis, still a very serious injury, but in Helmand terms, it was lucky!

At the same time the news came in that 'Timor', a senior Taliban commander, was in our Area of Responsibility, the morale was high knowing that we had a slight chance of either capturing or killing this individual. Then the grid of a booby trap was spread across the company group and out of bounds areas, and now FOB Inkerman were out conducting an Advance to Contact hoping to flush any Taliban towards outposts so we can kill or capture them.

The boss came into my hesco accommodation and we had a chat about the patrol that we were doing soon, the US MARINES were moving into the C(?) and would begin to conduct joint patrols into the Forward Line of Enemy Troops (FLET). This would be a shock to everyone but it needed to happen, I explained to him that I cannot get my head around not needing a weapon to walk around the camp, he just laughed and said that times were changing.

I made my way to the CSM and we discussed over a brew the Case vac plan for our patrol. I explained that when the platoon gets to certain checkpoints and RV points on the ground, then I will secure each point. Just in case of contacts with the enemy and if needs be will get my search section to secure crossing points to enable him to get a quad to that area. Either to extract a casualty or to resupply us with ammunition, we both examine every possible outcome and go through scenarios until we are both 100% happy with the plan. I can now go back and brief the platoon of the casualty extraction plan in the event of such an incident.

Orders took a long time in coming, a runner came across to speak to the boss, and I and we gathered the troops up for the OC to speak to them. He began like every other O Gp, weather and prelims. The guys don't care, they want to know when they are going, for how long, and when they will get back, oh, and what the rules of engagement are for this OP.

Once he was finished, the CSM stood up and went through his service support paragraph, this was my bread and butter, and I listened intensely to his plan even though I had sat down with him and the other platoon sergeants. There was always a chance that he had changed the plan due to other operations ongoing around our AOR and we had to fit into other units' plans. Or maybe at some stage we would be closer to another unit and they could take over our casualty extraction especially if we are near one of their HLS grids. The CSM had stuck to the plan, it was a go, now it's time for battle prep, the platoon were ready for anything, all I had to do was make sure they were equipped for whatever may come their way.

That night I sat down with Dave Heyhoe and his lifesaving dog TREO. Ronnie introduced me properly to him and we sat there having a brew while discussing the route for tomorrow's operation into the FLET. Dave was concerned about the time of day and the heat that might have an effect on TREO'S work pattern, this was a serious set-back, I did not think the OC had taken this into consideration. Dave should be from now on involved in the process when it comes to searching procedures, after all, his dog was setting the pace and proving the route for the company group. Our platoon will be on the outer extremity keeping an eye out for squirters from the inner cordon and looking out for possible trigger men.

That night I sat with the boss and Ronnie before I decided to go to bed. We chatted about moving into enemy territory and taking the fight to them, the guys were all pumped up and looking for a fight. I just thought back and worried about how it could be, as long as I get every man back to the DC I will be happy.

It's the morning of the op, it had been called OPERATION GHARTZE RANGE. This was the first time that the Royal Irish Regiment had conducted a company operation into enemy territory since Korea. It was exciting to be part of, and to be a platoon sergeant was a real honour when you consider some of the platoon sergeants of the Royal Irish that had gone before me.

I checked all the platoons serialized pieces of kit and made sure we had POW kit and enough countermeasures batteries and signals equipment. I had enough ammunition for a small war. Once the section commanders had carried out their kit checks and the boss had fully briefed us on the route he wanted us to take. We waited for the OC and his tactical party to give radio checks before we could move out into the wadi, it was another twenty minutes that we waited before everyone was on the all informed net, without further ado we left the DC and snaked out into the wadi and into the green zone.

The point section would stop and search every vulnerable point; this would enable the platoon to go in all around defence in case of enemy follow-up, and react with all firepower available.

At this point the Afghan Army took the lead and were to my front, this made us very nervous with our approach, the Afghan in front of my platoon seemed to be stoned on cannabis. Every few metres he would pretend to shake with fear and tiptoe forward pointing his weapon and say, 'Taliban Taliban', and then go, 'No, it is just a dog', and laugh. I could see that the guys hated this idiot, and we were supposed to accept these idiots open armed and fight alongside them, they were not worth the hassle.

The operation seemed to go without incident, we got intelligence updates every step of the way telling us how the Taliban where watching us and wanting to attack. But at the last safe moment couldn't get the attack in due to our patrolling and spacing out, they could have hit us but due to the formations that we used it would have been impossible for them to make a clean escape without taking casualties or being captured.

We did however discover bunkers that had been dug by the Taliban, there were a dozen or so that all faced towards the district centre and they were all evenly spaced. The OC plotted them on his map and passed this up the chain of command, so it turned out to be a productive operation after all.

This type of operation would go in every few weeks, it helped the OC gain vital intelligence and pay dividends on our hearts and minds mission, the locals could see that we meant no harm and would only engage if we were engaged. This began to work for a short period of time, that meant the locals would support us when we were out on the ground, when we returned to base and the Taliban were out, then guess what, they would support the Taliban.

All they wanted was an easy life and if that meant supporting the Taliban, then they would, we were only there for a short time and the Taliban were here for keeps so it made a lot of sense to support them. No matter what we could offer them, schools, shops, clean water and drainage, this meant absolutely nothing when the Taliban just had to say, 'I will kill your family tomorrow if you do not plant that bomb!'

WHAT WOULD YOU DO?

Chapter 14

A DETERMINED ENEMY

We continued to receive updates on enemy forces' activity from either our own intelligence sources or from the US Marines that were now embedded with us in Sangin DC. It seemed that no matter how hard we hit them, they would come back twice as hard, it was a never-ending battle to get the locals on the side of **ISAF**. Then there was the dysentery and vomiting (D and V), which took the company by storm, it seemed to just creep up behind us and attack from every angle.

I myself was be taken off to a remote part of camp with a box of rations and my camp bed to fester away for a few days, only to be meet by Maddy, the coy sniper, and a guy from Humint (SF). We all had the bug and were out of action for a few days, at one stage the guy from Humint stood up and said he was off to the toilet, only to then say, 'F——k it is too late, I have just been.'

It just makes you think what the hell is going on, this place is completely filthy, it is built by mud and dirt, they wash in rivers and do not want our way of life, and it makes you wonder WHY!

Then you think about the soldiers who have sacrificed everything for these people and that's the only thing that keeps you going, well, that and personal pride.

After a walk around the Sangers to see how the troops were getting on, I noticed that the Sangers were not 100% organised, and after speaking to the guys who stand there for twenty-four hours providing security for the rest of camp, they were not happy, we needed to sort out more than a means of alarm, the communications were not the best to the operations room and the panoramic sketches needed to be a lot better than what they currently were. I went back and explained about the sketch to be met by Ronnie who already had this in hand, typical that he seemed to be all over the administration side of the platoon as much as me.

H and Matt were both currently going over section admin, and I was finding a way to get the boss to approach Acky and tell him that H was taking over his section. He was more tactically aware and would command the section a lot better, and to be honest I was getting sick of Acky having to handrail the boss, he was currently ineffective as a commander due to his location out on the ground.

Just as the boss was about to explain to Acky, he came forward and asked to be inter-company posted to the Fire Support Group (FSG) and instead of explaining to him why he was losing his section, we just let him go, phew, job done!

Another O Gp being conducted and yet more rubbish being said, this time it had filtered down from the brigade, maroon turbans were now being given out to the locals, what the hell were they trying to do at brigade, funny how they were the same colour as the parachute regiment!

Even the paratroopers were disgusted at this, it was making a mockery of us all and now to top it all off, as we soldiers in the field were out fighting and trying to make a change to this goddamn country. The troops back in Bastion were doing their education for the next rank up, why not just send them bloody home. Or if they had a spare week on their hands, why not fly out to an outpost and help the fighting troops out.

The O Gp went on for the usual hour, the intelligence update was that the OC was getting frustrated that the Taliban were getting around the green zone too easily and hitting the camp with RPG and heavy machine gun fire. He was putting together a plan of action to interdict this, I was sure it will be something to tell the grandchildren.

We needed to start putting together wish lists, if the CQMS could get his hands on it, then it would be brought in by helicopter. The CSM kept bringing up his points, and to be honest, I was starting to get annoyed at the things that were highlighting my platoon in a bad way. It was basic stuff, like washing, surely the troops did not need me to stand beside them to get washed, but if that was what it took, I will, basic hygiene was letting certain personnel down, so I needed to grip this.

Just as I was digesting all this, a massive fire fight broke out at the end of the pipe range. We all grabbed our weapons and got into cover. The CSM got the Quick Reaction Force to move into the area and report back what was going on. Not long after that the QRF reports that the Afghan Army and the Afghan National Police had a blue on blue over who had jurisdiction over the area, just another reason why I did not trust them.

There had been a CAT A casualty in the DC, the Incident Response Team (IRT) was on route to this location to collect the casualty, then Joey managed to put everyone's backup on their arrival by rubbing his hands together and saying that he hoped the IRT bring some mail. Just a little bit insensitive, Joey, not the right moment to ask for mail, but I saw his logic!

Well, things just get better, if it was not the Taliban, it's us causing injuries. One of the young rangers was now stable in hospital after contracting an insect bite to his head, what next. Now we heard that the ANP general had arrested the Helmand chief of police, this place would always be lawless, and the Taliban were collecting poppy taxes.

Word had filtered around the AO that last night as the troops began to zero on the range at FOB ROBINSON, they hit a power cable that was running up the range, resulting in Kandahar going without electricity nearly 1.5 million people had no power.

It is now 8 May and things were moving along slowly, we now knew the ground around Sangin like the back of our hand, we knew the routes through the green zone very well and the Taliban knew we do. The thing we cannot help was that they can predict which way we patrol now.

News had been filtered down through the ranks that the Taliban in Musa Quala have agreed with commanders from Kajaki to give fighters to help with an offensive strike onto the FOB in Musa Quala for the first twenty-five days of the fighting season. This was not good news if you were based up there.

Garmasir Taliban had reinforced ready for an offensive onto ISAF troops and 4 x IEDS had been found in the bazaar in Sangin. B-Coy had been informed by the local nationals that the Taliban had greater numbers than them, not a great thing to hear when you know they will strike any day now.

And to top everything off, my platoon was being tasked to move into the FLET and occupy a compound for a few days. I was being given a few hundred pounds to use as influence money. Well, I was sure I could use that to good effect, I put together a list of items that I needed including a few claymores and a quad bike to carry most of the load. Due to the fact that the boss was away, I would step up to platoon commander and Ronnie will be the platoon sergeant.

The patrol moved out of the DC and made its way up north into the green zone, we came across a few obstacles that cannot be crossed by the quad bike. I quickly came up with a plan that made some of the guys laugh. I used some of the money to bribe the locals to lift our stores and bike across the river and reload the bike. I also paid for two crates of coke which I would dish out to the troops on arrival at our compound.

After a further 200 metres we arrived at a compound that the guys searched before we entered it. Cupples moved in and established communications back to the ops room. One of the sections conducted a clearance patrol and the other sections built up sentry positions and placed out the claymores. We had now established a short-term patrol base.

The US Marine snipers that were now attached to the platoon began to settle in. Tim decided to fire his Barrett sniper rifle into the compound wall to see if it can penetrate it, and this failed and only went in three quarters to the dismay of my OC and CSM.

We had been in position now for a few hours, I had put together a radio stag and Ronnie was cutting about the troops making sure we had good arcs of fire and that the sentry positions interlocked with each other. Toilets had been dug and we had a well that could be used for water, not a bad choice of compounds actually.

We got coms with zero and put together a patrol matrix, if we sent out two sections at a time, it will leave us vulnerable back here. So I decided to send out only one section, and they did not go out farther than 50 metres and even then one section would remain here dressed as QRF. It was a very dangerous decision to make, but I cannot afford us to be pinned down in this location. I had desert hawk on station to give me a live feed of any movement before we go on patrol. So it was as safe as I could make it, anyway we were only here to interdict their movement and close down one of their resupply routes.

The local kids started to bring us munitions, and I mean live high-explosive war heads and unexploded mortars. I quickly let the ops room know, my engineers attached were qualified to dispose of them. However they did not have the right equipment with them, then a pistol that had a British serial number on it got given to me by a local, I sent it across the net and got told that it belonged to the previous battle group's Marine who was killed in action. It sent a shiver down my spine.

I decided to tell the boss a lie and that we had the equipment to dispose of the ordinance, I got Nafrue to help me dig a pit and place the ammunition into it. I told the ops room that I was about to blow them. They gave me a countdown, two of us got L109 grenades and pulled the pins remembering to take off the safety clips, and we placed the grenades beside the ordinance and ran for cover. BOOOOOOOOOM! The loudest noise I had heard in a while, then I looked up only to be greeted by the ordinance coming down all around us. HOLY SHIT, we get under cover. Nothing detonated, thank God. I told the ops room that it had been destroyed, I then made my way over and personally collected every piece and then I decided to throw it in the Helmand river. JOB DONE!

That was a close call and now everyone thought I was a nut job. Well, no harm done. The Marines seemed to fit in very well, the stories started to come in that they would eventually take over Sangin and five more internet terminals would be up and running by the end of the month, the amount of kit and equipment that they had was unbelievable compared to what we had.

I spoke to Ronnie and we decided that one set of the countermeasure equipment was acceptable while we were in this compound, it would help save battery power for patrols, we doubled the gate and sentry positions just before last light, and I told the guys that they can use light after dark only inside the rooms, as we were hidden from outside.

It was at this time that H had gone down, he was pale and needed an IV drip. The CMT Caylie was now dealing with him, he needed evacuating ASAP. I informed the CSM who was putting together a plan to get him extracted from our location, if we were to come under attack, we would be screwed trying to get him moved. I knew he would still fight back but he would not be at his best for a proper contact, we now waited patiently for timings to meet at an RV point to hand over H.

The locals were now beginning to hang around our compound, it was a pain in the backside, but it had its advantages as the Taliban hopefully would not attack if we had young children with us, well I hoped not anyway.

As I looked up, I could see B1 Bombers dropping bombs to the east of my location, strong Taliban forces were grouping ready for an attack and we had hit them before they get the chance. Morale had slightly lifted on hearing the news, I was starting to get a lot of attitude from one of our officers across the net, and I would have words with him when we return to the FOB.

Our resupply had now been delayed and we were running low on fresh water and rations. I was sure we could make what we have lost, as long as we had water discipline everything would be okay. The CSM came across the chat net and explained that he had been rushed off his feet and wanted to RV at a given time. I said I will be there and secure the route for his arrival.

This short patrol had now turned out to be over seventy-two hours, not bad considering we only expected twenty-four to thirty-six hours. I would need to hand over two of my men during the resupply as they are going on R&R, so I wouldn't see them for another two weeks. Let's hope there is good news coming our way.

The resupply was a success as we got the boss back and H, it was good to have him back, his knowledge was what was needed here and the guys found it easier to relax knowing that we had a commander and sergeant back. Ronnie had done a great job so I informed the boss that he stepped up and done an amazing job, he told me about his leave and what he got up to. Then got down to business explaining the news back home and the new threat messages that the Taliban had been sending to ISAF.

We were not surprised at this; he then wanted to go out on a clearance patrol with one section just before last light, they were out for at least thirty minutes and returned. The boss came across and told me he was happy with where I had located the sentry positions but would like the rear one built up more, not a drama, I told him, after all, he was the boss, so we quickly rectified the problem and settled down for the night.

Today we extracted from our platoon location and made our way back to the district centre; we had notes on pattern of life and the bunker locations along with possible extraction routes from the bunker areas and a pistol belonging to the Marines MUD call sign, so at least we had some good news.

We had patrolled back only a few hundred yards when the Taliban attacked, I was at the back with the quad bike and stores. The noise of bullets whizzing past our heads and hitting the ground in front of the troops was deafening. Rat tat tat tat . . . Dud dud dud dud dud . . . CRACK . . . THUMP. BOOOOOOOOOM! There were now RPGs flying across the platoon, the boss was screaming to get a fire control order onto the enemy. I shouted across the radio that I had the back door secure. This would alleviate anyone worrying about being hit from the rear, I had it secure, I could hear the guys engaging enemy to the front. We had been caught out in the open and now we were in the Taliban's killing area. Only they knew our fate, but when you have thirty rangers with weapons and in the mood for a fight, you are not going to be a match on that day.

Matt had his guys well spread out, and hitting back with an awesome amount of firepower, the under-slung grenade launcher was hitting them where it hurt, the GPMG was direct, and after a few minutes the Taliban withdrew from the area. The boss was not happy and got the sections to exploit them, we followed up keeping one foot firmly on the ground, I moved up alongside the quad with my small band of men as rear protection.

After a short move the guys discovered blood trails from where the enemy had withdrawn from, it was great for morale, but the same old story, we didn't seem to find many bodies after a contact but lots of empty casings and blood trails, well, at least we were hitting them and that's the main thing.

The ops room was kept informed throughout the whole patrol, the CSM had the QRF on standby for a resupply of ammo and the desert hawk had been launched to pick up fleeing enemy. We had our backs covered by so many people, it would seem hard to not win a fight, but there were days that were just unwinnable.

On return to the DC, we went through the usual checks with serial numbered kit and batteries and water refills, weapons cleaned, then an after-action review with the OC and CSM with the FOO, FAC and MFC, the list was endless. So many moving parts in Afghanistan and that's just a patrol. We brain-stormed ideas for the next patrol and the OC was interested in the well that we had found and how we defended the compound. It was obvious that he was working on a plan of action for future operations.

The boss during his debrief explained that he at first was not sure of the direction of enemy fire but quickly moved into cover getting a steer from Matt, he was able to get the platoon into a base line and get accurate fire into the enemy. Ronnie was engaging from his position when an RG came straight across his guys, then they could identify that they had definitely hit one of the fighters and he went to ground. It got rather annoying for a platoon sergeant, in this incident my job was resupply and casualty extraction, I was rather unemployed throughout this whole battle.

It finished on a high and the guys were in good spirits their confidence had raised tenfold and I was rather pleased with their efforts, every man worked for each other. I knew I had something special with this platoon and the OC was pleased that we had a confirmed hit, another statistic for his report.

19 June and a lot to be done in the form of rehearsals and practice, the boss had told us that the OC was about to put together a company operation into the green zone. It would be for some time and that we would not return to the DC for a few weeks, the boss quickly let me know that our platoon would be stagging on in the DC. While the other two platoons carry out the operation, the task was for the company to occupy two compounds in the heart of the green zone. This was to purely disrupt the movements of the Taliban and let the

rest of the company conduct projects and hearts and minds in other areas of Sangin.

The main compound would be called Patrol Base (PB) Armagh, this would be the engine room of our patrolling, the other PB will be called Derry. After a few days conducting the task all that seemed to be drip, feedback was that we had seriously dealt the enemy a blow, they cannot move without us spotting them. Meanwhile back at the DC the troops were getting fatigued with all this stagging on, it would not be so bad if it was just that, but with Joey using the guys when they were on rest to unload the heli, and do basic tasks, it was wearing everyone down.

The information coming out of the ops room was that this would not last, we were now sitting ducks and very vulnerable, the amount of manpower that was needed just to secure it was overwhelming to say the least. Now we were on skeleton manning in the DC, with all the echelon left to become the CSM resupply group, not the way he would want it. But no one dared go up against the OC, even the 2i/c had been getting his ears bashed by everyone asking him to talk some sense into the OC.

The OC had his own opinion on the whole operation he was looking at the bigger picture, and if we achieve his end state on reconstruction of Sangin, it will be worth it.

Three days into the operation, 9 Platoon returned and went onto rest until the morning, this gave us a last-minute chance to get what comfy kit we needed. The next morning after a good comprehensive handover we left the DC and made our way towards PB ARMAGH, it took just over thirty minutes to make our way through the green zone. Every corner and compound was a possible firing position, we took our time to move cautiously towards the new compound, local children began to watch our every move, and it was nerve racking just getting there.

Having done a map recce, there were only three options to get there, one being straight down the 611 and through the tank park, not the best route as you will be watched the whole journey, and it lent itself to be taken on by the Taliban. The second was out through the HLS and handrail the Helmand river all the way through the green zone and into the back of PB ARMAGH, for this trip we decided to split the difference and use the green zone for as much of the journey to keep out of sight until the last safe moment.

On arrival at the new location, we were met by another officer from Ranger Company, he was from southern Ireland and had a lot to say, he took my boss around and gave a detailed brief of the area. I got the guys settled and met up with Stephen, the other platoon sergeant, he gave me a good brief and broke the camp down. I knew where our living area was and the arcs towards the enemy threat, it was actually a good set-up, I cannot help thinking that he had an attitude, I took myself off and spoke to my boss who was reluctant to agree with me.

The troops began by cleaning up our area; we had now established better arcs and got straight into a routine, I moved across to where Dave and Treo had settled in and they had a very chilled area. Just below where the fire support group had set up the guns, this would be a place that I can come over and relax, especially as Dave was a great host and always offered out cups of tea and coffee.

I settled in for the night knowing what radio stags I had, and now needed to get myself orientated with the layout of the new PB. The engineers started to build a shower in the corner and a spare generator was brought to our location to help charge the batteries. After a quick look, I decided to tell the CSM that an area for washing needs to be away from the living quarters and the toilets needed to be put into place ASAP, this was already in hand by Stephen who was all over the camp routine.

I then started to move around the PB which crossed over a stream into another compound, this needed to be cleared of all rubbish in order to have a clean casualty extraction route. The platoon was very quick to help this process along and began by clearing the place. Big Skillen was by far the hardest worker and started by pulling trees out by the roots, to my amazement, he had his area cleared in minutes and helped the others out.

Devine started to produce a hole in the wall so he could use it to scan his arcs with his .338 sniper rifle, he seemed to have everything in order on the rooftop sentry position. So I left him alone to get on with it. I just walked around the location to check that the extraction route was free from debris and at last it was, on my return to the ops room I noticed that Stephen had left now and was on R&R. Which meant

Robbie was now the platoon sergeant, he was a very good operator and a veteran from HERRICK 4, we had worked closely together before and I know he was a great choice to step up.

Only one slight drama, his boss will take full advantage of this and get Robbie to do whatever he wanted. I took a walk across to where his platoon were conducting admin only to find the boss wearing civilian shorts and a baseball cap. Already he was pushing the boundaries, if that was how he looked, the guys will copy him that's for sure. He smiled at me and said, 'Alright, Speedy', with that false grin that he had. He showed me that his guys were clearing trees and bushes from arcs with the use of phosphorous grenades. I nearly went mental at him, 'What the hell are you doing, boss, you are wasting ammunition and making a complete dick out of yourself.' He told me to watch my mouth and go back to my own platoon.

After trying my hardest not to punch him as hard as I could, I reported him to my platoon commander, who went straight over, he returned telling me that that man needed help and had become a liability. He was now stepping outside what Sandhurst would call the ten dimensions of leadership and function ability, I would report this straight to the CSM when I saw him next.

That night seemed to pass without incident, a lot of movement around our location and dicking of our sentry positions, but no attack yet, it was the calm before the storm. The next day just came and went with an intelligence update from the 2i/c telling us that the Taliban were going to attack our camp and cut us off from the DC, we already knew it was just a matter of time and placed the LASM and 66 mm close to hand.

That night Devine came down from the FSG position and asked me to have a look at something in the distance, he was a top-quality Mortar Fire Controller (MFC) and was just really asking for some advice. He already knew the answer, but it was always nice to get a second opinion, he wanted to know what I thought about two lights in the distance that seemed to be signalling to each other. I had a quick look and said, 'They are about 4-5 km away, mate, and I agree they are signalling to each other, what I suggest is that you log it and keep your eyes on them. There is nothing we can do, but good call, Dev, keep up the good work.' He smiled and said, 'Just as I thought, mate.'

As I was walking away, the boss of 8 Platoon came up and wanted to know what was happening. I said. 'Not much, sir, it is all in hand', but he insisted that we tell him. After hearing what we said, he was adamant that it was a Taliban hideout or even a weapons cache, and he wanted to call in fire onto the locations. I explained that he was not going to do that as people live there, at this stage Dev was shaking his head in disbelief and telling me that the boss was crazy. I began to swear at him and said he was not going to do it over my dead body.

I went to my boss and explained what the hell was going on; he shook his head and told me he would have a word, same old story as my boss returned to say that he was reporting him to the OC.

His platoon was a great platoon, but by now it was starting to cause a rift within the company; the platoon sergeant was in the UK and unaware of what was going on, and I knew he would go completely ballistic if he knew what his boss was doing.

After a few more minor errors by the platoon commander, the OC, CSM, and 2i/c had lengthy discussions with myself and my boss and Stephen, and decided to remove the officer from command. As soon as Stephen returned from his R&R, he was given the role of platoon commander of 8 Platoon, a role that he relished and did to a standard not matched by anyone.

We continued to conduct patrols from PB Armagh for up to two months and to be honest it had lost its surprise as the Taliban had now worked out how to get around us. We were in fact now fixed by the enemy, the Taliban had now placed IEDs around our location and effectively had now channelled us into where they wanted us to go. It was just a matter of time when we chose their route of choice.

And it was not long before that time came, during a routine resupply to the PB, the CSM had moved up the 611 and into the Tank Park. The troops had secured it by using their equipment and placing out troops into areas giving a 360-degree secure area for a resupply to be conducted. The WIMIK had moved across the ground being walked out by two guys 10 metres in front and two guys 10 metres behind. This was routine so as to not have too many troops on the vehicle at any one time. I was sorting out the kit back in the PB and the quad bike was being unloaded.

As I stopped for a cold drink, I heard a massive explosion from the area of I knew the troops were extracting back out of. I got my body armour helmet and rifle and screamed for a work party to follow me. I could hear shouting from the guys, 'Speedy, don't go without ECM.' It was too late, I knew the consequences if I walked on an IED, and to be honest at this time I was just thinking about the other troops.

When I arrived there, I could see two of the guys against the compound wall, one was bleeding heavily from the face, his eyesight was gone, and a team medic was dealing with him. I pointed out other casualties to my medics and off they went to help out, I do not think they needed me to point them out as my team medics were doing a great job. The vehicle was blown in half and the gunner was missing, he had been blown 30 feet into the air, and after a search for his body, he was found alive in an orchard, having bounced off a few trees had a broken back (very lucky).

The guys in front of the vehicle had superficial wounds, I ran back to the PB and jumped onto the quad bike. I thought I could use it to help extract the injured troops back into the PB. Well, it sounded better than I actually did, having carried out two runs and collecting all the equipment in, on my last trip I had a soldier who had been bitten by a scorpion so I got him to sit on the quad bike. Just as I was about to drive back, my rear wheel got stuck so I revved the throttle too much and the bike and the both of us flew into the river.

Breaking all the rules of first aid by becoming a casualty myself, the quad was on top of me and I was injured in the process, the weight of the quad underneath all that water was starting to hurt. I looked up and big Sam grabbed the quad and lifted it off me, I could see McDowell was in some sort of pain. I managed to get myself out of the stream and sat beside a tree. At this time the ops room was going mental with seven casualties to deal with, I was there for an extra ten minutes as the troops prioritised the casualties. I was then taken back to the DC and was now on a stretcher waiting for the IRT to arrive. I felt like I have let my troops down. Then I explained to the medic that my legs were sore, he cut off my combat trousers and stuck a morphine injector pen into my right thigh. After only twenty minutes, I was nearly asleep, all I could remember seeing was Davy Stewart standing over me asking if I was okay, then I drifted off asleep.

I drifted in and out of consciousness and woke up on the Chinook helicopter, I could see doctors and medics working franticly to make sure everyone was treated in priority and got us all into Bastion in good health. The wheels touched down and I could see four ambulances and crash-out teams waiting to get us into the operating rooms. Just as my stretcher was lifted, I could see a sea of people standing in a line taking pictures of this mass-casualty incident. This was a one-off and I knew that the garrison sergeant major would be mental when he found out, from this day forward cameras were now banned from the HLS.

I woke up the next day and I was in a ward, across from me was a Taliban fighter with a curtain around his bed space. It felt weird that we were both in the same ward. But I guess it had to happen, we were after all complying with the Geneva Convention even if we thought that it sucks a lot of the time!

A nurse came across and said how was I doing. I had wires and plugs all over me and I told her I was okay. She told me that I needed to rest and asked if it was okay to take a picture and fax it to my parents. I supposed she could, and then I spoke to my mother on the phone, she seemed relieved that I was okay. I was then greeted by a sergeant from 2 Para, it was only Lee Clegg. He came across as a nice guy and wanted clothing sizes from me, so he could get all my guys fresh combats, within the hour he returned with all new kit for us, fantastic guy, then I got a visit from my unit, they were just pleased that everyone was going to be okay.

After twenty-seven hours in Bastion hospital, I wanted to return to Sangin, I asked to leave and got given the thumbs-up with a caveat. I was told to rest and stay off my right leg, I agreed just to get out of there. I returned to Nigel the CQMS and waited for my flight back to Sangin. On arrival in Sangin DC, I could see the guys were chuffed to see me, the CSM had a word with me regarding why I was driving the quad bike without a licence. I explained that at the time I drove it, the situation dictated that I needed to extract the troops, so I made the decision to do it, he seemed to agree.

As I got up to walk away, he asked if I was all right, I turned and told him that the only thing that I hurt was my pride! He smiled and said, well, he was glad that I was okay and walked away. The OC had now gone on R&R, and now the 2i/c got his hands on the company, the first thing he did was collapse the PB and bring the troops back to the DC. Everyone praised him for having some balls to make that decision while the OC was away, it also gathered him more respect than he already had, and however not before things had gathered speed. As on my last trip out to the PB, I was manning the radio with the new platoon commander, he was taking over our platoon as Paddy Bury has picked up a promotion and returning to the UK. I told the boss that the CSM will be requesting a list from me for the resupply tomorrow at 1700 hours, I had everything written down and all he had to do was read it off the list.

It's now 1710 hours and we haven't heard from the CSM, I told the boss to get in touch with Zero and confirm that he still wanted our return. The officer that had lost command of his platoon had now been banished to the ops room. This was where he worked now, he came across the radio with one hell of an attitude. He told my boss, 'Hades 4 1 Alpha, when we are ready for you, we will be in touch, NOW STAY OFF THE NET!' To be honest this made me fume with anger, my new boss now felt like a prat having been belittled across the company net.

I got straight onto the net and asked for him, he ignored me, I asked again and he still ignored me. I got in communication with the FSG tower and they told me that my radio was fine and they knew I was trying to speak to that officer, I sent a message across the net that I will have a face-to-face with him when I return.

The next day came and I had been going over in my head what I was going to do on my return to the DC, I needed to back up my new boss and set some ground rules with this officer, we packed up our kit and fanned out, and began the patrol back to camp, I cannot get this officer out of my head.

We got into the DC and unloaded the troops, they all knew what jobs need to happen, the boss decided to go straight to the ops room. I told him to drop his kit off first and we will both go there. He looked at me and knew that I was about to snap, we made our way to the ops room only to find the CSM waiting on the wall, he just smiled at me.

As I approached the steps of the ops room, I saw the officer in question come up grinning at me, I launched myself down the steps and punched him square on the chin, and swore at him, 'Who the f——k do you think you are, how dare you speak to my boss like that, you pompous prick, do not ever try and degrade anyone, you waste of space.' It looked like he was about to strike, I got in first, he tried to fight back but hit like a girl. The OC came out wanting to know what all this was about, then the CSM split us up, he screamed at me and ordered me to follow him for a chat. Once we were away from everyone, he shook my hand and told me that that prick had it coming, but do not ever hit an officer again.

I had a brew with him and he agreed that the officer was a dangerous man and should never command men in battle. He thought this was all a game, his decision making and tactical acumen were that expected of a non-military man or that of a rogue.

Chapter 15

SAPWAN QUALA

The OC had returned from his R&R and was happy with the decision to extract from PB ARMAGH, he had other things on his mind. The brigade were about to mount an operation deep into enemy territory and he had insisted that 7 Platoon were going to conduct the operation. My boss was over the moon, we were going to fly into their own backyard and fight them on their own ground. It was a little bit daunting but great for the troop's morale.

The town of Sar Puzeh got mentioned at the orders group, it meant nothing to us right now but it will be etched on everyone's lips for a long time after this operation. The intelligence that was being filtered down to the troops suggested that there were over 250 Taliban fighters with an array of weapons from Dushka and ZPU .50 anti-aircraft guns to AK-47/AK-74, and 107 mm rockets and RPG through to SPG-9s. Not to mention areas that conceal possible IEDs where we could be channelled into, it will be a hell of a battle.

The brigade commander had stated that this area was Taliban occupied and deemed as a stronghold, we were to gain control of it. It would be a vital blow to the Taliban and gave us more control over the area which was classed as vital ground, it could also help shape the whole operation.

The wheels were now firmly set in motion to launch a large-scale air assault operation into the heart of the Taliban, the boss started to plan what he would like the platoon to rehearse. We were ready for whatever he wanted us to practice, the section commanders and the troops were buzzing, they cannot wait to get the job done. Everyone including me wanted the chance to conduct a live platoon attack into enemy territory, it was what we have waited for.

As the platoon sergeant, I started my preparation by checking weapons and night-vision optics. I wanted to be 100% accurate when the boss asks for a sit-rep on kit and equipment, the batteries needed to be fully charged and the ECM completely faultless, there was a lot to get done.

The boss let me know that it will consist of four platoons, 7 and 9 will move through the green zone, while our platoon will handrail the high ground with the FSG. This will enable us to identify the Taliban and put down heavy rates of fire into their position while remaining flexible for whatever task comes our way.

The boss went away to the O Gp, and after a few hours he returned to the platoon, he looked excited yet slightly worried. I left him alone to digest whatever news he had received. He eventually called me over for a chat about the operation. 'Speedy, this will make or break the platoon, it will not be easy, and to top it all off, we are about to drop into a hornet's nest with hornets everywhere.' I just stared at the boss with my mouth open, so we were to stay on the high ground, with the paratroopers below us, this could be a major problem, we will just have to wait and see. I can tell that everyone was now watching our platoon, depending on how well we perform will shape how the company gets used in the future. It will also show the wider army how good the regiment is under enemy fire.

That night as we prepared for the air assault, everyone was going through their job in their head. I was making sure we had enough ammunition for the job in hand. I decided to carry a Bergan in order to pack it with spare ammunition and bombs for the 60 mm mortar, I had a stretcher and spare batteries, just hope I had enough kit for the troops, I decided to head across with my kit and I noticed that the boss was awake already. He had not slept due to rehearsing every last thing in his head, he had a lot of pressure on his shoulders, but was trying not to show it.

We were now all standing on the HLS in Sangin waiting for the Chinook to arrive, the OC and CSM standing off to a flank talking.

They were gleaming with pride, both wishing it was them going in to do the assault. They were excited for us, the noise of the Chinook approaching made everyone stop talking, it landed and a gust of sand and dirt went across everyone. We bent over and struggled to our feet with the amount of weight that we carried. I broke into a gentle jog and boarded the aircraft, and we sat down in reverse order, so when we landed, we could run straight out into what fate awaited us.

The Chinook wasted no time to move off the HLS and into the night sky, it was early hours in the morning and we were hoping to surprise the enemy with a dawn attack. I started to get déjà vu, this felt like a repeat show. I looked around the Chinook in my night-vision goggles, everyone was in the zone, and no one dared to talk. We went through the plan in our heads and prepared for whatever was waiting for us, the news came down that it was a HOT LZ. Shit, I thought, the HLS was awashed with red and green tracer flying all over the place, this Chinook landing cannot come any sooner.

The door gunner told us it was going to be HOT, the boss shook his head, he was ready for it, but could do without it; this will be called as he saw it, everything now rested on the Quick Battle Orders that he will give in contact.

The Chinook lands and the door gunner was now engaging enemy fighters in the distance, we all run off behind the quad bike and the worst news possible happened, the Bowman radios across the ISAF troops had all dropped their fill. No one had communications to the CO, even worse we cannot speak to one another across the battlefield. It seemed that the ECM red once switched on ruined the signal on the radios, so we now had to fight this with just Personal Role Radios (PRR).

Already we were spread out across the open ground, the Chinooks had gotten off, sideways weaving in and out and keeping only 30 feet above the ground as they left us in what can only be described as hell on earth.

The boss made his way forward to a group of men, I sat there not knowing what the hell was happening, and at least we had 360 arcs of protection. He returned to tell us about the disaster with the communications, before pointing in the direction that he wanted us to travel in, and we then move off towards the high ground. Automatic fire and battles were taking place to our rear right, we began the climb onto a feature. I had the FSG with me at the back, and the boss had the FSG CSM with him at the front.

We had only moved 100 metres before we were forced to go firm in the dirt, bullets were whizzing past our heads and to the front of the platoon. The boss was now within the enemy's arcs and they responded in kind as I can hear bullets hitting around where he was.

He had now sent one of our sections to protect the commanding officer's tactical group, this just got better and better, our firepower within the platoon had dropped, however we did have the FSG, so it balanced itself out.

The boss was now relaying everything back to me at the back, it seemed like only five minutes into the battle when I heard the APACHE opening up into enemy positions. A-107 mm rocket flew over my head, it was very close to the boss, and then I heard the boss screaming, 'MAN DOWN, MAN DOWN, SPEEDY, GET THE MEDIC UP HERE!' My CMT tried to run forward to assist but I grabbed her, she was keen to get the casualty treated. I refused to let her move forward, we were taking too much enemy fire and I cannot afford her to become a casualty. I needed the troops to suppress and win the fire fight before we can move forward, the boss was shouting for heavy fire. The section commanders were pinned down at this moment, a few seconds later I heard FCOs being screamed and a heavy rate of fire going down.

We were winning the fire fight; I moved forward with Caylie, she began to conduct basic life support onto the casualty, we moved him slightly into a bit more cover, some of the FSG group sat there with their hearts in their mouths, and I thought they already knew the outcome.

After a few minutes, Caylie looked at me and shook her head, without hesitation I began to distribute his ammunition and serialized equipment, I took his Garmin GPS and left my broken one in his backpack. The boss's radio was broken, so I took his Bowman and gave it to the boss, he needed it, I cannot leave his backpack there, so I decided to strap it onto my already-heavy equipment, at times like this, you seem to get extra strength from somewhere.

I got Joe and a few others to help me extract the casualty back into cover, I let the boss know that he was KIA, he looked pissed off, and I used my new radio to find out where the RSM was located. The enemy fire was still coming in and now I and my band of men were carrying a soldier killed in action all over the battlefield to the doctor. My back was about to break with the extra kit and now my platoon had no platoon sergeant until I returned from handing over the FSG CSM.

I got back to find the platoon had moved forward slightly, the boss was now furious that we kept taking enemy fire from our right flank, and we cannot engage back due to the paratroopers in the low ground. It felt like we were being used by the CO to draw in enemy fire so they can identify the enemy and then kill them. We asked can we come off the high ground and were refused point blank by the CO, he wanted us to stay there.

This was a nightmare! Matt had taken his section forward and was now controlling the fire fight, we had a slight reprise for a few minutes, the incoming enemy fire towards our location was relentless, this was something out of a war movie, and I had never felt so helpless, not being able to return fire.

I met up with Tony, he was mentoring the Afghan Army and had his team of merry men from the Royal Irish with him, and they were spread thinly across groups on Afghan soldiers, Tony was trying to keep a cool head while everyone around him was going mental. He tried to beckon me to go to his location, but there were bullets and RPGs flying towards us, we stood and argued over who was going to go to who, we ended up laughing, this was bloody crazy.

I managed to crawl into a broken compound wall where I found a dozen or so soldiers sitting in cover. I dropped my Bergan down and joined them for a drink. The bullets were hitting the wall near my Bergan, I can see the guys were laughing at the fact that my US Marines Bergan could be destroyed. I looked at my Bergan and looked at them, Caylie shouted it was not worth it. I got up and ran towards my Bergan and bent over to pick it up. Just then a bullet hit the wall in front of me, I rolled down into cover and now I had my Bergan, everyone just stared at me and thought I was f——king mental. I knew, but I had my Bergan intact.

We continued to move across the hillside for a few more hours, every step was vital, an RPG flew straight towards Bubbles, he was stunned for a few minutes but continued to dodge bullets across the open ground. This was becoming surreal, an APACHE directly above us fired the 40 mm rounds and the empty casings were landing on top of us, it seemed like the whole world was exploding around us. The boss was keeping the troops motivated at the front, we dared not take our eyes off the ball for a moment.

We continued to move forward in short bounds, Matt had now been tasked to secure a possible HLS for the T4 to be extracted from the ground, his section was taking heavy fire from all directions, he managed to control and secure the area with his section, after all he was a very experienced veteran from the Iraq war.

This seemed that it will never end, we continued to skirt around the high ground, it had been nearly fifteen hours now and we had not been able to return fire onto the enemy in the green zone. The frustration was etched across everyone's face, then after a further hour and ten minutes the firing faded away. We had had a great effect on the Taliban, due to our platoon being used as target practice, we had helped the paratroopers to pick off the Taliban like sitting ducks, well, I was glad someone was happy!

From my perspective this had been an eye opener for me, it probably did not mean to look like it did, but for me I felt used and abused, I will not let the platoon know what just happened, but I was sure they already knew, we had been used as cannon fodder, just something to attract the enemy's fire while the paratroopers dealt with the Taliban. I feel the commanding officer was a disgrace and to think he was ex–Royal Irish, well, he let us one section down in order to protect him, and then left us for dead on the side of a feature.

The commanding officer decided to call an end to the operation once there were no enemy left to engage; he moved the whole entire fighting force onto the 611 and patrolled us to a pre-designated HLS, I can see the frustration etched on everyone's face, what the hell was the point in this, what did we achieve?

We sat in chalks waiting for our lift to arrive, not many of the guys were talking, we were still stunned at being fired upon for seventeen hours and not being able to fire back, it had been the biggest disappointment I had ever been involved in, and for one unlucky paratrooper, well he didn't even get to look through his sight, God rest his soul.

Within a short time, we boarded the Chinook and headed back to the DC, it was late at night and the guys were exhausted through battle and drained from concentration, it had been an experience they will never forget. Young Armstrong had proven to be worthy of a medal, he was giving target indications and putting down fire like a veteran from Vietnam, I was impressed with his knowledge.

As the Chinook came into the HLS, we were welcomed by the OC, CSM, and Joey. They shook our hands and praised the platoon for a job well done. Joey gave every man a cold can of Coke and we sat and discussed how mental the whole thing was, the CSM told me it sounded like a nightmare. 'Speedy, I am really proud of how you all handled it, the guys need a pat on the back.' And I said thanks and made my way back to my accommodation for a well-earned rest.

The OC was already there praising the platoon for what they had just been through, he knew we were hung out to dry by the CO, and the fact that we conducted ourselves with the pride of the Irish Rangers, showing guts and determination expected of a ranger from the Royal Irish Regiment.

This will never be forgotten, and the fact that no matter what anyone says, this was a complete cluster of a battle. With no communications, no end state, and a commanding officer who sat in a doorway of a shop drinking tea from a china cup as he was protected by a Royal Irish section of eight men as the rest of their platoon were being used as target practice.

Chapter 16

DAY OF DAYS

The air assault operation was the talk of Sangin DC for a few days, the other platoons wanted their bit of action, and the OC was determined to share out these rare opportunities so that everyone got a taste of the action. He was bringing a lot of changes to the Sangin bazaar and the locals were beginning to come on side with ISAF, but we all knew that this wouldn't last long. As we had now collapsed back from PB Armagh, the Taliban had used the time to good effect by planting dozens and dozens of IEDs, we were now actually fixed.

The Taliban had us exactly where they wanted us, no one would admit how vulnerable we had become, our patrolling formations had to be tweaked to perfection. Dave and Treo had now got twice as much pressure on their shoulders, we took them for granted a lot. Treo was now the company's answer to every IED, and the poor dog was working around the clock.

I think we expected far more from Treo than anyone else had ever, Dave had bags below his eyes and looked completely shattered. He and Treo would never let anyone down. It was as if they were robots, I would make a point of popping across and chatting to him, hopefully gaining not just a work asset but a great friend into the bargain.

He would go through every detail of the forthcoming patrol in fine detail until he was happy with the route and that Treo had rest and time to have some water. Treo was now part of the team, everyone loved him, and if he was a soldier at 6 ft tall, I am sure he would have been a highly decorated war veteran for his bravery.

Having now been fixed with the IEDs, the OC was determined to push us all out and try to gain ground from the enemy, we were nearly at the end of our tour and it looked like we had lost ground. This was not going down well with the troops, we knew the enemy were crafty but now they had stooped to a new low.

The OC began to send the platoons out at last light, this did not go down well with any of the soldiers in Ranger Company, we knew that we needed light to search the route we were patrolling, especially with the possibility of IEDs dug in, and the Taliban knew this too.

I made the command decision after the OC had given orders to carry out his plan, but in a way that made sense to my soldiers and our new platoon commander. We would patrol out as the OC had requested and occupy a compound close to the DC and lie up there until first light and then continue with the task given. This would mean that my platoon was in fact safe and that the troops trusted you even more than they already did. The sad thing about this whole tactic was that it was not just me that carried out these actions; it was across the company group. The idea of going on a long patrol at night in Sangin during the IED crisis would have frustrated any soldier, for god's sake, we are talking about lives unnecessarily being put at risk, why not put up the desert hawk or unmanned aviation if you want to know what's there.

This was the task given for a few patrols, each platoon carried out the same drills, and IEDs were being found every hundred or so metres by either the Valon men or by Treo. The company found all in all during our six-month tour over 110 IEDs, the majority of them found by Treo, saving countless lives and helping to reconstruct Sangin town.

The morning had come for 7 Platoon to be relieved from guard by 8 Platoon, the guys needed a long rest, and I and the boss went to the ops room for a brief from the 2i/c on the forthcoming patrol's matrix. He was a trusted guy who oozed combat experience from HERRICK 4, where he had been surrounded for a long period of his tour and spent the entire time in contact. Now a seasoned veteran, he was in charge of us.

He wanted our platoon to leave the DC at last light and make our way towards monkey, we would leave through the pipe range and skirt around the school, it sounded easy, apart from moving at night. We marked the route on our maps and moved away to have a chat about the outcome, this was now my new boss, Paddy had now returned to the UK, Sangin had gone crazy with every corner and vulnerable point and area having either an RPG pointed at it or a bomb awaiting us.

I was feeling uncomfortable every time we left he DC now, I just didn't show it, that night before we left the DC the phone rang in the ops room, it was my old boss, he asked how everyone was keeping. I told him fine but the place was awash with IEDs, he was shocked but also knew that PB Armagh had overstayed its welcome and we should have withdrawn a week earlier, I agreed and he told me to pass on his best wishes to the troops.

Time came far too soon as it seemed like we had only had a few hours off before we were all assembled near the pipe range. We accounted for every man before the section commanders loaded their sections. The boss had already briefed the platoon on our task, Dave and his trusted dog Treo were ready as per usual, and he knew that it was just a matter of time before he found yet another IED to add to list of finds.

We left the DC in sections, I sat at the gate and counted every last man out, paying attention to what they were wearing. I grabbed guys who did not have their sleeves rolled down, I shouted at others who did not have their infrared mocking birds on. Basically checking how they were dressed and making sure they were wearing suitable clothing for the job in hand, they all hated me at that precise minute in time, but on return they always praised me for being such pain in the ass, it's my job, I told them.

With Joe and Jordan, my 60 mm mortar men, and Caylie, my combat medic technician, I had my platoon sergeant group sorted. We all left together and not only more behind the platoon as their medic and firepower, we also acted as rear protection, we had patrolled only a few hundred yards before the guys at the front stopped and went firm. They had a reading with the expert nose of Treo, and along with tell-tale ground sign, Dave seemed very unhappy about what could be there, he was almost certain it was an IED, we reported it to the ops room and got told to mark it and box around it, we must continue with our task.

We continued on with the patrol and found a second IED, the guys were not happy, again we marked it and boxed around it, we came to a compound and we secured it by sending in Ronnie and his search team. Davy looked pretty pissed off with the whole situation, he knew he was dicing with death at the front along with the rest of his team, there was nothing I can do about it, and orders are orders.

We put sentries on and spent the night getting some valuable rest, I decided to cook some hot food and check up on the guys. The new boss, Mr Ward, had begun to find his feet and very fast. I took a picture of him sleeping to be used as ransom in the near future, he just laughed, I began to take the piss out of Chips, we called him that because he ate junk food and it also annoyed him.

He was enjoying this time and relaxing with the rest of the guys, Cupples had still not put any food on, he walked from radio to radio checking to make sure not only we have enough batteries left but also making sure the ECM had been switched off and that we were only using one set while we were static.

The next morning the sentries had woken everyone and the guys did not make breakfast as we were about to return to the DC, we all packed away our kit and got ready to leave this compound. The boss surprised me by packing up first and was waiting for the rest of us.

He gave the section commanders a quick set of QBOs and we left the compound, again I sat near the exit counting everyone out, checking dress and equipment. I sent a radio message to the DC, our interpreter was full of energy, I had asked him to carry a video camera to film the patrol and the route we took back to the DC, this I will use to help brief the Marines on how we conducted patrols.

I had changed the patrol matrix about, for some reason I had decided to put Conroy who was a CMT 3 with the boss at the front, that way if we take casualties, then it gives me a better option and we can react a lot sooner than having to run from the back. It was something I have learnt from Sapwan Qala.

T and Davy were at the front with Dave and Treo, they were searching every last grain of dirt, a lot rested on them doing their job to the highest of qualities. The platoon snaked out and followed in the footsteps of all three men and one dog. I saw the platoon began to disappear right down an entry, the walls were over 15 ft in height and were now channelling us into alleyways, there was nowhere else to go, it was right on the edge of the green zone.

The new boss was happy to be going back into the district centre, only a few hundred metres from the pipe range, then out of nowhere I first saw a mushroom black cloud to my front, then I heard the most deafening explosive to date. I looked with pure panic etched across my face, I knew it was right in the middle of the platoon, I started to run forward shouting at Caylie. She already knew what had happened, I could hear the boss sending a message to the ops room screaming, 'HADES 4 1 ALPHA, CONTACT IED, WAIT OUT!'

I could hear screaming from the platoon, we got to the guys and I could see the interpreter lying a few feet away from the rest of the platoon, the high cornfield around him had been cut away by the large explosion. I could see his face was badly marked, his nose had been blown completely from it, his fingers had all been blown off, his hand leaving just his index finger and thumb, and he was covered in blood and screaming for help.

I know this sounds terrible, but I left him and prioritised who needed help first, and it wasn't him, it was my radio operator Justin Cupples. Conroy was already working on him. Caylie got down and assisted in treating him, it was a token gesture, she was a great medic but not a miracle worker. Justin had stood on what the IED report claimed to be three 105 mm tank shells that had all been placed together, to cause one massive explosion.

It had been intended for the boss, with the fact that Justin had a large antenna and so did the boss, they initiated it at the wrong person, and he just happened to take the blast, I will never forget looking at him and seeing so many people trying to save his life. Tourniquet applied to his left leg and his left arm, both been blown off from the blast, the cornfield half been torn from the ground and claret everywhere.

We managed to get Justin and Rock onto stretchers. The CSM, always true to his word, had grabbed anyone that was available and ran to our position to assist in the extraction of the casualties, one of them now being a T4. Which meant injuries so severe he was not going to survive, in fact he had died right there as the impact had taken place, and the only thing that was a saving grace was that he would not have felt a thing.

Dave and Treo had been at the front of the patrol trying to detect signs of an IED, Treo had found everything up to date, the poor dog had worked wonders, however we must remember Treo was not a robot. If the Taliban decide to dig in an IED deep in the ground, then not only will he find it hard to detect, but the equipment we use cannot detect it either, in fact a whole section of men had walked across it before it went off!

The CSM was fuming, I think having given him the chance, he would have killed someone at that moment when he spoke with me, we were both ready to kill. As both parties were extracted, I could not push the troops out to exploit the area due to possible secondary IEDs, I had to keep everyone where they were, which meant they all had seen what was going on.

I do not know why I decided to do this, but as out of pure respect, I asked some of the guys to check around where Cupples had been lying in order to maybe find his wedding ring, I was not thinking about his wife and what we were going to do when we see her.

I did not have to ask the guys to clear up, they started to cover up all the blood with sand and dirt, we did not want to leave any sign that we had been dealt a massive blow, this will take a long time for the guys to get over. I had been conducting myself to what everyone expects from a platoon sergeant, there was no time for crying, you remain strong, not only for your men, but because that is what is expected from you, you cannot ever let your men see you are weak.

The CSM and OC spoke to me when we have returned from the patrol, they knew I was at breaking point and encouraged me to continue being the strong person that I am. I now get asked to keep an eye on the new boss, he was nearly killed and he knew it, I knew they were telling him the same story and to keep an eye on me, it was what you do.

This was where the CSM started to add bullshit into the company, the guys were all now complaining about tasks being given out and shit jobs from the CSM, this was where only the veterans understood why. The CSM was keeping everyone busy with tasks, it was because if they were busy and bitching at him, it stopped them from thinking about Ranger Justin Cupples. No one had time to reflect and the job continued to be done without fear, I respected the CSM for his pure drive and how this whole situation was conducted, I do not think anyone else could have done it better.

The OC waited a few days and then visited our platoon to find out how the guys were coping after such a blow within the ranks, he told the platoon that when Ranger Cupples in being repatriated from Bastion onto the flight home, he will be sending eight men from our platoon to help carry the coffin. There was an instant smile across the guys' faces, I needed to sit down with the boss now and discuss who we can let go, we must remain focussed and have firepower to remain operational, yet I need to be flexible and understand.

After a shuffle of troops and dropping to only two sections, we managed to get guys away for what was a very important day in Ranger Company, the last chance that the guys have to say goodbye to a brave soldier and very good friend.

Chapter 17

PB PYLAE

It had taken the platoon a few days to recuperate before we had digested our new Orbat and re-cock for the next task, the platoon were on a high at the minute having been able to send Justin Back with a sense of pride, I could see that the platoon had not fully recovered from the death of a colleague.

The OC knew this and with his next task will help in rebuilding the morale within 7 Platoon, he gave us a task to move south of the DC and occupy a compound, it will interdict the Taliban movement towards the DC. It will also be overlooked by our FSG Tower on top of the platoon house, this sounded like any other plan we had received in the past.

There was a method behind his plan, one which he will not tell us until we return. I had my reservations but cannot let the guys know what I think, and we moved out the following day. I had managed to get two disposable saws from the engineers, these will be used to cut branches from trees that obscure the line of sight to the FSG Tower. The compound was in need of defending, it was wide open to attack, with my OCD, I began to clean around the area that will be the new ops room.

We have established communications with Zero and now it was sentries into position, a section went on a clearance patrol just around the immediate area as not to be vulnerable to attack. I got the troops to start building Sangers out of the fifty sandbags that we had brought, after over an hour of constant digging, all sandbags were filled and up on the roof. We had a 1 foot barrier now around the compound and we have all arcs interlocking, the platoon's 66 mm rocket launchers were now on the roof spread out facing south.

The enemy knew we were here and I knew they will be coming for us as for when, well whenever they want, if they hit us before we get settled, it will destroy whatever morale is left. If we get this place sorted and quick, we could deal them an almighty blow, the platoon will need to hit back in kind.

Once we started to get into a routine, I decided to walk around the compound to find two of the guys cutting down branches with the saws, they were throwing the branches into the river and all the branches were building up on green 12, which was a crossing point for locals, to be honest there was nowhere else to put them.

They informed me that they now have eyes on the FSG Tower, and through the radio we got word that they now had us marked on their map as a place of interest. Out of nowhere we were engaged by the Taliban, the guys scrambled for their rifles and tried to engage back, but the Taliban had already disappeared into the green zone.

With all this going on and defending of a new compound, the OC told my new boss that he wanted this compound named after Ranger Justin Cupples, it was to be called PB PYLAE, PYLAE meaning in Pastuni the word Cupples. It put a smile onto everyone's face, with the new PB now up and running and toilet area in place, I started to design a sign that said PB CUPPLES. The guys were now bonding and talking about Justin, I can see that some of them were finding it hard to come to terms with his death.

We had been there just over a day, when the OC decided to call in and see how we were all coping, it was just by chance he was there when we got attacked from the other side of the river. We took a heavy rate of fire towards the Sanger, big Joe was on sentry, the OC looked at me and the boss as if to say was this really happening.

We both looked up at Joe when a massive explosion took place in his position, the roof was completely destroyed and his position was in pieces. I cannot see Joe, I shouted up at him, but nothing, his position had taken a direct hit by an RPG. The rest of the guys grabbed whatever they had at hand and began to get on the roof and engage the enemy, then I heard Joe laughing his head off, he was firing everything he had got into the enemy.

I was amazed that he was still alive, it just goes to prove that if you build up your position properly, then it will withstand most things that is thrown at it. Joe explained to me that he had killed six Taliban fighters by hitting them directly with a 66 mm rocket, and that he stated when he fired it, it blew the Sanger roof off.

The OC waited for a soak period before he extracted back to the DC, he was happy with what he had seen and now returned to sing our praises, even with what had happened, we still were undefeated, we continued to take sporadic enemy fire throughout the night and into the third day. I got onto the net and requested a resupply of ammunition from the CSM, he agreed to meet me at a pre-designated RV point 100 metres to our rear and near a crossing point.

I got Ronnie and his team to search and secure the route for the arrival of the CSM, after what happened to the Sanger, I requested another hundred sandbags, the guys knew they will need filling once they arrive. The drama we had was when Ronnie had left, we got attacked again, this time we had less firepower to return so anti-tank rockets get fired into the enemy and we killed a few more fighters in the process, we had the upper hand.

The resupply took just thirty minutes and the CSM had safely got his team back to the DC and Ronnie had returned with his team, Davy explained that it was very dodgy and a very easy place to take us on by the Taliban. I discussed the extraction plan with the boss, we needed to get the platoon out of here without incident, no one now was talking about young Justin, we were now remembering him in our own way, there will be time to reflect on our fallen comrades once we get the hell out of this shithole.

That night went with more sporadic gunfire coming in from the green zone, apart from putting up light and keeping our eyes on stalks, there was nothing else we can do.

The next morning we were told that John was bringing his platoon in to replace us; we were being extracted back to the DC for what I could only describe as a chance to do admin and re-cock for whatever was next.

The boss explained how he would like the relief in place to go, he will remain here while I go with the point section, and we will leave all 66 mm and anti-tank missiles along the roof top facing south. So the new platoon can use them. As we patrolled towards the crossing point, I could see the other platoon well spaced out, John was kneeling at the other side of the river trying to get eye contact with me.

Then Ronnie stopped, his point men T and Davy came walking back shaking their head, they had picked up a reading with the equipment, the ground sign was different from its surroundings. Someone had been there and moved the soil, I think IED, holy shit, not at this stage in the game, and we decided to send it up to the OC informing him of what we had.

Then out of the right side Skillen spotted someone moving, he engaged with the GPMG, he hit him, I now shouted, 'CONTACT HADES FOUR ONE BRAVO WAIT OUT!' I told Skillen and Dev to move in, if he moves towards them then to engage, they agreed and slowly moved forward towards him, I waited patiently for the outcome.

Then I heard the GPMG firing again along with the single shots from Dev, they returned to tell me he was dead, he was what Skillen had seen moving on the right. I moved in for a closer look and saw he was dead. I checked his pulse and breathing, I could see his sharp shattered and exposed hips where the GPMG has blown away the flesh from the hip to expose the bone area, his clothing now bloodstained, I got the troops to help me place him onto a stretcher which I had been carrying.

I got onto Zero and explained that I have one times enemy force KIA at my location and I will bring him back with me during the changeover with John's platoon, I got told quickly to change channel to the chat-net, this was where we can talk freely without being listened into by the battle group.

The CSM then explained to me that I was in no certain terms to bring back the body of the enemy fighter to the district centre as it was like a circus there at the minute, with the radio 1 road show, Bill Nealy from ITN, and the deputy brigade commander, the last thing the army top brass needs is for a dead enemy fighter to appear in the press. Because that is what would happen if I bring him back, I agreed and he told me to get rid, now I did not know he actually meant leave in situ.

I took it for granted and did what I thought was right, as I stated the situation dictated that I get rid of the body, I knew that if I was to leave it just lying out in the open, then the locals would think we were barbarians. So I got one of the guys to help me with the stretcher, we walked towards the edge of the river and set it down, I could see the look on his face, he was in shock at what I was about to do, I explained that after three I would launch him into the river, now grab his arms and I will grab his legs, after three, ready, one, two, three go. We threw this motionless body high into the air and he landed with a hell of a splash face up in the river.

Then I was worried as it did not sink, it just floated in a circle, I got the troops to throw mud boulders on top of it to help it sink, eventually it met up with another current and sank below the surface of the river to my relief. By this time the other platoon was shaking their heads at my actions, I did not care as I had gotten my platoon back and safe through this incident.

We arrived back at the DC in one piece and I had a few things running through my head now, Jesus Christ, what next, the members of my platoon knew I had no choice in what I did, and today I still stand by that. The CSM asked if I left the body and I explained I got rid of it, he looked at me and explained he said leave in situ, I looked white now. I walked off with him and explained what I had done. He just held his head and said, 'What the f——k did you do that for, Speedy?' I explained I carried out the actions that I deemed was necessary at the time, to this day we both disagree, but then again he was not there with me.

That night the troops had a great sleep only to be woken up in the early hours in the morning by yet again another large contact, I could hear explosions and automatic fire to the south, I grabbed my helmet, rifle, and body armour and ran to the ops room. Telling the guys to stand to, when I arrived there, I could see everyone was there around a map looking at the multiple firing positions that John's platoon was being engaged from.

I stupidly then asked what's going on, just then the CSM turned around and said, 'Really, Sergeant Coult, what's going on, YOU ARE

WHAT'S GOING ON, FU——ING YOU, what did you do with all those branches that you cut off the trees in that PB?' I said we threw them in the river. 'And what happened to them?' They got stuck at green 12. 'And what did you do with that dead Taliban fighter?' I threw him in the river also. 'Guess what, Sergeant Coult, he is stuck at green 12 wrapped up in branches, and now 9 Platoon are running low in ammunition, and you are going to resupply them, NOT ME!'

At that time my backside nearly fell out, he was just pissed off; he did resupply them and gave me a few dirty jobs to carry out, it was the last time I left camp, we continued to carry out low-level patrols with the US Marines and finish off our job in Sangin. It was only a few more days before we handed over to the Royal Marine Commandos, I was completely exhausted with this way of life and promised myself that I would never return to Sangin again!

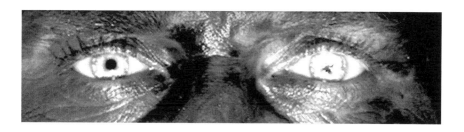

DOES THIS PICTURE GRAB YOUR ATTENTION?

This was me not that long ago. I was in a place where I felt I had no way out, I would sit and stare into space. Anyone who was watching me thought I was daydreaming. I was far from it! A smell, a noise, or a movement would send me back to a place where I feared to return; it was back into combat and I had to relive the same terrible things over and over again. There were days when I would break down crying and wonder if it would ever end.

Well, the truth is, it never ends. I have found ways to cope and now with the help of Veterans in Action and the team, I enjoy each day and look to the future. Veterans in Action have made me a very proud man by giving me the honour of being one of their distinguished patrons, and I now try and raise awareness for what they do.

Veterans in Action help veterans who have suffered the effects of war or who have found the transition to civilian life difficult by helping them to rebuild their confidence, self-esteem, and self-belief on adventurous events and expeditions.

VIA is the difference that makes the difference, committed to rebuilding effective interaction towards the future of Britain's armed forces veterans.

If you would like to help us by giving up your time or donating, then please get in touch using the following contact details.

Phone: **01264 771658**

Out of Hours: **07889 400830**

Website: info@veteransinaction.org.uk

http://www.veteransinaction.org.uk/

Registered Charity No. 1128026

INDEX

A

ACM (Anti-Coalition Militia) 96, 168
administration 42, 98, 100, 123, 138, 163-4, 222, 226, 228
Afghanistan 17, 19, 23-6, 33, 39, 46, 56, 60, 63, 80-1, 83-6, 180-1, 198-9, 201-3, 243-4
aircraft 5, 14, 21, 24, 26-7, 68-9, 71, 79-82, 87-9, 91, 93, 181, 200, 244-5, 273
ANA (Afghan National Army) 48-9, 59, 77

B

B-Company 2, 13, 34, 63, 102-3, 170, 173
Baghdad 4-6, 10-11, 13-14, 16-19, 129, 190, 198, 212, 225
Bastion 38-9, 67-8, 71, 88-9, 104, 106, 123, 127, 130, 163, 170-1, 174-5, 177-80, 244, 246
battalion 2, 13, 15, 17-18, 24-7, 55, 89, 91, 165, 168, 184, 197-9, 216, 219-21, 237
battle group 34-5, 44, 46, 59, 63, 67, 95, 100, 116, 124, 137, 248, 288
battlefield 25, 41, 46, 69, 78, 81, 89, 92, 110, 177, 227, 273, 275
BE (battle exercise) 223

Belfast 21, 55, 57, 77, 83, 183, 193, 197-201, 203-4, 210
belt kit 3-4, 36, 50-1, 92, 171, 221, 228, 234, 245
Berry, Jim 166, 173
BL (battle lesson) 223
Bloodhound camp 182, 188
Brecon 23, 220, 225, 230, 232, 235, 237-8, 241, 250
BSU (Baghdad support unit) 4, 6-7, 9-11, 14-17

C

C-Company 22, 68-9, 103, 107, 111, 189, 193, 207
Camp Bastion 28, 68-9, 73, 77, 95, 100, 132, 137
Camp Victory 6, 18
Caylie (CMT) 274-5, 280, 282
CEFO (combat equipment fighting order) 4, 21
checkpoints 5-8, 12, 48-9, 251
Chinook 35, 67, 70-1, 89, 91-2, 96, 99-100, 106-7, 111, 127-8, 163-4, 168-72, 174-6, 272-3, 277
clearance patrol 248, 258, 261, 285
CMT (combat medic technician) 38, 69, 93, 274, 280-1
Colchester 17, 22-3, 27, 187, 189-90

293

command appointment 230-1, 235, 237-8

commanders 6-7, 10-11, 13, 18, 22-3, 30, 53-4, 56, 73-6, 94-6, 100-2, 116-17, 121, 235-6, 249-50

commanding officer 4, 8, 17, 25, 65, 101, 108, 137, 163, 172, 193, 212-13, 230, 274, 276-7

COP (Close Observation Platoon) 85

Craig 47, 84, 125, 202

Cupples 250, 258, 281, 283

D

Danish soldiers 96, 99

Dave 250, 252, 264, 278, 280-1, 283

Davey 39, 55, 60-1, 68-9, 71, 102, 121, 124-5, 128, 131, 133, 177, 184, 187-8, 228

Davy 29, 34, 37, 196, 209, 247, 281, 287-8

decompression 179, 183, 186

Dougal 21, 24, 46, 112, 114, 121, 129-31, 171, 175, 187-8, 191, 196, 200

Driscol 22, 30-2, 38, 42, 46, 48-9, 71, 98, 102, 108-9, 164, 175, 196

E

enemy fighters 24, 97, 171, 288

enemy forces 4, 28, 33, 43, 53, 97, 104, 122, 124, 237, 248, 255

enemy positions 75, 107, 109, 119, 241, 274

enemy strength 101, 103

enemy territory 70, 115, 217, 252-3, 271-2

engineers 115-16, 131, 134-5, 248, 259, 264, 285

escort tasks 13, 16

F

Farmer 224-7, 234, 238-9

FIBUA (Fighting in Built-up Areas) 230-1

fighting troops 7, 34, 256

films 45, 183, 230, 234, 281

fitness 21, 26, 28, 32, 185, 219-21

FLET (Forward Line of Enemy Troops) 251-2, 258

FOB (Forward Operating Base) 29, 36, 42, 63, 110, 112, 115, 119, 172-3, 177, 260

FOB Price 49, 93, 95, 175, 177

FOB Robinson 35-7, 39-41, 136, 246, 257

FOO (Forward Observation Officer) 40-1, 248, 262

FSG (Fire Support Group) 171, 256, 272, 274

FSG Tower 114, 120, 269, 285-6

FUP (forming up point) 25, 239-41

G

Gereshk 31-4, 41, 44, 54-6, 59, 61, 75-7, 93, 137, 175-8

Gereshk camp 43, 53

good soldiers 3, 21, 42, 55, 224, 230

GPMG (general purpose machine gun) 59, 70, 114, 116, 120, 172, 261, 288

GPS (global positioning satellite) 178

Grant 62, 191-2, 209

green zone 5-7, 9, 14, 64, 71, 103, 107, 170, 172, 176, 253, 256-8, 262-4, 272, 286-7

grenades 8, 38, 59, 64, 71-2, 94, 97-8, 109, 259

grip bags 4, 14, 170, 177, 179, 194-6, 221, 247

guardroom 6-7, 11, 15, 200

gunfire 3, 10, 34, 71, 74, 77, 115, 117

H

HC (highly competent) 237

HCR (household cavalry regiment) 63, 93, 96, 127, 134, 164

Helmand 17-18, 39, 83, 115, 120, 133, 168, 187, 204, 236, 243-4

HLS (helicopter landing site) 22, 39,
    42, 44, 67, 77, 104, 107, 127-8,
    164, 169-70, 172, 229, 272-3,
    276-7
HLZ (hot landing zone) 92
holiday 188, 213-14, 216
home 1, 16, 19-20, 79, 81-2, 122-4,
    132-3, 169-70, 176-7, 180-3,
    189, 193-5, 199-202, 204-5,
    213-16

I

ICFT (Infantry Combat Fitness Test)
    220, 223, 231-2
instructors 224-5, 227, 230, 250
insurgents 6, 9-10, 14, 33, 60, 65-6,
    73
Inverness 18, 21, 193, 207-9, 217,
    221
Iraq 2, 6, 14, 16, 60, 205, 210, 220,
    224
Ireland 196, 200, 203, 212, 214-15,
    220
IRT (Immediate Response Team) 35-
    6, 90, 92-4, 127, 174, 257, 267
ISAF troops 258, 273
ISO containers 36, 78, 112-13, 247

J

JOC (Joint Operations Cell) 28, 35,
    73, 91, 95, 104, 116
Joey 247, 257, 263, 277
John 201, 204, 287-9
Justin 282, 286

K

Kabul 28, 78-80, 88, 180
KIA (killed in action) 1, 33-4, 46, 89-
    90, 111, 116, 122, 130, 165, 246,
    251, 259, 275, 288
knowledge 13, 15, 55, 70, 190, 219,
    221, 251, 260, 277

L

LFTT (Live Fire Tactical Training)
    221-2
locals 9, 24, 32, 45, 49, 51-2, 54-6,
    59, 63, 74, 76, 133-4, 254-6,
    258, 260
loss 67, 174, 209
Luba 213-16, 219, 244-5
Luke 30-2, 42-3, 46, 48-9, 57, 69,
    71-2, 93-4, 97-9, 120-1, 124-31,
    171, 175-6, 179, 208-9

M

machine gun platoon 43, 47
mail 34, 133, 137, 165, 207, 245-6,
    257
Marines 168-73, 177-8, 259, 281
Matt 250, 256, 261-2, 275-6
Maude house 6, 8, 11
MCCP (Movement Control
    Checkpoint) 79, 179
meals 7, 80-1, 86, 88, 181, 210, 213-
    15, 238, 248
media 63-4, 173-4
medic 38, 126, 128, 230-1, 238, 267-
    8, 274, 280
MFC (Mortar Fire Controller) 262,
    265
Mickey 84, 187, 202
mission 40, 61-2, 120, 133-4, 240,
    248
mortar platoon 55, 117
mortars 39, 58, 64, 70, 96-7, 107,
    113-15, 118-19, 122, 127, 130,
    137, 167, 171-2, 250
MREs (meals ready to eat) 36
MSR (main supply route) 41, 44, 54
Musa Quala 91-2, 94-6, 98-9, 116,
    119, 122, 130, 134-5, 163, 165,
    168, 171, 199, 248

N

NAAFI   1, 78-9, 175, 177, 179, 195-7,
   209, 246
NBI (Non-Battle Injury)   35
Neil   220, 222, 224
nightclub   191-2, 208

O

OC (officer commanding)   4-6, 8,
   10-11, 69-70, 74-5, 93-4, 108-
   11, 163-5, 168-9, 219-20, 252-4,
   262-3, 268-71, 277-9, 283-8
OCD (obsessive cleaning disorder)   4,
   14, 30, 81, 186, 194-5, 285
Oman   23-4, 187, 206
operation   2, 7, 22, 26, 41, 46, 63,
   65-7, 69-70, 83, 102-3, 227-8,
   252-4, 262-3, 271-2
operations room   30-1, 45, 50, 57, 65,
   67, 114, 127, 132, 136, 169-70,
   176, 256

P

Pablo   207-8, 213
Palace   210-12
parade   27, 200, 209, 223
paratroopers   22-3, 25, 56, 78, 103-4,
   110, 113-14, 173, 179, 186-8,
   190, 193, 256, 272, 275-6
parents   19-20, 31, 54, 83-5, 88, 135,
   183-4, 200-5, 207, 210-17, 243-
   5, 268
pathfinder platoon   30, 34, 50
PB (patrol base)   101, 124, 258, 263-4,
   266-7, 269, 290
PB Armagh   263, 266, 271, 278, 280
PCBC (Platoon Commanders Battle
   Course)   231
pilots   35, 89, 100, 136, 164, 181, 187
pistols   68-9, 76, 79, 259, 261
PJ   230, 236, 247-51
plane   13, 24, 82-3, 181, 189, 243-4
platoon area   4, 30

platoon commander   13, 18, 57, 101,
   128, 166, 206, 227-8, 236, 238-
   40, 258, 265-6
platoon house   41, 74, 102, 285
platoon sergeant   2, 12, 18, 23, 76,
   110-11, 206, 217-20, 226-7, 233-
   4, 236-7, 242, 249-50, 252-3,
   264-6
PPW (personal protection weapons)   15
PRR (personal role radios)   9, 12, 236,
   273
PSBC (Platoon Sergeants Battle Course)
   222

Q

QRF (Quick Reaction Force)   30-1,
   55, 58, 60, 112-13, 131, 257,
   259, 262
Queen   183-4, 205, 209-11, 216

R

radio operator   29, 58
RAF camp   87, 188
Ralf   30, 92, 102, 109, 196, 199, 202
Ranger Platoon   20, 22, 59, 66, 86,
   133-4, 136, 166, 186
recce platoon   55, 64, 85
Remembrance Day   199, 203, 207-8
RHA (Royal Horse Artillery)   46, 93
RMP (Royal Military Police)   58, 62,
   191-2
Robbie   18, 24, 29, 34-5, 37-9, 61, 69,
   125, 128, 130-1, 175, 177, 196,
   200, 265
ROE (rules of engagement)   29, 99,
   134, 245
Ronnie   250, 252, 256, 258-60, 262,
   281, 287-8
Royal Irish   23, 53, 91, 94, 116, 122,
   135, 173, 178-9, 204, 253, 275,
   277
RPGs (rocket-propelled grenades)   58,
   97, 108, 113-15, 117, 119, 130,
   136-7, 164, 167, 256, 271, 280,
   286

RSM (Regimental Sergeant Major) 4, 165, 173-4, 217, 220, 222, 275
runners 47, 65, 91, 129, 224, 230, 252

S

Sangers 73-6, 91-2, 95-6, 101, 111-21, 123, 128, 131, 135-6, 167, 171-2, 255, 286-7
Sangin 39, 46, 63, 65-7, 72-4, 95, 100-3, 112-13, 122-4, 132-3, 136-7, 167-9, 171-2, 245-8, 257-9
Senior Brecon 217, 220-2, 233
Sergeant Coult 228, 238, 242, 289-90
Sergeants Mess 187, 209, 222, 229-30
serial number 95, 168, 178, 228-9
SFSG (Special Forces Support Group) 222, 224
signals 49, 51, 240, 273
snipers 67, 76, 92, 96, 241
soldiers 3-5, 13, 35-6, 76, 85-7, 89-91, 93, 101, 126-7, 136-8, 165-6, 168-71, 174, 204, 279
  infantry 220, 222
Spalding (instructor) 224
Spence 7, 21-2, 27-8, 30, 33-5, 50-3, 56-7, 60-1, 69-76, 93-5, 102, 112, 117-20, 124-8, 186-92
Stella 58, 124-6, 129, 165, 187, 189, 196
Stephen 264, 266
suicide bombers 5, 14, 61-2, 176, 246-7

T

Taliban 33-4, 54-5, 57-60, 94-9, 101-3, 107-9, 113-15, 118-20, 126-8, 134-7, 163-72, 253-4, 256-8, 260-3, 271-2
Taliban fighters 49, 77, 101, 131, 174, 268, 271, 287
Tam 9-10, 55, 102, 129, 175, 187, 196, 198
television crews 56-7, 189-90

TF (Task Force) 248
track plan 226-7, 237
training 18, 24, 26-7, 178, 250
transport 80-1, 89, 226-7, 230, 233, 235, 238-9

U

UAV (Unmanned Aerial Vehicle) 46, 63, 76, 171, 187
UDR (Ulster Defence Regiment) 197-8, 204
UKSF (United Kingdom Special Forces) 116, 232
Ulster Defence Regiment (UDR) 197-8, 204
US camp 9-10, 18
US Marines 5-6, 15-16, 180, 251, 255, 290

V

VCPs (Vehicle Checkpoints) 12, 54
vehicle convoys 14, 48-9
vehicle patrol 177, 251
village 1, 3, 33, 47-51, 59-60, 73, 80, 134, 194, 230-1

W

weapons 7-9, 15, 17-18, 32, 44-6, 51-3, 60-1, 94, 98, 104, 174-7, 229, 241-2, 261-2, 271-2
wedding 85-6, 283
Whitstable 85-6

Trevor Raywood Coult MC joined the Royal Irish Regiment on the 4th July 1994 after passing out of ITB Strensal he was posted to his unit who were based in Episkopi Garrison Cyprus. He then went onto serve in N.Ireland, Canada, Oman, Brunei, Kenya, UAE, Kuwait, Bahrain, Germany and Afghanistan. He completed 10 Operational tours and was awarded the Military Cross by her Majesty the Queen on the 6th December 2006 for actions he carried out in Baghdad; He was also presented with the Presidential seal by the President of the United States of America George W Bush on 17th March 2008 while at the White House. Here is his Citation: L/Cpl Coult has been employed as a Team Commander in the 1st Battalion The Royal Irish Regiment throughout his tour of Iraq. He was a member of the UK Protection Force based in Baghdad, providing security for and escorting the senior British Military representative- Iraq and senior UK service personnel. At the time of his tour, Baghdad was a scene of very numerous and lethal insurgent attacks against coalition forces on a daily basis.

On the 6th November 2005 L/Cpl Coult was a member of an escort task travelling along route IRISH Baghdad International Airport to the Green Zone, assessed to be the most dangerous road in the world. L/Cpl Coult was top cover sentry in the rear vehicle, a role he was conducting for the first time. Approaching checkpoint 540 the lead snatch stopped due to a suspicious vehicle parked at the side of the road. With the other top cover sentries now engaged in trying to move the vehicle it quickly sped up and began to reverse towards the vehicles. With a clear and unambiguous threat towards life three warning shots were fired. Despite this activity L/Cpl Coult was not drawn in and continued to observe his arcs.

While all the attention was focused to the front, 3 gunmen opened up with extensive automatic fire aimed at the stationary vehicles, L/Cpl Coult quickly realised the complex and dual nature of this lethal ambush. He scanned his arcs and quickly identified the gunmen. Amidst considerable incoming small arms fire, with tracer striking the ground to his front he calmly controlled the other top cover sentries and gave precise target information on his personal radio, returned fire and controlled the movement of his vehicle. L/Cpl Coult's accurate and effective fire supressed the gunmen and enabled the vehicles to extract from the killing zone. Thereby undoubtedly saving the lives of the other vehicle crew, He then kept his vehicle in the killing zone while the other vehicles extracted and in which 1 vehicle had stalled. He ordered his vehicle to be driven along the stalled vehicle attracting considerable additional incoming fire. This selfless act saved the stalled vehicle from being immobilised and the crew from becoming casualties. Throughout this complex and well prepared insurgent ambush L/Cpl Coult returned proportional accurate and justified fire, remained totally focussed and acted in a considered professional and courageous manner.

L/Cpl Coult's actions undoubtedly saved the lives of the logistic soldiers. On his first day of top cover in Baghdad, he showed outstanding judgement, bravery and restraint n returning fire against the enemy. His life saving actions, personal and tactical control, with total disregard for his own safety are the indictment of the highest qualities of a British JNCO in the face of the enemy and are richly deserving of official recognition.

Printed in Great Britain
by Amazon

75274804R00184